easy
OS X®
Mavericks

Kate Binder

que®

800 East 96th Street
Indianapolis, In 46240

CONTENTS

CHAPTER 3   INSTALLING AND USING APPLICATIONS ... 56

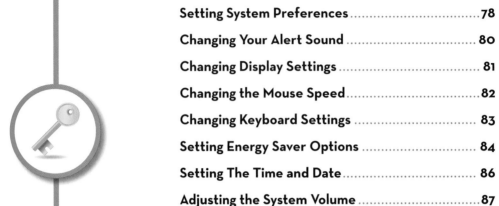
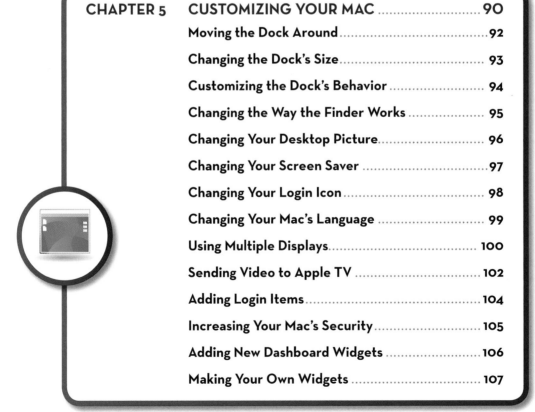

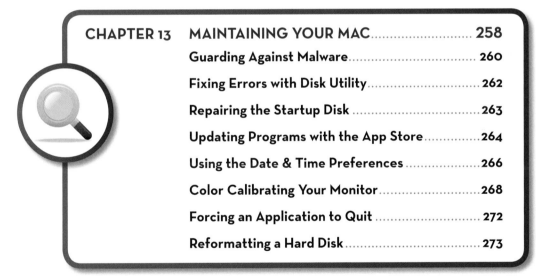

TRADEMARKS

WARNING AND DISCLAIMER

SPECIAL SALES

For information about buying this title in bulk quantities, or for special sales opportunities (which may include electronic versions; custom cover designs; and content particular to your business, training goals, marketing focus, or branding interests), please contact our corporate sales department at corpsales@pearsoned.com or (800) 382-3419.

For government sales inquiries, please contact governmentsales@pearsoned.com.

For questions about sales outside the U.S., please contact international@pearsoned.com.

Editor-in-Chief
Greg Wiegand

Acquisitions Editor
Laura Norman

Development Editor
Charlotte Kughen

Managing Editor
Kristy Hart

Project Editor
Katie Matejka

Indexer
Lisa Stumpf

Technical Editor
Paul Sihvonen-Binder

Editorial Assistant
Cindy Teeters

Cover Designer
Alan Clements

Composition
TnT Design, Inc.

Proofreader
Dan Knott

ABOUT THE AUTHOR

Kate Binder is a longtime Mac lover and graphics expert who works from her home in New Hampshire. She has written articles on graphics, publishing, and photography for magazines including *Publish*, *PEI*, and *Desktop Publishers Journal*. Kate is also the author of several books, including *The Complete Idiot's Guide to Mac OS X*, and coauthor of books including *Sams Teach Yourself Adobe Photoshop CS4 in 24 Hours*, *Microsoft Office: Mac v.X Inside Out*, *SVG for Designers*, and *Get Creative: The Digital Photo Idea Book*. To those interested in a successful career as a computer book writer, Kate recommends acquiring several retired racing greyhounds (find out more at www.adopt-a-greyhound.org)—she finds her own pack of greyhounds extraordinarily inspirational.

DEDICATION

This book is for my amazing husband Don Fluckinger, who is forced to put up with authorial crankiness while I'm trying to meet deadlines, and who still makes me popcorn at night despite it all.

ACKNOWLEDGMENTS

Profuse thanks are due to Laura Norman for shepherding me through yet another one. Thanks, too, to the awesome editorial, design, and production people at Que—and especially my favorite tech editor, Paul Sihvonen-Binder—for making it happen once again.

WE WANT TO HEAR FROM YOU!

As the reader of this book, you are our most important critic and commentator. We value your opinion and want to know what we're doing right, what we could do better, what areas you'd like to see us publish in, and any other words of wisdom you're willing to pass our way.

We welcome your comments. You can email or write to let us know what you did or didn't like about this book—as well as what we can do to make our books better.

Please note that we cannot help you with technical problems related to the topic of this book.

When you write, please be sure to include this book's title and author as well as your name, email address, and phone number. I will carefully review your comments and share them with the author and editors who worked on the book.

Email: feedback@quepublishing.com

Mail: Que Publishing
         ATTN: Reader Feedback
         800 East 96th Street
         Indianapolis, IN 46240 USA

READER SERVICES

Visit our website and register this book at www.quepublishing.com/register for convenient access to any updates, downloads, or errata that might be available for this book.

IT'S AS EASY AS 1-2-3

Each part of this book is made up of a series of short, instructional lessons, designed to help you understand basic information.

① Each step is fully illustrated to show you how it looks onscreen

② Each task includes a series of quick, easy steps designed to guide you through the procedure.

③ Items that you select or click in menus, dialog boxes, tabs, and windows are shown in **bold**.

Tips, notes, and cautions give you a heads-up for any extra information you may need while working through the task.

How to Drag: Point to the starting place or object. Hold down the mouse button (right or left per instructions), move the mouse to the new location, and then release the button.

Click: Click the left mouse button once.

Click & Type: Click once where indicated and begin typing to enter your text or data.

Selection: Highlights the area onscreen discussed in the step or task.

Double-click: Click the left mouse button twice in rapid succession.

Right-click: Click the right mouse button once.

Pointer arrow: Highlights an item on the screen you need to point to or focus on in the step or task.

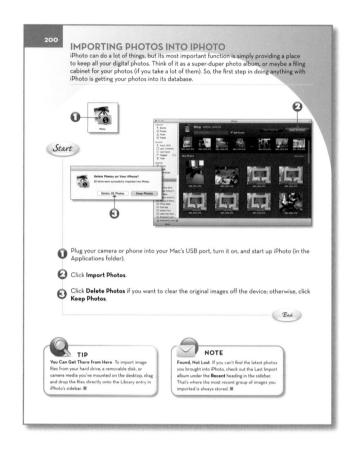

200

IMPORTING PHOTOS INTO IPHOTO

iPhoto can do a lot of things, but its most important function is simply providing a place to keep all your digital photos. Think of it as a super-duper photo album, or maybe a filing cabinet for your photos (if you take a lot of them). So, the first step in doing anything with iPhoto is getting your photos into its database.

Start

① Plug your camera or phone into your Mac's USB port, turn it on, and start up iPhoto (in the Applications folder).

② Click **Import Photos**.

③ Click **Delete Photos** if you want to clear the original images off the device; otherwise, click **Keep Photos**.

End

🔍 **TIP**
You Can Get There from Here To import image files from your hard drive, a removable disk, or camera media you've mounted on the desktop, drag and drop the files directly onto the Library entry in iPhoto's sidebar. ■

✉ **NOTE**
Found, Not Lost If you can't find the latest photos you brought into iPhoto, check out the Last Import album under the **Recent** heading in the sidebar. That's where the most recent group of images you imported is always stored. ■

INTRODUCTION TO
EASY OS X® MAVERICKS

OS X is like no other computer operating system: It's incredibly stable and powerful, and it looks amazingly sleek. But underneath the glitz and sparkle, it has the same old friendly nature that Mac users have enjoyed since 1984. And it's all about enabling you to do whatever you want to do with your Mac.

With *Easy OS X Mavericks*, you'll learn how to take advantage of powerful and useful OS X features such as the built-in instant messaging program Messages, built-in access to cloud storage and backup, and the ability to stream video right from your Mac to your TV. Along the way, you'll get used to being able to run a dozen programs at one time on a stable system that doesn't crash. This book's step-by-step approach tells you just what you need to know to accomplish the task at hand, quickly and efficiently. All the skills you need to get the most out of OS X, both online and on the desktop, are covered here.

If you want, you can work through the tasks in *Easy OS X Mavericks* in order, building your skills steadily. Or, if you prefer, use this book as a reference to look up just what you need to know *right now*. Either way, *Easy OS X Mavericks* lets you see it done, and then do it yourself.

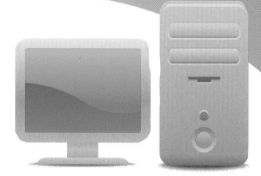

GETTING STARTED

With the advent of Mac OS X 10.9 Mavericks, Mac users get a good view of both the future and the past. Innovative features such as the Notification Center combine with the Mac's traditionally intuitive interface to provide a user experience that's both new and comfortably familiar. Mac OS X 10.9 is still many times more powerful than older systems, completely modern, capable of handling the latest innovations in hardware, and as easy to use as any Mac system that has gone before. But Mavericks has a few surprises in store for you.

The starting point for any exploration of Mac OS X is the desktop: what you see when your Mac has finished starting up. The desktop is operated by a program called the Finder, and it's a central location where you'll gain access to your disks and their contents, move files around, and keep track of what your computer's up to—sort of like a hotel or office building lobby. This section covers the basics of working with the Finder, as well as other functions that work the same no matter what program you're using.

MAC OS X DESKTOP

Control your Mac with the Apple menu's commands, 5

Maximize windows, 13

Drag the title bar to move a window, 12

Check messages and updates in the Notification Center, 8

Set System Preferences, 18

Restart and shut down your Mac, 6

Close windows, 12

Minimize windows into the Dock, 13

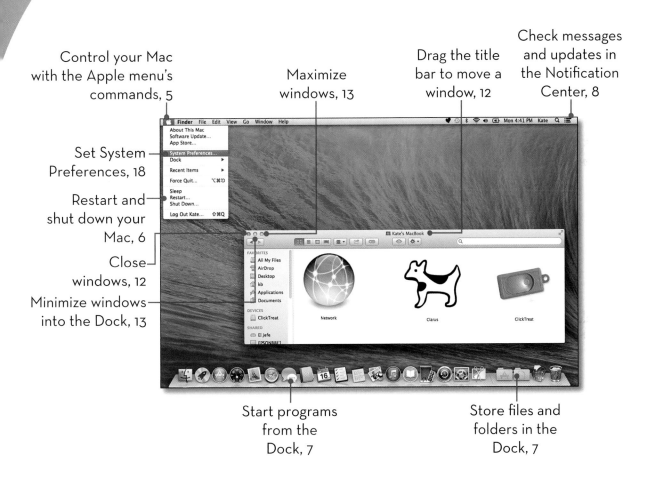

Start programs from the Dock, 7

Store files and folders in the Dock, 7

TOURING THE DESKTOP

If you've used an older version of Mac OS before, the desktop in Mavericks won't look completely new to you—just a bit unfamiliar. On the other hand, if you're new to computers, concepts like *windows*, *icons*, and *menus* need a little explanation. Either way, this tour of the Mac OS X desktop should set you on your way.

Start

Continued

1. Double-click to view a window showing the contents of a drive or folder.

2. Click and drag to move icons on the desktop.

3. Click objects in the Dock to activate them.

4. Click a menu name, drag the mouse down, and release the mouse button when the menu item you want to use is highlighted.

NOTE

It's Okay to Explore If you're not sure what something on the desktop does, try clicking or double-clicking it—it's safe to explore and experiment. If something *does* go wrong, you can usually undo the last thing you did by pressing ⌘+Z or choosing **Edit, Undo**. ■

NOTE

Making the Desktop Your Own Turn to the task called "Changing Your Desktop Picture" in Chapter 5, "Customizing Your Mac," to learn how to change the desktop picture so you'll truly feel at home when you sit down in front of your Mac. ■

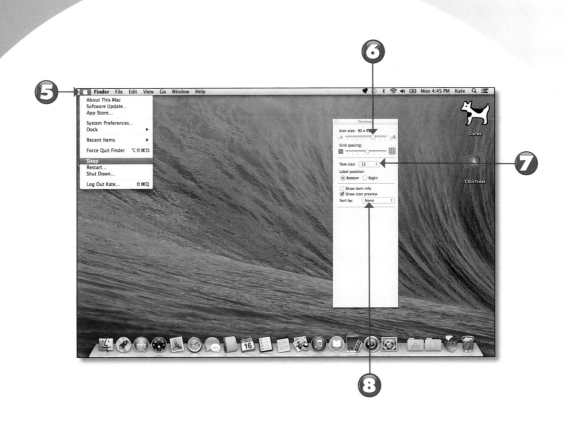

5 Click the **Apple** icon in the upper-left corner of the screen to access the Apple menu, where you can perform tasks that affect your whole computer.

6 Choose **View**, **Show View Options** to open the View Options dialog box. Drag the **Icon size** slider to change the size of desktop icons.

7 Change the **Text size** and **Label position** settings to change the appearance of icon labels.

8 Check any of the other options or choose an option from the **Sort By** pop-up menu to set other options for files, folders, and drives on the desktop.

End

TIP

Cleaning Up the Place When your desktop gets cluttered with files and folders so that it's impossible for you to find anything, choose **View**, **Clean Up** to line up all the icons on the desktop in neat rows, so you can see what you've got. ■

NOTE

Where's the Trash? If you've used pre-OS X Macs, you're probably looking for the Trash, which used to live on the desktop. It's in the Dock now, but you can put it back on the desktop if you like by using a little program called Trash X (www.northernsoftworks.com). ■

RESTARTING OR SHUTTING DOWN THE MAC

Because they're commands that affect the entire system, Restart and Shut Down are located in the Apple menu, so you can access them from any program rather than having to switch to the Finder, as in pre-OS X versions of the Mac OS. You'll use Restart most often after installing new software, and you'll use Shut Down when you want to turn off your computer.

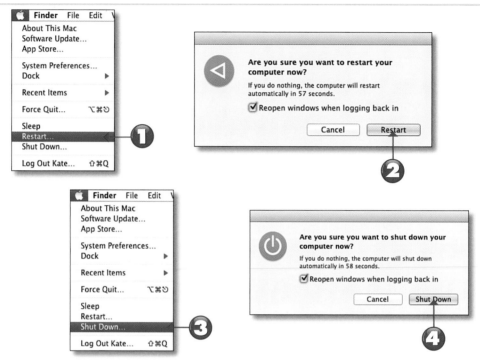

Start

End

① To restart the Mac, choose **Apple menu**, **Restart**.

② In the dialog box, click **Restart**. Click **Cancel** to exit the dialog box without restarting.

③ To shut down the Mac, choose **Apple menu**, **Shut Down**.

④ In the dialog box, click **Shut Down**. Click **Cancel** to exit the dialog box without shutting down.

TIP

No Fresh Start Needed You don't have to restart the Mac if you only want to switch users. Instead, choose **Apple menu, Log Out**; this command quits all running programs and presents you with the login screen, but it doesn't require the computer to completely reboot. ■

TIP

As Easy as Pressing a Button Press your Mac's Power key briefly to bring up a dialog asking you whether you want to restart, shut down, or sleep the Mac. ■

USING THE DOCK

The *Dock* serves more than one function. First, it's where you can see which programs are running and switch among them. The Dock contains an icon for each active program at any given time. Second, it's a good place to store things you use often, whether they're programs, folders, or documents. And finally, it's where you'll find the Trash. The Dock has a line dividing its two sides. Program icons are stored on the left side, whether the programs are running or not, and folders and documents that have been added to the Dock are stored on the right side.

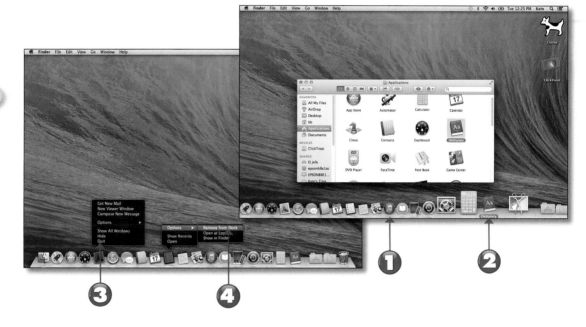

 Click a program icon in the Dock to switch to that program (if it's running) or to start it up (if it's not running). Running programs are indicated by glowing dots under their icons.

2 Drag programs from the desktop into the Dock's left side and documents or folders from the desktop into the Dock's right side to store them for easy access.

3 Click and hold an icon in the Dock to see a menu of actions you can perform on that object or a list of folder contents. If you don't like waiting, you can Control-click or right-click.

4 Choose **Options**, **Remove from Dock** from an icon's contextual menu to remove it from the Dock in a puff of virtual smoke.

End

NOTE

Disappearing Act When you remove programs or documents from the Dock, they disappear in a puff of smoke. But don't worry about the original files—they're still on your hard drive. Dock icons are just pointers to the files, not the files themselves. ■

TIP

Moving Day If you don't like the order of the icons in the Dock, you can drag and drop them into an order that suits you better. ■

CHECKING YOUR NOTIFICATIONS

With Mavericks, you can check your Mac's messages, so to speak, in one central location called the Notification Center. Here you'll find lists of new email and chat messages, software updates to download, event alerts and to-do reminders, and much more—neatly hidden when you don't want to be bothered and easily available when you need the information.

Start

1 To check notifications, click the **Notification Center** button at the right-hand end of the menu bar.

2 To go to the subject of a notification, click that notification in the list.

3 Take any needed actions in the original program.

Continued

NOTE

A Banner Day Some notifications appear as banners or alerts in the upper right-hand corner of your screen. Banners disappear after five seconds, whereas alerts require you to acknowledge them before closing. Either way, they're also listed in the Notifications Center. You can set what type of alert appears in the Notification Center preference pane. ■

TIP

Take a Swipe at It If you're using a trackpad, you can also bring up the Notifications Center by swiping from the trackpad's right edge toward its center with two fingers. Swipe to the right with two fingers to close the Notifications Center. ■

4 To change settings for Notification Center, choose **Apple menu**, **System Preferences**.

5 Click **Notifications** in the Personal section of the System Preferences window.

6 Click the type of notification you want to modify and make settings to change how this type of notification displays.

7 Choose **System Preferences**, **Quit System Preferences**.

End

TIP

Do Not Disturb If you need to concentrate for a while and don't want to be distracted by notifications popping onto your screen all the time, click the **Notification Center** button, grab the scroll handle at the right edge of the screen and scroll upward, and then click **Do Not Disturb** to turn it on. Don't forget to turn it off when you're done! You can also use Notification Center to automatically turn on Do Not Disturb for specified time periods. ■

NOTE

I Love iOS Notifications are one of the features that Mac OS X inherited from iOS, the operating system used by iPods, iPhones, and iPads. If you like how they work on your Mac, you'll love iOS. ■

USING CONTEXTUAL MENUS

The more you use your Mac, the more you'll appreciate time-saving techniques. Contextual menus pop up right where you're working, instead of requiring you to mouse up to the menu bar or take your hands off the mouse to use the keyboard. Their contents vary depending on what you're doing at the time, and even according to what programs you have installed.

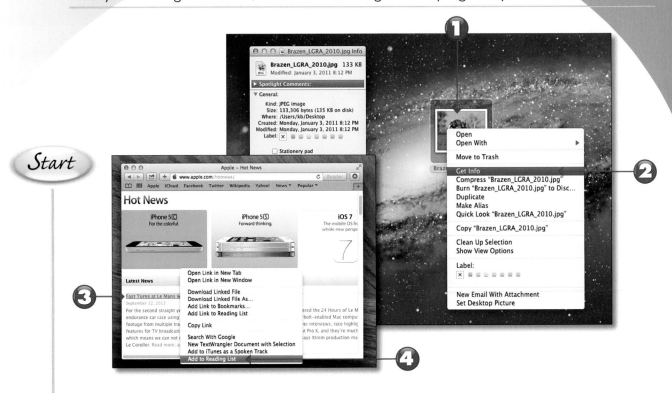

 Press **Control** and click any object on the desktop.

 Click the contextual menu command you want to perform.

3 In an application, such as Safari, Control-click any object such as an image or a text link, to see if it has a contextual menu.

4 Choose a command from the contextual menu to perform that function, or click elsewhere to dismiss the menu.

TIP

Remember the Context Contextual menus contain different options depending on what you click to see them. Try Control-clicking the desktop itself, and don't forget to Control-click objects in document windows, such as pictures or misspelled words. ■

NOTE

The Easy Way If you have a multibutton mouse, you can use the software that came with it to program one of the buttons to perform a Control-click. Most people use the right mouse button. ■

GETTING HELP

Macs are very easy to use—that's probably one of the reasons you own one in the first place—and, of course, you've got this book to help you out when you do get stuck. But we don't have room here to cover everything you might need to know about how your Mac works, so it's a good thing that Apple has included its Help Center right in OS X Mavericks. A quick trip to the Help menu, maybe a search for a few relevant words, and you've got step-by-step instructions for any task that's puzzling you.

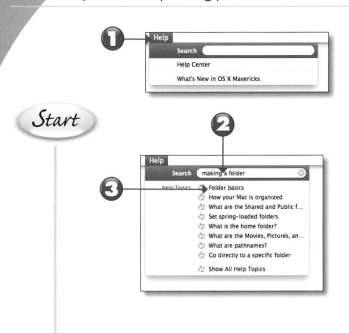

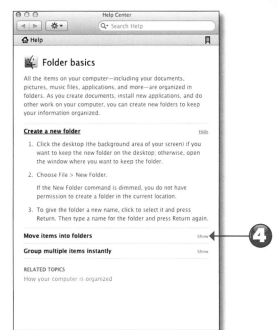

Start

1 In the Finder, click the **Help** menu.

2 Enter the words you want to search for in the **Search** field.

3 Choose a topic from the resulting list.

4 In the Help Center window, click **Show** to reveal details about the topics covered.

End

TIP

At a Loss for Words If you're not sure how to word the topic for which you want to search, click **Help Center** in the Help menu to open the Help Center's main screen. Then you can click through a table of contents to see what help is available. ■

TIP

You Have Options Click the gear menu at the top of the Help Center window to see options such as printing and changing the text size. You can also bookmark Help topics that you think you might want to return to often. ■

MOVING AND RESIZING WINDOWS

Mac OS X is full of windows: document windows, folder windows, more windows than you can count. The Finder shows you the contents of each folder or disk in a window. Each of your open documents—a picture, a text file, a web page, and so on—appears in a window, too. All these windows, whether they belong to the Finder or to the program in which you're viewing or editing a document, have certain features in common. Knowing how to get windows to go where you want them is an important skill you'll use every hour of your Mac's life.

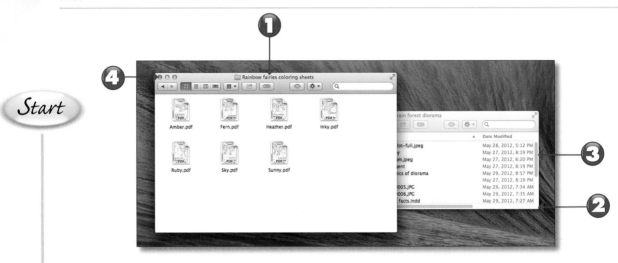

Start

① To move a window so you can see what's underneath it, click its title bar and drag the window to a new position.

② Click and drag either side, the bottom, or a corner of a window to change the window's size.

③ View the remaining contents of a window by clicking and dragging the scrollbars.

④ To close a window, click the red button at the left end of the window's title bar.

End

NOTE

More to Windows Than Meets the Eye Keep reading for more about wrangling windows. The next task shows how to minimize and maximize your windows, and the results might not be quite what you're expecting. ■

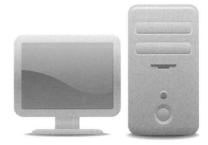

MINIMIZING AND MAXIMIZING WINDOWS

Although windows are a great way to look inside folders, they never seem to open at just the right size for what you're trying to see. Getting the most from your windows requires learning to maximize their size when you need them and minimize them out of sight when you don't.

Start

1 Click the green or **+ button** at the left end of a window's title bar to size the window so that it shows its entire contents—or as much as will fit on the screen.

2 Click the green or **+ button** again to return the window to its previous size.

3 Click the yellow or **– button** at the left end of a window's title bar to shrink the window downward into the right side of the Dock.

4 Click the window's thumbnail image in the Dock to put it back onto the desktop.

End

NOTE

Window Identification Each minimized window in the right side of the Dock has a small icon attached to its lower-right corner that identifies the program to which the window belongs. Folder and disk windows belong to the Finder, so they have a Finder logo. ■

NOTE

The Wonders of Windows The Dock continuously updates the appearance of minimized document windows. For example, if you minimize a movie window while the movie's playing, you can monitor the movie's progress while its window is in the Dock. ■

MANAGING MULTIPLE WINDOWS

By combining the features of Spaces (see the next task) and Exposé, and then adding a few tricks, Mission Control gives you a handy way to cut through window clutter instantly, no matter what program you're using. And if you tend to use a lot of programs at the same time, you'll definitely find these little magic tricks very useful. To invoke Mission Control, you can use the function keys, the row of F keys at the top of your keyboard.

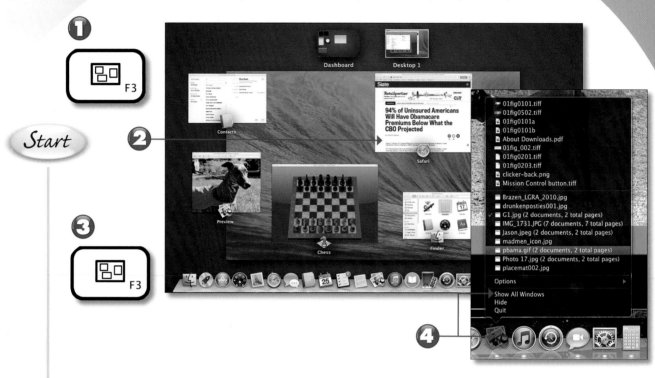

Start

To see all the open windows on your Mac, press the Mission Control button on your keyboard, or press **Ctrl-↑** if your Mac doesn't have a Mission Control button.

Click a window to select it and return all the windows to their normal size.

To close Mission Control without choosing a new window, press the Mission Control button or **Ctrl-↑** again.

To show all windows in a single application, click and hold the application's icon in the Dock; then choose **Show All Windows** or **Show Recents** from the shortcut menu.

Continued

TIP

Change It Up To change the shortcuts for Mission Control and Exposé, choose **Apple menu, System Preferences**, and then click **Mission Control**. ■

TIP

You Have Options If you have a multitouch-capable trackpad, swipe up on your trackpad with four fingers to open Mission Control. Swipe down again with three or four fingers to close Mission Control. ■

5 Click a thumbnail to move to that window; larger thumbnails represent the most recent files that you worked on.

6 To hide open windows from all programs so that you can see the desktop, press **Cmd-Mission Control** or **Fn-F11**.

7 When you're not in Mission Control, you can make a window active and hide the current application by pressing **Option** and clicking either the window or the Dock icon for its application.

End

TIP
Just Around the Corner The fastest way to invoke Mission Control is to simply move your mouse to a particular corner of the screen—using a hot corner. You can specify functions for hot corners in Mission Control's System Preferences. ■

TIP
Yours to Command You can switch applications quickly by pressing **Cmd-Tab** and, within many programs, you can switch document windows by pressing **Cmd-`** repeatedly until you get to the window you want. ■

USING CUSTOM DESKTOPS

Time to quit work and take a Solitaire break! But wait—if you close all your Finder and document windows, you'll have to open them all back up again when you return to work. There's a better way—change Desktops. You can set up custom configurations of programs and documents that appear when you switch to the appropriate Desktop, and slide neatly off the side of the screen when you switch to another Desktop. Switch back to the first Desktop, and there are all your windows, just waiting for you.

Start

① Press the **Mission Control** button on your keyboard, or press **Fn-F9** if your Mac doesn't have a Mission Control button, to open Mission Control.

② Move your cursor to the upper-right corner of the screen and click the + button that appears there to create a new Desktop.

③ Open programs and documents, and arrange windows to set up your custom workspace.

④ To move back and forth among Desktops, open Mission Control again and click the Desktop you want to use.

Continued

NOTE

Space for a Dashboard When you first open Mission Control, you'll notice that you already have two Desktops. The one on the right is your regular desktop, and the one on the left is Dashboard. Turn to "Adding New Dashboard Widgets," in Chapter 5 to learn more. ■

TIP

A Spacey Shortcut Flip back and forth among your different Desktops by holding down Control and pressing the arrow keys. Or press Control and a number to move directly to the Desktop with that number (as seen left to right on the Mission Control screen). Or, if you have a multitouch trackpad, just swipe back and forth with three fingers—how easy is that? ■

5 To move a window from one Desktop to another, click and drag the window off the edge of your screen toward the Desktop to which you want to move it.

6 To delete a Desktop, move the cursor over the Desktop's thumbnail and click the **X** in the thumbnail's upper-left corner.

7 To control which Desktop an application opens in, click and hold the application's Dock icon to show its contextual menu.

8 From the contextual menu, choose **Options**, **This Desktop** to keep the application in the current Desktop, **All Desktops** to make the application available in all Desktops, or **None** to make the application open in whatever Desktop you're currently using.

End

TIP

Too Much of a Good Thing Desktops are exciting when you first start using them, especially if you do several types of work on your Mac. How about a Desktop for work, with project folders open and Mail running? Or one for web surfing, with your browser and iChat open? Or even a minimalist Desktop with nothing at all open? But for efficiency's sake, don't set up more Desktops than you're actually going to use. With too many Desktops, it becomes too hard to remember what's where. ■

SETTING BASIC SYSTEM PREFERENCES

You can't customize everything about your Mac, but you can get darn close (for more customization techniques, turn to Chapter 5). Here's a look at the most basic preferences you'll want to set on a new Mac.

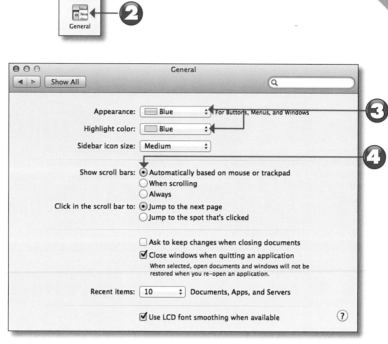

 Start

1 Choose **Apple menu**, **System Preferences**.

2 Click **General** to display the Appearance preferences.

3 Choose colors from the **Appearance** pop-up menu (for scrollbars, buttons, and menus) and the **Highlight Color** pop-up menu (for selected text and objects in list view).

4 Click a radio button to choose whether scrollbars always appear or only when they're needed. The Automatically setting makes the choice for you based on what kind of mouse or trackpad you use.

 Continued

NOTE

Blue Versus Graphite Your Appearance color preference starts out set to Blue. If you switch it to Graphite, all your dialog box buttons, menu highlights, and window components turn graphite gray. The only problem you might encounter with that setting is that the Close, Minimize, and Maximize buttons—normally red, yellow, and green, respectively—also turn gray. You can still tell them apart by placing the cursor over them; an X appears in the Close button, a minus sign in the Minimize button, and a plus sign in the Maximize button. ■

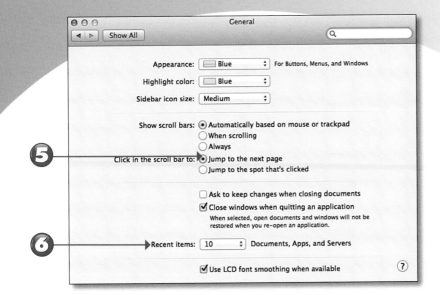

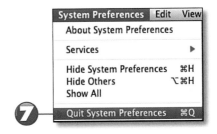

5 Click a radio button to choose how far clicking in the scrollbar scrolls the window.

6 Choose the number of recently used applications and documents that will appear in the Apple menu.

7 Choose **System Preferences**, **Quit System Preferences** to apply your changes.

End

TIP

Scroll, Scroll, Scroll Your Window Here's how the scrollbar settings work: **Jump to the next page** moves the view up or down one screen when you click in the scrollbar. With long documents, you might prefer **Jump to the spot that's clicked**, which moves the view to the location within the document that approximates the location of your click. In other words, click halfway down the scrollbar to see the document's midpoint. These settings apply within both application windows and folder windows in the Finder. ■

SETTING UP YOUR INTERNET CONNECTION

To set up your Internet connection, you'll need to find out a few things from your Internet service provider (ISP): your login name and password, possibly the ISP's DNS (Domain Name System) server addresses, and definitely the preferred configuration method.

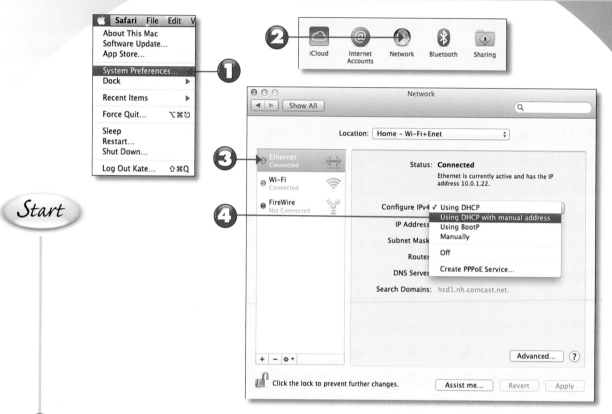

Start

1. Choose **Apple menu**, **System Preferences**.

2. Click the **Network** button to see your connection settings.

3. Choose your connection type from the column at the left of the window.

4. Choose your ISP's configuration method from the **Configure** pop-up menu: usually **Using PPP** for phone modems, **Manually** for LAN connections, or **Using DHCP** for cable and DSL modems.

Continued

NOTE

Talk to Me Transmission Control Protocol/Internet Protocol (TCP/IP) is the language in which your Mac communicates with the other computers on the Internet. The choices in the **Configure IPv4** menu are different ways of setting up a TCP/IP connection. PPP (Point-to-Point Protocol) is used for phone line connections, and DHCP (Dynamic Host Configuration Protocol) is used for broadband connections and internal networks. If your ISP doesn't use DHCP, you need to enter settings manually. ■

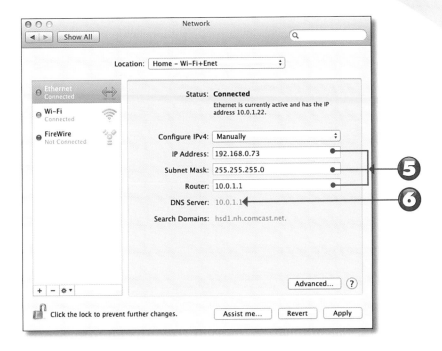

 If your configuration method is **Manually**, enter your IP address, the subnet mask, and the router address for your network.

 If the field is blank, enter your ISP's DNS server in the **DNS Server** field.

Continued

NOTE

Getting Help When You Need It If any of these settings don't make sense to you, get in touch with your ISP's tech support people. It's their job to help you make the connection, so stick with it until you have what you need. ■

NOTE

Don't Worry, Be Happy You might notice different tabs in the Network preferences pane, but don't worry. For example, when you're configuring Wi-Fi, you see Wi-Fi settings that don't appear when you're configuring Ethernet. ■

Click **Assist Me** if you're having trouble and want your Mac to walk you through the steps to set up your network.

Click **Diagnostics** if your existing network settings aren't working; click **Assistant** if you want help making the settings.

Follow the remaining steps in the Network Setup Assistant.

End

NOTE

If Your Mac Is a Laptop If you connect using different methods in different places, you should definitely look into creating custom locations so you don't have to change all these settings every time you switch connections (see Chapter 5). ■

NOTE

Status Quo After your network settings are in place, you shouldn't need to change them unless you buy new hardware (such as a router for Internet connection sharing) or your service provider changes the way its service is set up. ■

CONNECTING TO YOUR ISP

If you use a phone modem or a DSL modem with PPPoE, you need to initiate a connection when you want to go online. You can store more than one configuration, in case you connect in different ways at home, at work, and on the road. System Preferences always remembers the last connection you made.

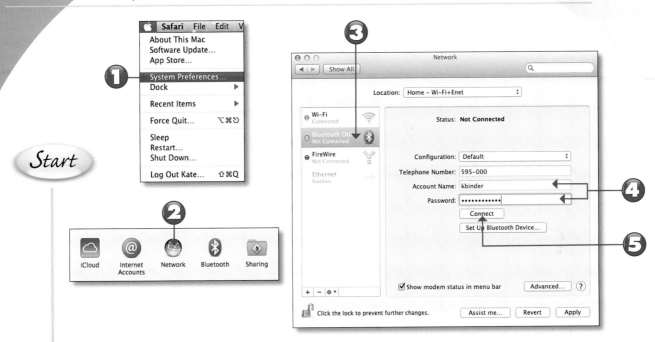

Start

1 Choose **Apple Menu**, **System Preferences**.

2 Click the **Network** button to see your connection settings.

3 Click to choose your modem.

4 Type in the connection data, including your username and password.

5 Click **Connect**.

End

TIP
Getting Offline You need to disconnect when you're done surfing and checking your email. Go back to System Preferences and you'll find that the **Connect** button has changed to a **Disconnect** button. Click that and you're offline again. ■

TIP
Status Symbol In System Preferences, check the box labeled **Show modem status in menu bar** to add a Modem Status menu to your menu bar. And in the **Modem Status** menu, choose **Show time connected** to display how long you've been online. ■

USING UNIVERSAL ACCESS

Universal Access provides alternative ways of viewing the Mac's screen, hearing the sounds it makes, using the keyboard, and using the mouse. For example, if you can't hear alert sounds, you can set the screen to flash instead, calling your attention to what's happening just as clearly as an alert sound would.

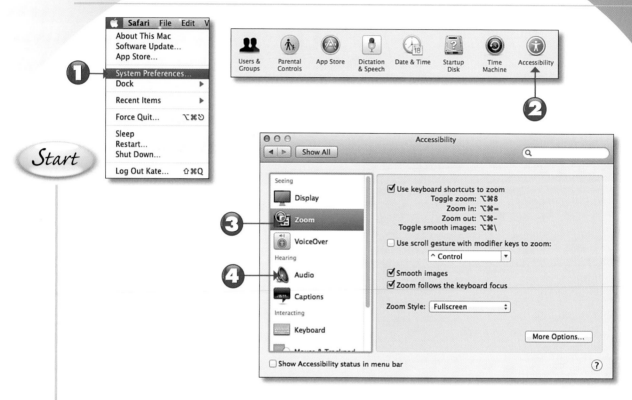

Start

1. Choose **Apple menu**, **System Preferences**.

2. Click **Accessibility**.

3. Click **Zoom** under Seeing and click to turn on the Zoom feature; to switch to white text on a black background, click **Display**.

4. Click **Audio** under Hearing and click the check box to flash the screen when an alert sound is played.

Continued

TIP
Universally Useful Universal Access is truly for everyone. Consider using its features to enlarge your cursor while giving on-screen presentations, to zoom in on tiny text while editing, and to enable you to continue working while you walk around your office for a bit of exercise. ■

NOTE
Yakkety Yak VoiceOver is the third setting in the Seeing section of the Universal Access preferences. This feature enables you to control your Mac with voice commands. Turn to the next task to learn more. ■

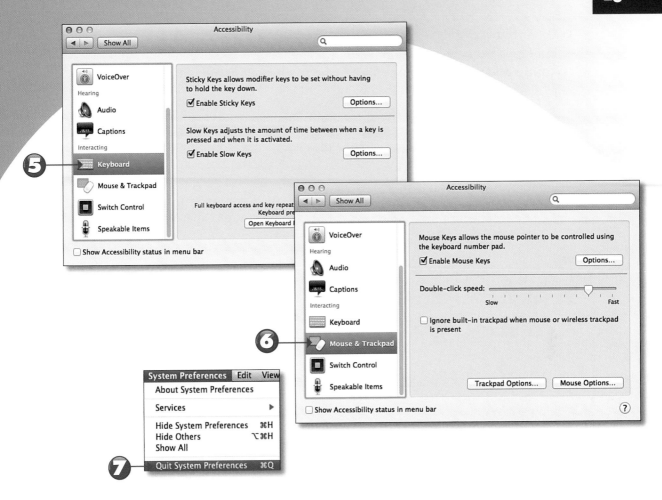

5 Click **Keyboard** under Interacting and choose from the various keyboard options.

6 Click **Mouse & Trackpad** under **Interacting** and choose from the various mouse options.

7 Choose **System Preferences**, **Quit System Preferences** to apply your changes.

End

NOTE

Devising Access for Devices If you use an assistive device such as a Braille screen or an alternative pointing device, you'll need to enable access for it in System Preferences' Security & Privacy panel. Click the **Privacy** tab, and then click **Accessibility** and choose which applications should make use of your device. ■

SETTING UP VOICEOVER

With VoiceOver, you can use the keyboard and Mac speech features to control your computer. Standard keyboard commands are augmented by special commands to enable you to start up, switch, and control programs, and to move around your hard drive.

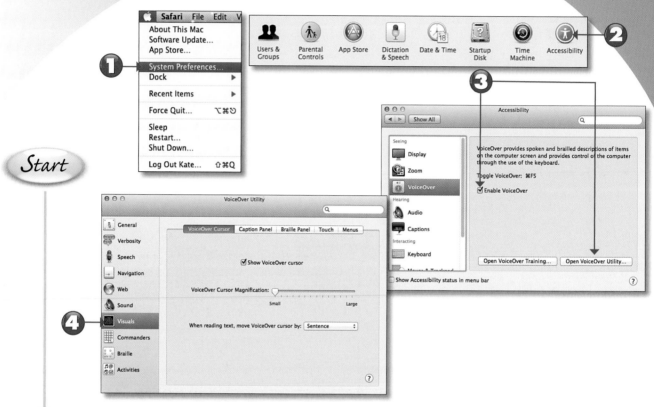

1 Choose **Apple menu**, **System Preferences**.

2 Click **Accessibility**.

3 Click the **Enable VoiceOver** check box to turn on VoiceOver, and then click **Open VoiceOver Utility** to configure VoiceOver settings.

4 In VoiceOver Utility, click **Visuals** to control when and how the VoiceOver feature is invoked.

Continued

NOTE

More or Less The Display settings determine how evident VoiceOver is as you use your Mac. For example, you can turn on the VoiceOver cursor to hear spoken descriptions of the objects and dialog boxes under your cursor, or you can turn off the cursor to hide this feature. ■

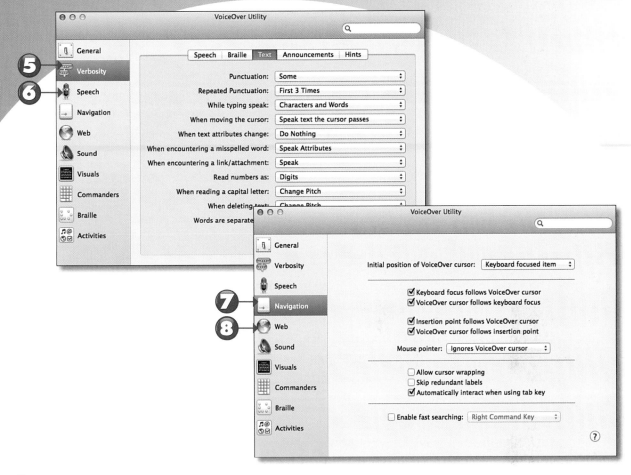

5 Click **Verbosity** to control how much VoiceOver talks.

6 Click **Speech** to change the voice VoiceOver uses.

7 Click **Navigation** to control how VoiceOver moves around your screen.

8 Click **Web** to set how VoiceOver interprets web pages for you.

End

TIP

PatienceOver The level of your Verbosity settings should be proportional to your patience. If you want to get moving without listening for very long, lower the **Item Description** and **Punctuation** settings. ■

Chapter 2

WORKING WITH DISKS, FOLDERS, AND FILES

The tasks in this chapter might not be glamorous or exciting, but they're the foundation of everything you do on your Mac. It's all about files, folders, and the disks that hold them. Every time you create a new document or receive an email attachment, that information is stored in a file on your hard drive, and the file is in turn stored within a folder. Mac OS X provides many ways for you to view and modify folder contents and file attributes, so you're in complete control of your Mac.

The tasks in this part teach you how to create new folders and view their contents in different ways, how to move and copy files, how to organize your hard drive and keep it uncluttered, and how to back up your hard drive with Time Machine.

You might notice that windows on your Mac OS X desktop have two distinct guises—a "plain" dress that looks like any document window and a "fancy" version that includes racks of buttons down the side and across the top. These are, respectively, multi-window mode and single-window mode. Don't be deceived, though—you can have windows of both types open at the same time. This important aspect of Mac OS X is covered in the first two tasks in this part.

VIEWING YOUR FILES AND FOLDERS

Use single-window mode, 30

Use multi-window mode, 31

Find files, 48

Change folder views, 34

Access favorite folders, 41

See a quick preview of any file, 45

Get information about files and folders, 47

Use Time Machine to back up and restore files, 52

USING SINGLE-WINDOW MODE

Traditionally, the Mac spawned a new window for each folder or disk you opened. Mac OS X introduced single-window mode, in which the contents of each folder or disk appear in the same window, like each successive page in a web browser displays in the same window. It took a little getting used to back when it first came out, but it's a better way of working.

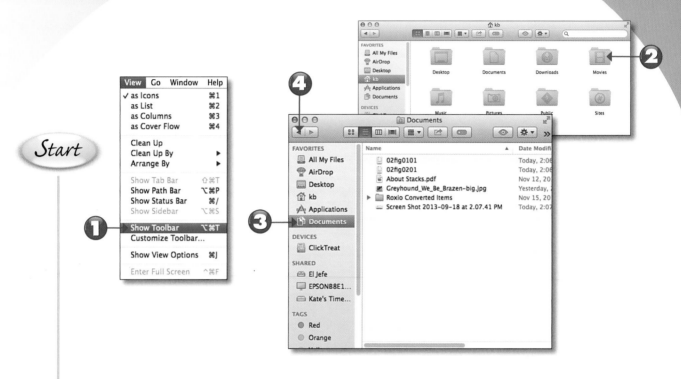

1. If you're using multi-window mode, choose **View**, **Show Toolbar** to switch to single-window mode and display the toolbar and sidebar.

2. Double-click folders in the main window to see their contents.

3. Click a folder or disk in the sidebar to see its contents.

4. Click the **left** and **right arrows** to go back and forward in the series of windows you've viewed (similar to the Back and Forward buttons in a web browser window).

End

TIP

Single Versus Multi Single-window mode is at its most useful when you need to see the contents of only one window. If you're copying or moving files from one folder to another, you'll probably find multi-window mode a better bet. Don't forget that you can switch window views in single-window mode by clicking the **Icon**, **List**, **Column**, and **Cover Flow** view buttons at the top of the window. Re-sort items in any view by choosing an option from the **Item Arrangement** menu. ■

USING MULTI-WINDOW MODE

Sometimes you need to see the contents of two windows at once, and it's easier to focus on what you need to look at without the sidebar and toolbar in single-window mode. Multi-window mode makes copying or moving files from one folder or disk to another easier.

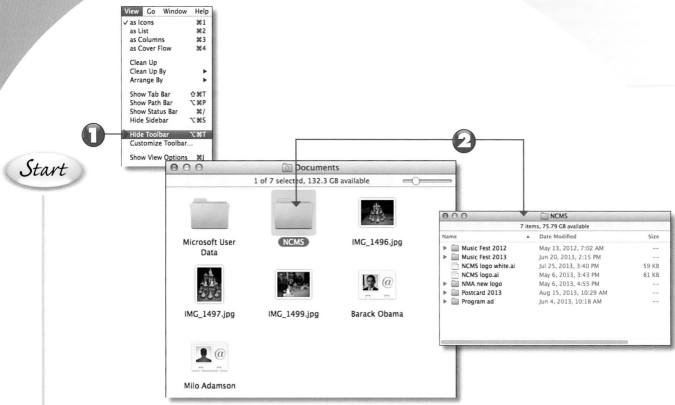

1 If you're using single-window mode, choose **View**, **Hide Toolbar** to switch to multi-window mode.

2 Double-click a folder in the window to open a new window showing its contents.

End

TIP

Quick Switch Even without the single-window mode toolbar, you can switch quickly from one window view to another. Click in a window and press ⌘-**1** for Icon view, ⌘-**2** for List view, ⌘-**3** for Column view, and ⌘-**4** for Cover Flow view. ■

TIP

Buttoning Up The other buttons in the toolbar include the **Share**, **Edit Tags**, **Quick Look**, and **Action** buttons. With these you can share files online via social media, customize your file tags (see "Creating and Editing Tags," later in this chapter), view a file in the Finder, and take various context-sensitive actions on your files. ■

USING THE TOOLBAR

In single-window mode, each window contains a toolbar that provides shortcuts to common tasks in the Finder, such as switching folder views and searching for files. After you get to know the toolbar, it quickly becomes your best friend. You can even customize it with your favorite buttons, too—see the next task.

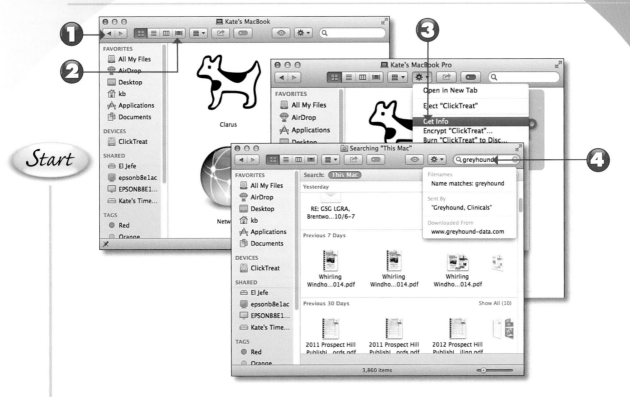

Start

1 Click the **Back** and **Forward** buttons to see the contents of folders you've looked at before in this window.

2 Click the **Icon View**, **List View**, **Column View**, or **Cover Flow** button to change your folder view.

3 Choose an option from the **Action** menu to perform one of several common tasks.

4 Type in the **Search** field to search for files and folders by name.

End

NOTE

Where to Look The toolbar's Search field automatically starts out by searching your entire system. But as soon as the search begins, a toolbar pops up, giving you a choice of other locations. If you can narrow down the search location, the search will go faster. ■

TIP

Action Figures The commands available in the **Action** menu vary depending on what's selected. For example, if you click a disk icon, the **Action** menu adds an **Eject** command. Be sure to explore your **Action** menu options. ■

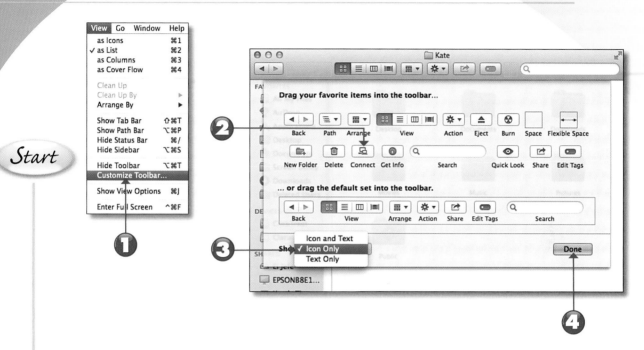

CUSTOMIZING THE TOOLBAR

Because the toolbar is intended to make life easier for you, the individual Mac user, you can choose the buttons you want to display in the toolbar. You can also change the appearance and contents of the icons in the sidebar that's visible whenever the toolbar is visible; see "Accessing Your Favorite Files and Places" later in this chapter.

1 Choose **View**, **Customize Toolbar**.

2 Drag buttons onto the toolbar to add them.

3 Choose an option from the **Show** pop-up menu.

4 Click **Done**.

End

TIP

Back Where You Started When you're customizing your toolbar, you can restore the default set of buttons by dragging the whole set from the bottom of the Customize dialog up to the toolbar. ■

TIP

Cutting Back To remove buttons from the toolbar, choose **View**, **Customize Toolbar** and drag the buttons you don't want off the toolbar. ■

USING DIFFERENT FOLDER VIEWS

You can view Finder windows in four ways. Icon view is convenient when a folder contains just a few files and you want to be able to tell them apart quickly. List view enables you to sort the contents of a window, and column view provides a quick way of burrowing down into a series of nested folders. The glamorous Cover Flow view speaks for itself.

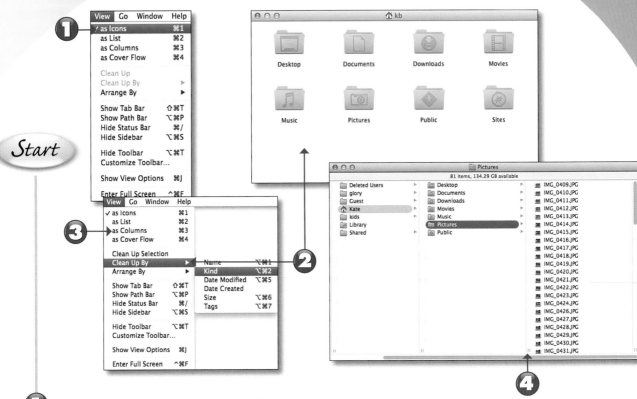

Start

① To switch to icon view, choose **View**, **As Icons**.

② If the icons are stacked on top of each other, choose **View**, **Clean Up By** to space them out so you can see them all.

③ To switch to column view, choose **View**, **As Columns**.

④ Drag the bar between two columns to adjust the columns' width.

Continued

TIP

Wide Angle View To adjust column widths in column view, drag the small divider line at the bottom of the column divider. It's only visible if the column contains a list of files and folders; you can't adjust empty columns. ∎

TIP

Getting There Via Buttons In single-window mode, you can click the buttons in the upper-left corner of the window to switch window views. Turn to the task "Using Single-Window Mode," earlier in this chapter, to learn more about using single-window mode. ∎

5 To switch to list view, choose **View, As List**.

6 Drag the right edge of a list column header to change that column's width, or drag a column header to a different position to change the order of the columns.

7 To switch to Cover Flow view, choose **View, As Cover Flow**.

8 Click an image at the top of the window to see its information in the lower half of the window.

End

TIP
If you want to change which columns are visible in List view, choose **View, Show View Options** and check boxes to choose which columns show up in the active window. ■

TIP
Switch Hitting Lists can be sorted in ascending or descending order. Click the active column header to switch from ascending to descending order or vice versa. A triangle in the active column header indicates which way the list is sorted. ■

SELECTING FILES

It might seem obvious, but before you can do anything with a file, folder, or disk in the Finder, you must select it so that the Finder knows which object(s) you want it to act on. A couple of selection methods enable you to select more than one item at a time while leaving out those you don't want to use at the moment.

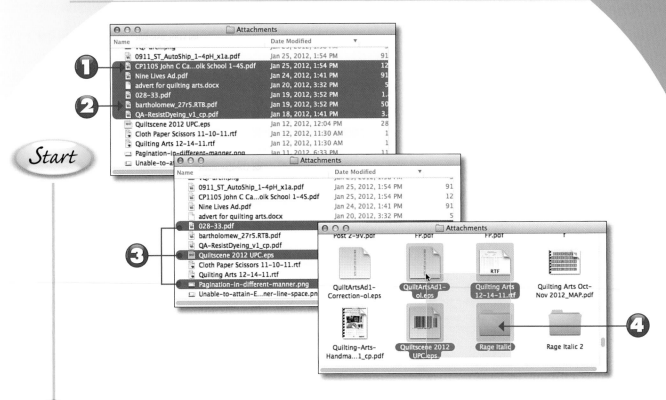

Start

1 In any folder view, click a file or folder to select it.

2 **Shift-click** another file or folder to select it along with all the items between it and the first object you selected.

3 ⌘**-click** to select noncontiguous items.

4 In Icon view, click and drag to select a group of icons.

End

TIP

Selecting Everything at One Time To select all the items in a folder (or on the desktop), click the folder's title bar to make sure it is the active folder; then either press ⌘-A or choose **Edit, Select All.** ■

MOVING AND COPYING FILES AND FOLDERS

Keeping your computer tidy is mostly a matter of putting things where they belong. That means moving and copying files and folders to different locations. You have to be authorized to open folders to which you're copying items, which means you can't put files in other users' folders, for the most part.

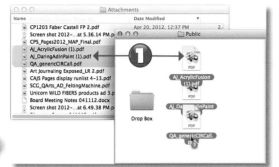

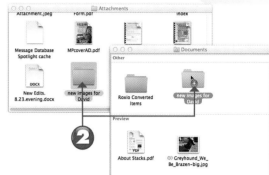

Start

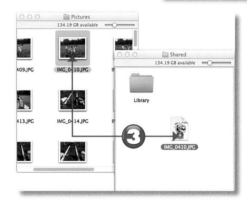

① To move an item to another folder on the same disk, drag and drop it into the folder's window.

② To copy an item to a location on a different disk, drag and drop it into the folder's window. The green + on its icon indicates that you are copying rather than moving.

③ To copy an item to a different location on the same disk, press **Option** while you drag and drop it into the folder's window.

End

TIP
Another Way to Copy To make a copy of an item in the same place, press **Option** and drag the icon a little away from its current location or choose **File, Duplicate**. ■

TIP
Using Copy and Paste to Copy Files Control-click the file you want to copy, and choose **Copy** from the menu. **Control-click** in an open area of the folder's window where you want to put the copy and choose **Paste Item**. ■

MAKING A NEW FOLDER

This is one task that often trips up people who are used to older Mac systems in which you used to press ⌘-N to create a new folder. Now that keyboard shortcut brings up a new Finder window instead of creating a new folder. You'll get used to the change, and you'll find that being able to create new Finder windows this way is pretty useful, too.

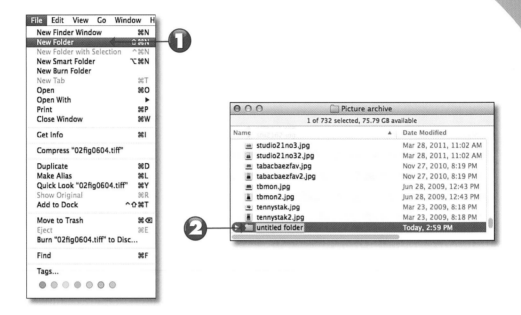

1 To create a new folder, choose **File**, **New Folder** (or press ⌘-**Shift-N**).

2 Type a name for the untitled folder; to change the name, see the next task.

TIP

You Don't Have to Start from Scratch If you need several folders with the same name and, perhaps, a different number tacked onto the end of each, create the first one and create copies of it as described earlier in the task "Moving and Copying Files and Folders." Then replace "copy" in the folder name with the numbers or text you want. ■

RENAMING FOLDERS AND FILES

Some people like to include dates and similar information in filenames so anyone can tell what's inside; others don't care if anyone else can make sense of their filenames. Whichever camp you fall into, you'll need to know how to change the names of files and folders so that they make sense to *you*.

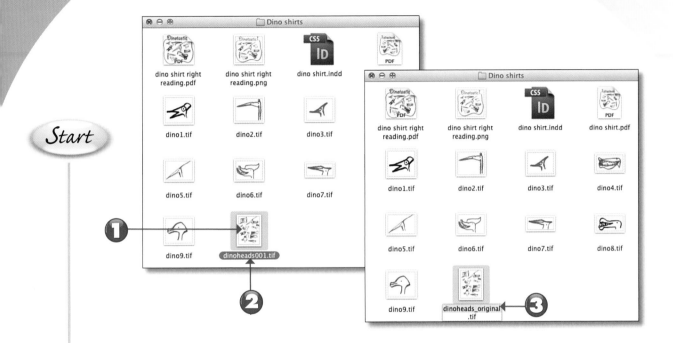

1 Click to select the item whose name you want to change.

2 Keep the mouse cursor positioned over the name.

3 When the item's name becomes highlighted, type to replace the old name with the new one. Press **Enter** when you're done.

End

TIP

Extended Filenames Each filename has two components: the name and the extension, such as .pdf or .doc. Mac OS X uses extensions to determine which program can open which files, so don't change an extension unless you know what you're doing. ■

CAUTION

Adding Extensions Hate documents with blank, white icons? You can't open them by double-clicking because your Mac doesn't know which program to use. If you know which kind of document it is, add the correct filename extension. ■

USING TABBED WINDOWS

Tabbed folder windows are like tabbed browser windows (see page 180), all about efficiency. When you want to look at two different places on your hard drive, but you don't want to have two windows open cluttering up your screen, you can now try out this new feature introduced in OS X Mavericks.

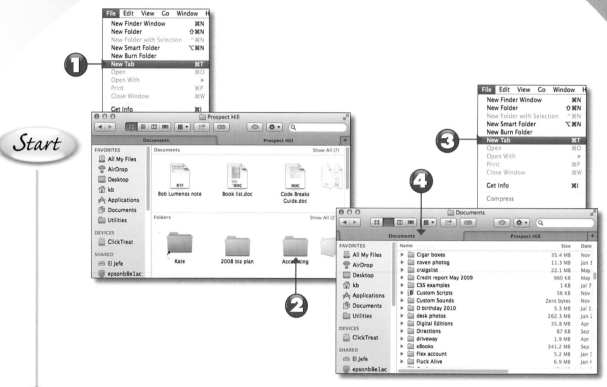

Start

End

1 With a Finder window open in single-window mode, choose **File**, **New Tab** or press ⌘-T.

2 Navigate to any folder location within this tab.

3 Choose **File**, **New Tab** again to add another tab. You can choose the content of new tabs in the Finder preferences.

4 Click a tab to view that location's contents.

TIP

E Pluribus Unum If you've already got a lot of windows open in the Finder, you can merge them all into a single tabbed window by choosing **Window, Merge All Windows**. ■

TIP

Getting It There To move a file from one window tab to another, just drag it over the second tab's title bar and release. ■

ACCESSING YOUR FAVORITE FILES AND PLACES

Mac OS X offers a way to store and access your favorites. They're visible in a column called the Places sidebar at the left side of every window when you're using single-window mode. The lower section of the Places list contains disks attached to your Mac, and the top section contains anything you want.

Start

End

1. If you don't see the Places sidebar, choose **View**, **Show Toolbar** to enter single-window mode.

2. Click a disk or folder to view its contents in the window.

3. Drag files or folders into or out of the upper section of the Places sidebar, labeled Favorites, to customize it.

NOTE

Quick Copy, Quick Move You can move or copy files to disks or folders in the Places sidebar by dragging them from the main section of the window over a disk or folder icon in the sidebar. ■

TIP

Customizing the Custom List To change the order of items in the top half of the Places sidebar, just drag and drop them into the order you prefer. Drag items out of the upper section of the Places sidebar to remove them from the list. ■

TAGGING FILES WITH CATEGORIES

The Mac OS Finder is very, very good at finding things using Spotlight, either from the menu bar or right in a Finder window. And now Spotlight has gotten even smarter because you can assign your own categories—called *tags*—to files to group them in a way that makes sense to you. Each file can have multiple tags, and you can assign tags in any of several ways.

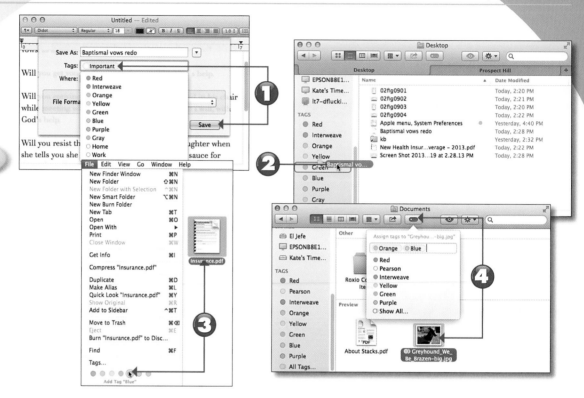

Start

1 When saving a file, click in the **Tags** field and choose a tag to assign it to that file, then press Enter.

2 Drag a file to a tag in the **Places** sidebar to assign the tag to it.

3 Select a file, then choose **File** and pick a tag from the bottom of the menu to assign that tag to the file.

4 In single-window mode, select a file and click the **Edit Tags** button to assign a tag to that file.

End

NOTE

Wait, What? Not sure what the point of tags is? Think of them as similar to the categories assigned to posts on your favorite blog. You can click the Recipe tag to view all the posts containing recipes. Similarly, you can categorize your files in a way that makes sense to you—for example, you might have categories for your work, the kids' school, your church, a social club, and your personal projects. That way you can quickly find all the files relating to each of those subjects without having to keep them in the same place on your hard drive. And it's easy to assign tags when you first save a file, so you really don't have an excuse not to be organized any more. ■

SEARCHING FOR TAGGED FILES

When you want to locate a group of files that you've tagged, you have a choice of ways to search for that tag. Your Mac will show you all the files on its hard drive that use the tag or combination of tags on which you're searching, and it will include any files you have saved in iCloud using the iWork programs (Numbers, Pages, and Keynote).

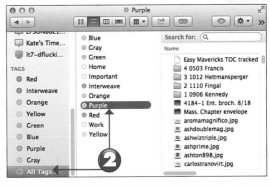

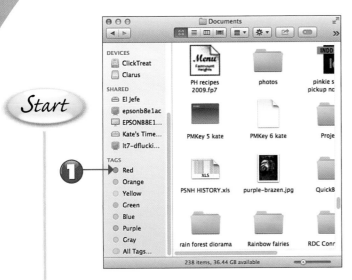

Start

 Click a tag in the Places sidebar to view all files using that tag.

 If you don't see the tag you want to search for in the Places sidebar, click **All Tags**, and then click the tag on which you want to search.

3 To search for multiple tags at once, type their names into the **Spotlight** search field.

End

NOTE

What's Old Is (Not) New Versions of the Mac OS before Mavericks didn't support tags, but they had a similar but limited feature called Labels. So, if you move a tagged file to a Mac running an older system, that file shows up as labeled with the most recent tag color you applied. ■

TIP

Here and There Don't forget that the Places sidebar and the Spotlight search field appear in Open dialogs—so you can search for files using their tags or any other attributes without having to go back to the Finder. ■

CREATING AND EDITING TAGS

If you've taken a liking to tags for their organizational prowess, you'll be pleased to know you can create as many tags as you want—although they'll all have to share the same limited number of colors. Apple's default set of tags includes seven color names (which you can change to suit your needs) and three basic categories: Home, Work, and Important.

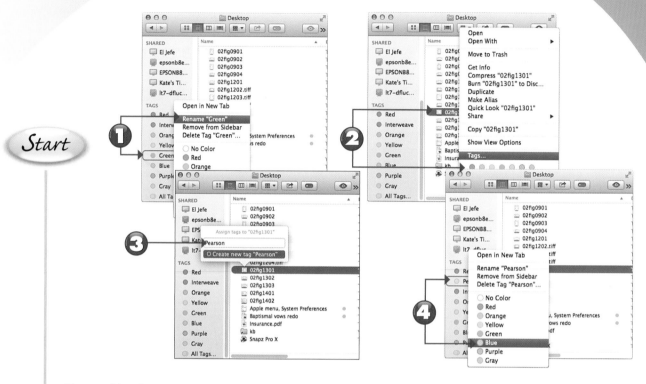

1. To quickly change a tag's name, Ctrl-click it in the **Places** sidebar and choose **Rename** from the contextual menu, then type your new name and press **Enter**.

2. To create a new tag, select the file and choose **File**, **Tags**.

3. Type the new tag name into the text field and press **Enter**.

4. To assign a color to the new tag, Ctrl-click it in the **Places** sidebar and choose a color from the contextual menu.

TIP

First Among Equals All tags may be important, but some are *definitely* more important than others, so you can choose which tags show up by default in your Places sidebar. Choose **Finder**, **Preferences** and click the **Tags** tab, then drag the most important tags to the Favorite Tags row at the bottom of the window. ■

NOTE

One More Than a Rainbow Having only these basic colors to choose from for your tags may feel limiting. But remember, you can apply multiple tags, which means you can search on tag combinations as well as single tags. ■

PREVIEWING A FILE

If you're looking through a lot of files at one ⸻ ⸻ ⸻ t be enough to help you figure out exactly what's ⸻ ⸻ a Mac OS X feature that enables you to see the c⸻ ⸻ can flip through each page, and you can even s⸻ ⸻ look.

1 Click a file to select ⸻

2 Choose **File**, **Quick Look** ⸻

3 To view the document in full-screen mode, click the double arrows at the upper-right corner of the window.

4 To close the Quick Look window, click the **X** button.

End

TIP

Quick Navigation To enlarge the preview image, drag the corner of the window to make it bigger—the image will expand to fill the window. Use the scroll bar on the window's right side to move through the document's pages. ∎

TIP

Give Me My Space A quick way to take a Quick Look at one or more selected files in the Finder is to press the spacebar. Press the spacebar again to close the Quick Look window. ∎

OPENING A FILE

When you're looking at a file's icon in the Finder, you can open that file in the correct program without having to first start up the program. Conversely, if you're already using that program, you can open more files without having to return to the Finder to locate them.

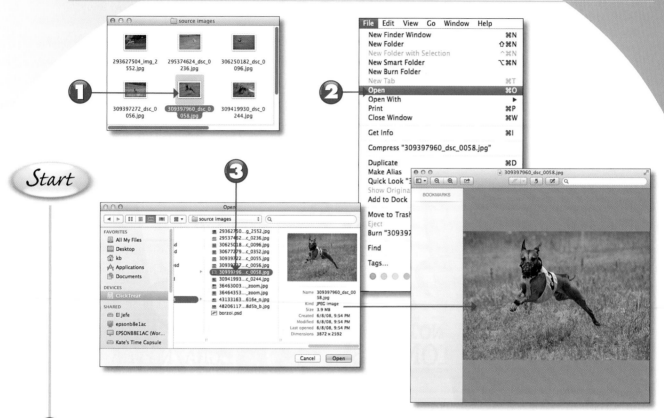

Start

 In the Finder, double-click the file's icon. The file opens in the program that created it or the program that it's currently assigned to.

 Or, to open a file from within a running program, choose **File**, **Open**.

3 Navigate to the file in the pick list and double-click it or click the **Open** button. The file opens in the program.

End

TIP

Programs Some programs are picky about which types of files they'll open, so your file might be unavailable in an Open dialog box. If a pop-up menu below the pick list has an option such as Show All Files, choose this option to make your file available. ■

NOTE

It's a Drag A third method of opening a file is to drag it on top of a program icon, either in the Finder or in the Dock. The program starts up, if it wasn't already running, and opens the file if it can. If it can't, its icon won't darken. ■

VIEWING FILE INFORMATION

Each file or folder on your computer has a lot of information associated with it—not just the data it contains, such as recipes or pictures or programming code, but also data about the file, such as when it was created, the last time it was modified, and which program made it.

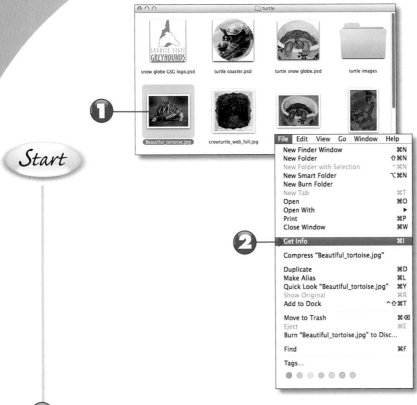

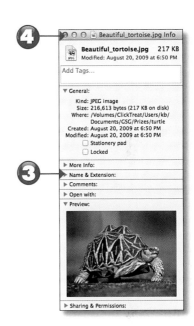

 Start

1 Click a file to select it.

2 Choose **File**, **Get Info**.

3 The Info window opens to the General pane; to see the contents of another pane, click the gray triangle next to its name.

4 Click the **Close** button to close the Info window when you're done.

End

TIP

Avoiding a Trip to the Menu Bar You can also press ⌘-I or use a contextual menu to get information about an item. ■

NOTE

Getting Info You can change some file information in the Info window, if you're the owner of a file. You can change the name and extension, the program that opens a document, and the file's ownership (if you're an admin user), and you can add tags and comments to help you find that document in Spotlight later on. ■

FINDING FILES WITH SPOTLIGHT

Spotlight is a powerful and speedy search utility. Built into the Finder, it's always waiting for you in the upper-right corner of the screen. After it finds what you're looking for, Spotlight doesn't stop there; it organizes its results into categories and sorts them any way you like.

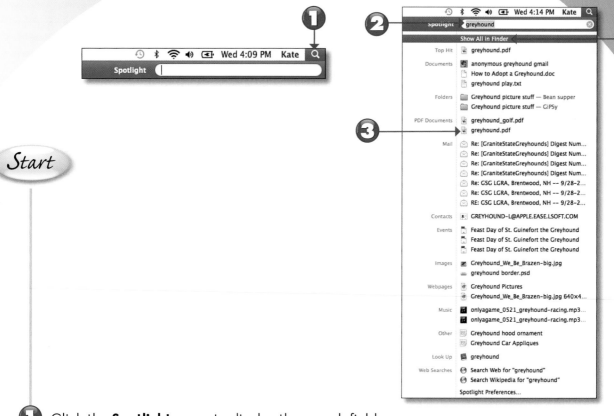

Start

1. Click the **Spotlight** menu to display the search field.

2. Enter search terms in the field.

3. Click a document in the results to open it.

4. Click **Show All in Finder** to see more results.

Continued

TIP

Talking Your Language Spotlight is even smarter than it looks. Try adding natural-language search terms, such as "yesterday" (for files modified yesterday) or "image" (for image files), to narrow your searches. ■

5 Click **Add** to display a filter menu for your search results.

6 Use the menus at the top of the window to filter the search results by time, location, or other criteria.

7 Click a column header to sort the results differently.

8 Double-click an item in the list to open the file.

End

TIP

What's It Look Like? You can use any of the four view modes to sort through your results; Cover Flow and Icon view work particularly well when you're searching for an image. ■

TIP

It's a Long Way to the Menu Bar If you don't want to make the trip all the way up to the right-hand end of the menu bar with your mouse, you can also perform a Spotlight search in any Finder window that's in single-window mode. ■

CREATING A SMART FOLDER

A smart folder collects related files into a single folder without moving the files from their original locations. One way to use a smart folder is to collect all the text modified in the last week so you can keep track of the files you're currently working on.

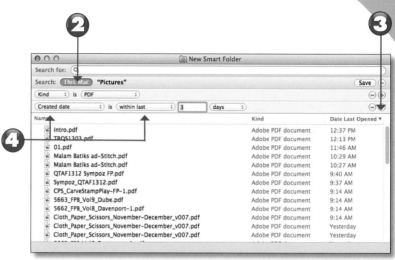

Start

1 Choose **File, New Smart Folder**.

2 Click to specify a location for the files you want to track in this folder.

3 Click **Add** to display filter menus for the files that will be shown in the smart folder.

4 Select a search criteria category and make a setting within that category; after you've created your filters, you can click **Remove** to delete a folder.

Continued

TIP

On-the-Fly Smarts The system adds files to the smart folder as soon as you start setting search criteria. Don't worry about ending up with the wrong files in your smart folder, though; as you change the criteria, the folder's contents are updated to reflect the new criteria. ■

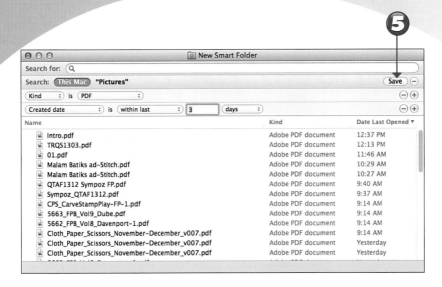

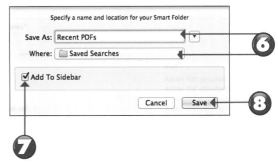

5 Click **Save**.

6 Enter a name and select a location for the folder.

7 Check **Add To Sidebar** if you want the folder to appear in the sidebar when you're using single-window mode.

8 Click **Save**.

End

TIP

Narrowing It Down In addition to a file's attributes, you can filter files for a smart folder based on text search terms. For example, to include files that contain the word *Apple* in the folder, enter that text in the search field at the top of the folder's window. ■

TIP

For Geeks Only (Not!) To get really specific about the kinds of files in your smart folder, choose **Other** from any search attribute pop-up menu. In the dialog box, choose attributes. To add the selected attribute to the pop-up menu, check **Add to Favorites**. ■

SETTING UP BACKUP DRIVES

If you were to learn only one thing from this book, that thing should be how to back up your files. Fortunately, Mac OS X puts Time Machine at your disposal, which makes it utterly simple to back up and retrieve files on your Mac. It keeps copies of all the versions of each file, so you can see exactly how your Mac looked in the past and retrieve files from that date.

Start

1 Choose **Apple menu**, **System Preferences**.

2 Click the **Time Machine** button to see your backup settings.

3 Click **Select Backup Disk** to choose a hard drive where Time Machine can store backed-up files.

Continued

TIP

Better Safe Than Sorry If at all possible, use a drive for Time Machine that doesn't have any files already stored on it. For one thing, you want the maximum amount of room available for backup files. For another, it's a remote possibility that Time Machine might overwrite your files. ■

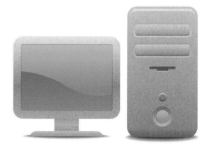

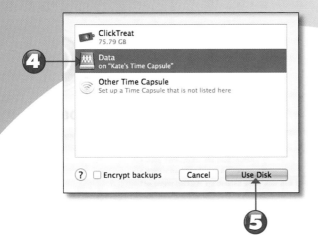

4 Choose a disk in the list.

5 Click **Use Disk**. If your backup drive is a Time Capsule, you'll be asked to enter its password.

6 To add another backup disk, repeat steps 3 and 4.

7 In the resulting dialog, click **Use Both** to use each backup disk in rotation.

End

TIP
More Is Better Your backup disk won't do you much good if it turns out to be corrupt—and you won't find that out until you need the files it contains. Always use multiple drives and rotate them if you can possibly swing it. ■

TIP
I Said No To save space on your backup drive you can add disks or folders to the Exclude list in the Time Machine preferences—click **Options** to get there. These items will be ignored when Time Machine backs up the rest of your files. ■

RESTORING BACKED-UP FILES

You know right where the file was. You're sure of it. You even know when and why you deleted it—but now you need it back. Fortunately for you, your Time Machine can solve your problem. All you have to do is take a look at past versions of your hard drive and choose the files you want to resurrect.

Start

1 Open the folder where the file you want was previously located; then click **Time Machine**.

2 Click back and forth through the previous versions of that folder to find a backup in which the file still exists.

3 Click to select the file you want.

4 Click **Restore** to return the file to your present-day Mac.

End

TIP

Take Me There If you know exactly what date you're looking for in Time Machine, click the bars on the right side of the screen to choose a specific backup date. You'll zoom right to the state of your Mac on that date. ■

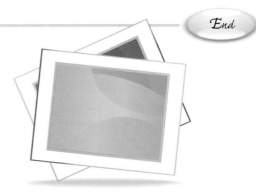

DELETING A FILE

Mac OS X stores files you don't want any more in a trash can. You can rummage through the Trash to retrieve files you didn't mean to discard, just as you can in the real world. But—again, just like the real world—the Trash doesn't empty itself; you have to remember to empty it to truly delete the discarded files.

Start

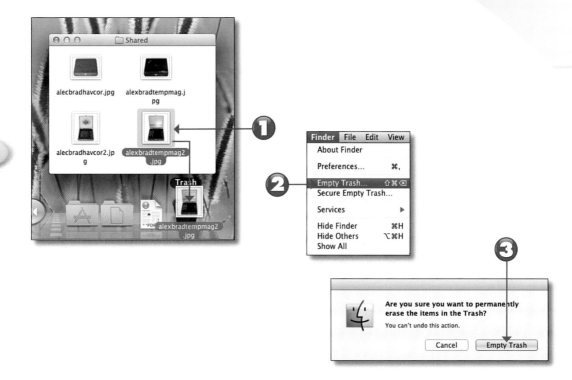

1 Drag the file to the **Trash** icon on the Dock and drop it when the Trash icon is highlighted.

2 To delete all the objects in the Trash, choose **Finder**, **Empty Trash**.

3 Click **Empty Trash** in the confirmation dialog box or **Cancel** to keep the items in the Trash.

End

NOTE

Here a File, There a File Applications leave files all over the place, so if you want to uninstall a program, you may need to do more than just drag the program's icon to the Trash. Consider using a clean-up utility such as AppCleaner (www.freemacsoft.net/appcleaner/). ▪

TIP

Deleting Files Securely To make sure your files are removed from your hard drive, choose **Finder**, **Secure Empty Trash**. Secure Empty Trash writes gibberish data over the files so they can never be found, even by "computer detectives." ▪

INSTALLING AND USING APPLICATIONS

It's the programs that make using your Mac worthwhile, whether they're the applications that come with Mac OS X (such as Preview, TextEdit, and Safari) or the ones you buy and install yourself (such as Microsoft Word, Adobe Photoshop, or your favorite games). Apple even sells two collections of programs designed just for home and business users, called iLife (with iMovie, iPhoto, and GarageBand) and iWork (featuring Pages for page layout, Numbers for spreadsheets, and Keynote for presentations).

Some programs come with a special installer program that puts all their pieces in the right places. Other programs are so simple that you can just drag and drop them into your Applications or Utilities folder, and programs you buy in the App Store are downloaded and installed automatically. You can store programs in any folder you want, technically, but it's easier to find everything if you stick to the designated folders.

Some applications are, of course, commercially produced, with thick manuals and lots of shrinkwrap. But you may find your favorites turn out to be freeware or shareware—programs you download, try out, and then pay for if you keep using them. Be sure to pay your shareware fees, and check out MacUpdate.com for the most comprehensive listing of downloadable Mac software anywhere on the Web.

MAC OS X PROGRAMS

Create text documents with TextEdit, 68–69

Buy and install new applications from the App Store, 60–61

Apply text formatting with the Fonts panel, 70–71

Switch programs with the Dock, 74

Locate and start up programs, 62

INSTALLING PROGRAMS

Some Mac programs that you download or install from a disc are small enough that you can drag them off their discs right into the Applications folder, but others require an installer program to make sure all their pieces get to the right places. When you run Installer, you have to enter an admin password to authorize the installation. Of course, you should never run an installer program that you didn't download yourself!

Start

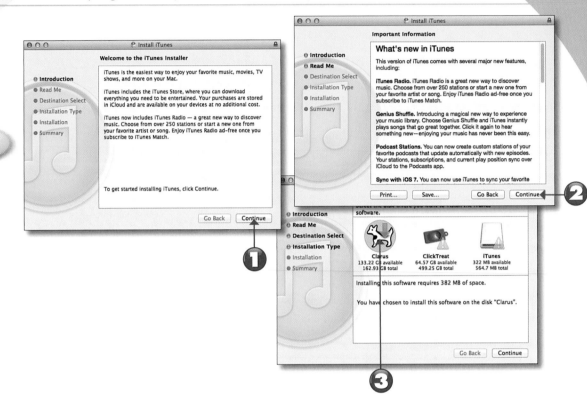

After you read each screen of the installer, click the **Continue** button at the bottom of the window to move to the next screen.

Read the program information and the license agreement; then click **Continue**.

If you have more than one hard drive, choose the drive where you want to install the software.

Continued

NOTE

Applications in the Applications Folder You can install programs anywhere you want, but it's best to put them in the Applications folder on your startup drive. That way, all users of your Mac can run the programs. ■

NOTE

Just Checking Many installers start out by asking your permission to run a program to see whether the program can be installed on your Mac. If you see a dialog like this, just click **OK** to confirm that you downloaded and want to install the program. ■

 Click **Install** to begin the installation process.

Enter an admin username and password to authorize the installation and click **Install Software**.

When the installation is complete, click **Close** to quit Installer.

 The application's icon now appears in the Applications folder (or whatever folder you chose).

End

NOTE

Installation Options Many installer scripts ask you to choose whether to install optional software such as sample files, fonts, or bonus features. The Easy Install or Full Install option usually installs everything that's available. ■

NOTE

Easy Uninstalling Some installer programs have an Uninstall option in case you decide you no longer want the software installed on your Mac. Using an installer to uninstall programs ensures that all the extra pieces scattered through your system are uninstalled. ■

SHOPPING IN THE APP STORE

In the App Store, Mac users can shop for fun and useful applications with the click of a mouse, then download and install new programs automatically, and keep them updated to the latest versions. Be sure to watch for sales and promotional offers for free apps!

Start

1 Find App Store in the Applications folder and double-click to start it up, or click the App Store icon in the Dock (if it's there).

2 Click **Featured**, **Top Charts**, or **Categories** to browse through the selection of applications.

3 Enter terms in the search field to search for a particular app.

4 Click an app's icon to see more information about it.

Continued

NOTE

You Gotta Pay The App Store works just like iTunes—you can pay for your purchases with gift cards or a credit card, and your account uses your Apple ID. Click **Account** or **Redeem** under Quick Links to enter your credit card information or redeem a gift card. ■

TIP

Wishing on an App If you think you've purchased an app in the App Store before and then deleted it from your computer but you're not sure, try adding it to your wish list. The App Store won't let you add previously purchased items. ■

5 Click the price to purchase and download an app. (Some apps are free.)

6 Click **Purchases** to see a list of the apps you've already downloaded via the App Store.

7 Click **Install** to redownload an app.

8 Click **Updates** to see whether any of your App Store purchases have new versions that you can download and install.

End

NOTE

You Got It The App Store figures out what Apple programs you already have installed on your Mac and adds them to your Purchased list. This way you don't accidentally buy apps you already have, and you can update those apps through the App Store. ■

NOTE

Getting Around Use the arrow buttons at the upper-left corner of the App Store window to move back and forth from screen to screen, just as you would in Safari or iTunes. On app description pages, you can see screen shots at the bottom of the page—click the thumbnails to see each screen shot at full size. ■

STARTING APPLICATIONS WITH LAUNCHPAD

Launchpad provides a quick and amazingly intuitive way to see what programs you've got installed on your Mac and start up any of them with a single click, displaying all your apps in a neat grid that disappears as soon as you make your choice. Launchpad adds and deletes apps automatically to match what's installed.

Start

esc

1 Click the **Launchpad** icon in the Dock to see all your applications.

2 Click a dot to move to another screen full of apps.

3 Click an app's icon to start up that program.

4 Press **Esc** to exit Launchpad without starting any app.

End

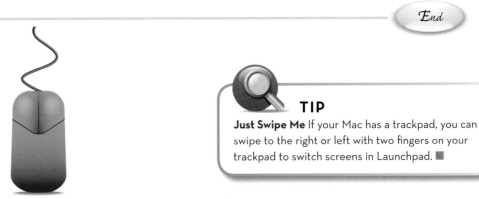

TIP

Just Swipe Me If your Mac has a trackpad, you can swipe to the right or left with two fingers on your trackpad to switch screens in Launchpad. ■

ORGANIZING APPLICATIONS WITH LAUNCHPAD

Even though Launchpad is about as neat a presentation as you could wish for, if you have a lot of apps, it can still be hard to get a handle on what you've got and find what you want. Fortunately, you can arrange the Launchpad screens to suit your own organizational preferences, and you can add as many screens as you want.

Start

End

1 Click the **Launchpad** icon in the Dock to see all your applications.

2 Click an app's icon and drag it off the right or left edge of the screen to move it to another screen of apps.

TIP
Begone, App! If you want to delete an application from your Mac completely, you can click and hold its icon in Launchpad until you see an X at its upper-left corner. Click the **X** to delete the program. Be careful! Don't click the **X** unless you're absolutely sure you don't want that app anymore. ■

TIP
Folded Space Combine related apps into folders by dragging one icon over another. Launchpad suggests a name for the folder, but you can change the name to whatever you like. Click a folder to see the apps it contains. ■

USING APPS IN FULL-SCREEN MODE

Years ago, Apple's Multifinder was an incredible innovation—you could run more than one program at a time, and you could see windows from all your running apps simultaneously. Now that computers can run dozens of programs at the same time, though, all those windows can really clutter up your screen. Full-screen mode fixes that.

 Click the double arrows in the corner of a window to expand that window to fill the whole screen.

Continued

NOTE

Where'd That Come From? OS X has borrowed its full-screen mode from iOS, the system that runs on Apple's smaller devices such as the iPhone, iPad, and iPod touch. ■

TIP

Full-Screen Spaces For distraction-free multitasking, which may be an oxymoron, try combining full-screen mode with Spaces to set up multiple workspaces, each focused on a single app. ■

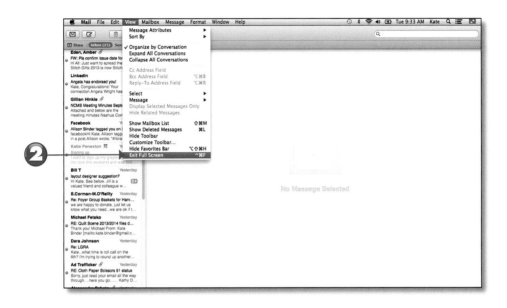

  Choose **View, Exit Full Screen** (or press **Esc**) to shrink the current window and see the rest of your windows.

End

SAVING FILES

Every program is different, of course, but some operations work almost the same no matter which program you're using. One of those is saving a file. Each program saves files in different formats, depending on which type of data that program works with, but the general process is the same no matter what. Here's how it goes.

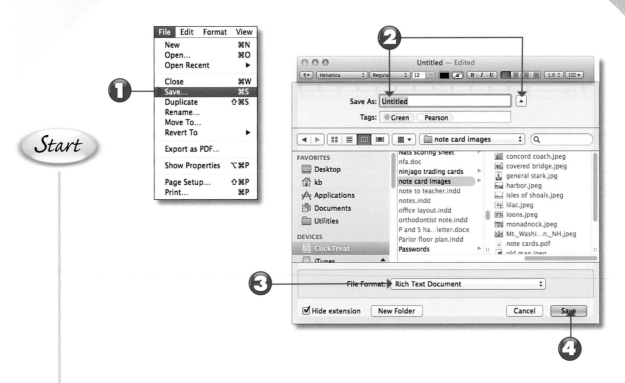

Start

1 In the application in which you're working, either choose **File**, **Save** or press ⌘-**S**.

2 Give the file a name and choose a location in the pick list. If you don't see the pick list, click the arrow button to the right of the **Save As** field.

3 Choose file options such as format and compression (the available options vary depending on the program).

4 Click **Save**.

Continued

TIP

Pay Attention! Save dialog boxes usually open to the last place you saved a file in that program, which is unlikely to be the same place you want now. To save to the desktop, press ⌘-**D**—you'll have to put the file away later, but you'll be able to find it for the moment. ■

NOTE

Save Early, Save Often Don't wait until you're done working on a file to save it—start early and keep using the Save command as you continue to work. That way the file will be stored on your hard drive in case of a drive crash or power outage. After the first time you save a file, many apps—including Apple's own programs—automatically save your changes whenever you pause working. ■

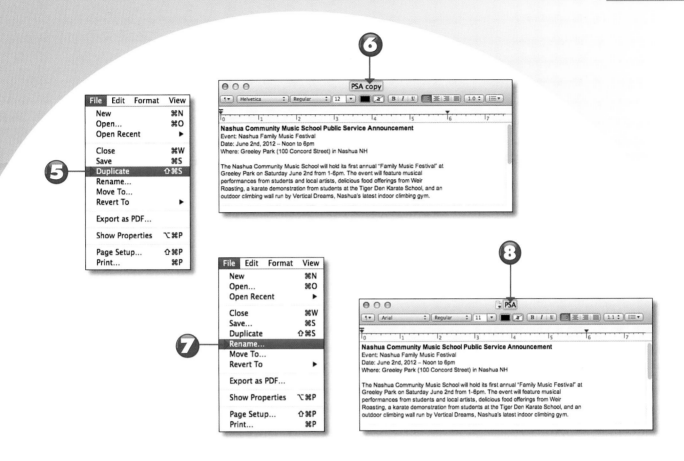

5 To create a new copy of the file on your hard drive, choose **File**, **Duplicate**.

6 Enter a name for the new file.

7 To change the name of the file you're working on, choose **File**, **Rename**.

8 Enter a new name for the file.

End

TIP

When in Doubt If you think there's a chance you may ever want to go back to the original version of your document or image, then use the Duplicate command. You can always delete the versions you don't need later, but better safe than sorry. ■

NOTE

Sometimes It Works The two commands shown in steps 5 and 7 may not appear in all your programs. They're made available to developers by Apple, but not all developers choose to use them in their applications. Apple programs such as TextEdit always have these commands. ■

WRITING WITH TEXTEDIT

Mac OS X's TextEdit program can do a lot more than its remote ancestor, TeachText. It's really a very compact, fast word processor with a lot of formatting options and tools as well as the capability to read and write Microsoft Word documents.

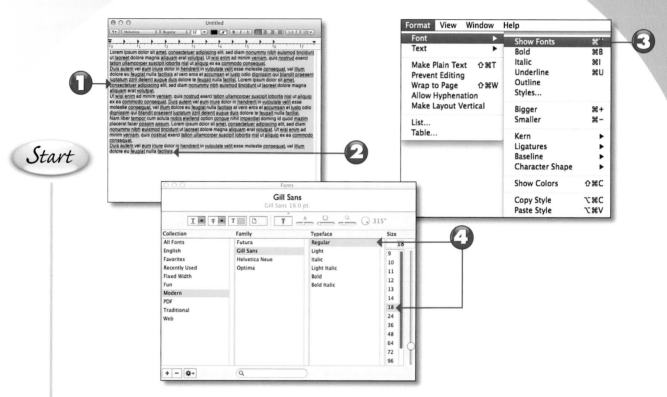

Start

1. Start TextEdit (located in the Applications folder) and begin typing in the new document window.

2. To copy text to another location, click and drag to select the text and press ⌘-**C**; place the cursor where you want the text to appear and press ⌘-**V** to paste it.

3. To change the font, select the text and choose **Format**, **Font**, **Show Fonts**.

4. Choose a new typeface and size in the Fonts panel. The change is applied immediately.

Continued

TIP

Learning How to Spell TextEdit gives questionable words a red underline; **Control-click** each and choose an option from the contextual menu. The **Learn Spelling** command adds the word to a system-wide dictionary. ∎

NOTE

What's Not in There TextEdit is capable, especially with features such as automatic bulleted lists, but it's not a full-featured word processor. If you need to use outlining or HTML conversion, you should use a program such as Microsoft Word. ∎

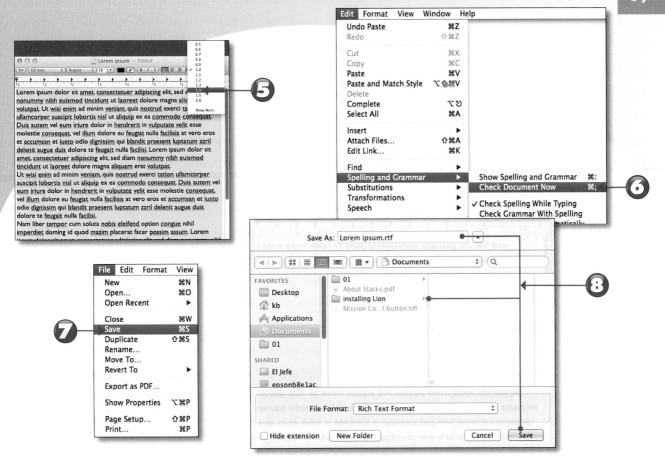

5 To change the text alignment or spacing, click and drag to select the text and choose an option from the controls at the top of the document window.

6 To run a spell check, choose **Edit**, **Spelling and Grammar**, **Check Document Now**.

7 Choose **File**, **Save** to save the file.

8 Give the file a name, choose a location for it, and click **Save**.

End

NOTE

Getting What You Pay For TextEdit's capability to open and save files in Microsoft Word format could keep you from having to invest in Word. Some complex features such as hyperlinks can be lost when you edit a Word file in TextEdit, though. ■

NOTE

Word Compatibility When you're saving your document in step 8, you can choose Rich Text Format or Word format. Either way, your document can be opened in Microsoft Word and retains all its formatting. ■

USING THE FONT PANEL

Mac OS X handles fonts very well. Apple's engineers have put a lot of thought into designing ways to make excellent typography more accessible to the average Mac user. The Fonts panel, which is the same in all the built-in applications, contains a wide variety of settings, from basic to advanced, for modifying the way text is formatted.

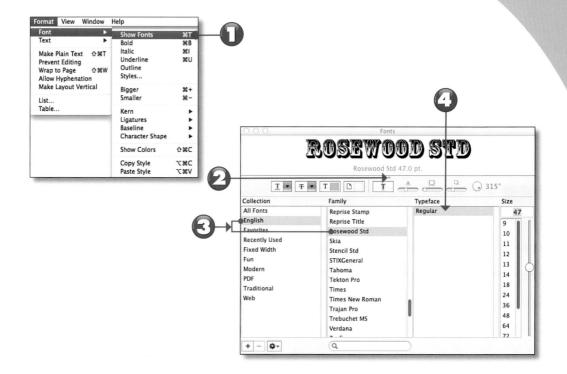

Start

1. In TextEdit, choose **Format**, **Font**, **Show Fonts** to display the Fonts panel.

2. Click the dot below the window's title bar and drag downward to reveal the preview area.

3. Click a font collection in the Collections column and choose a font family from the Family column.

4. Choose a style from the Typeface column.

Continued

TIP

Favorite Type Styles If you create a combination of type settings you plan to use again in TextEdit, click the **Action** menu at the bottom of the Fonts panel and choose **Add to Favorites**. Then you can apply this style to other text selections by choosing **Font**, **Styles** from the menu bar. ■

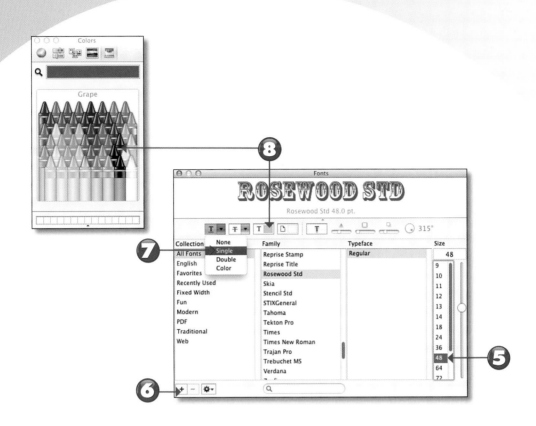

5 Choose a size from the Size column, or enter a value above the column.

6 Click the **Add** button to create a new font collection.

7 Click the **Strikethrough** or **Underline** button and choose an option to add strikethrough or underline style to the selected text.

8 Click the **Text Color** and **Paper Color** buttons to open the Colors panel; then choose a color for the text or the background.

End

NOTE

Beyond the Font Basics If you're interested in working more specifically with type, check out the Font Book program (located in the Utilities folder within Applications). This utility helps you install and manage fonts. ■

NOTE

Collectible Fonts Collections of your corporate fonts or the fonts for a particular project enable you to access those fonts without digging through a long list of fonts. To add a font to a collection, just drag its name from the Family column on top of the collection name. ■

WATCHING DVDS

Who needs a TV to watch DVDs? Not you! If you're looking for some entertainment while you work in the office, or if you just don't feel like getting up and moving to the living room, you can play DVDs right on your Mac. Mac OS X includes a full-featured DVD Player program that can do at least as much as your living room DVD player.

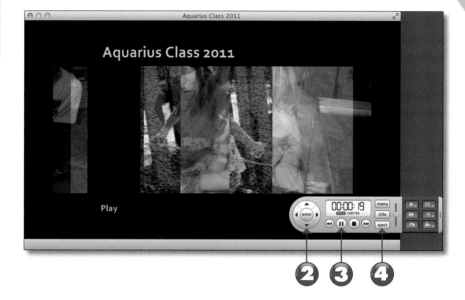

Start

① Insert a DVD disc; DVD Player automatically starts up.

② Click the navigation buttons on the remote control to make choices in the DVD's menus.

③ Click **Pause** on the remote control to stop playing the DVD.

④ Click **Eject** on the remote control to eject the disc.

Continued

TIP

Size Matters Use the **Video** menu to control the size of the virtual TV screen. Choose **Half Size**, **Normal Size**, **Maximum Size**, or **Enter Full Screen** (to get rid of the window and hide the desktop entirely). ■

TIP

Zoom, Zoom, Zoom Choose **Window**, **Video Zoom** to zoom in on an area of the screen as the video plays or while it's paused. Click **Auto Zoom** to resize the window to hold the video image at the current zoom level. ■

5 Place the cursor over the bottom edge of the player window and drag the **Time** slider to skip to any part of the video.

6 To add a bookmark so you can skip right to a particular moment in the video any time you play it, choose **Window**, **Bookmarks**.

7 Click the **Add Bookmark** button.

8 Enter a name for the bookmark and click **Add**.

End

TIP

Playing Around Whether your real DVD player can play in slow motion, your Mac can do it! Using the commands in the Controls menu, you can play in slow motion, scan forward or backward, and even set a sleep timer. ■

SWITCHING PROGRAMS WITH THE DOCK

The Dock acts as central storage for running programs and frequently used programs, but it has other functions, too. One of those is as an application switcher—a method of bringing different programs to the foreground so you can use them in turn. The Dock's location at the bottom or side of the screen makes it the most convenient way to switch applications.

① Move your cursor to the bottom of the screen and click a program icon on the Dock.

② To hide windows belonging to the current program when you switch to the new program, press **Option** as you click.

③ To quit a program you're not using, click and hold its **Dock** icon (or **Control-click**) and choose **Quit** from the contextual menu.

Start

End

TIP

Don't Touch That Mouse! If you prefer to use the keyboard to switch programs, press ⌘-**Tab** to see a list of the currently running programs in the center of the screen. Press ⌘-**Tab** as many times as needed to cycle through the list to the program you want. ■

HIDING PROGRAMS

Mac OS X enables you to run many programs at the same time because it hands over memory to each program as it's needed. But if you do like to run multiple programs, your screen can get pretty cluttered. Hiding program windows and palettes is a lifesaver for people who never quit programs until they shut down their Macs.

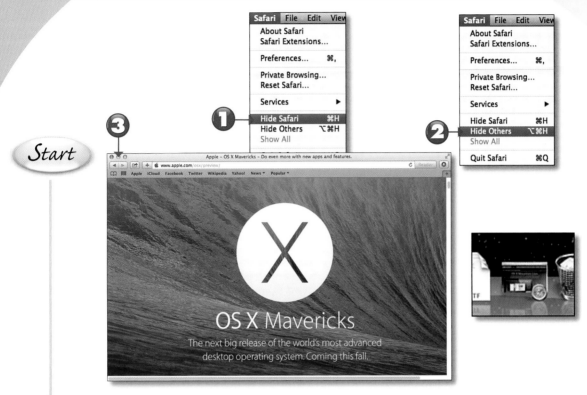

1 In the Application menu, choose **Hide** (or press ⌘-**H**) to hide the program you're currently using.

2 In the Application menu, choose **Hide Others** (or press ⌘-**Option-H**) to hide all other programs that are currently running.

3 To get one window out of the way instead of hiding the program, click the **Minimize** button to send it to the Dock.

End

TIP

Another Way to Hide   Another way to hide programs is to **Option-click** the desktop or a window from another program to simultaneously switch to the Finder or the other program, respectively, and hide the previous program. ■

NOTE

Remain in Control   Yet another way to maneuver among running programs and open windows is to use Mission Control. Turn to "Managing Multiple Windows" in Chapter 1, "Getting Started." ■

Chapter 4

SETTING SYSTEM PREFERENCES

The System Preferences command in the Apple menu opens a command center for preferences. It contains buttons for each preference pane, organized into categories.

Preferences make the world go round—or, at least, they are what make your Mac into *your* Mac. You can control so many aspects of your everyday computing experience that it's worth a trip to the System Preferences window every once in a while just to remind yourself what's there. Be sure to explore all the tabs of each preference pane, too, to make sure you know what all your options are.

In this chapter, you'll learn how to set preferences for everything from how your mouse or trackpad works to what size objects are displayed on your monitor. A couple of tasks—"Setting Trackpad Preferences" and "Monitoring Battery Use"—deal with preferences for laptop users only; if your Mac isn't a MacBook, you won't even see these settings, so don't worry about them.

THE SYSTEM PREFERENCES WINDOW

Minimize energy
consumption, 84

Customize
mouse and
keyboard
settings, 82–83

Change monitor
settings, 81

Manage sound
effects, 87

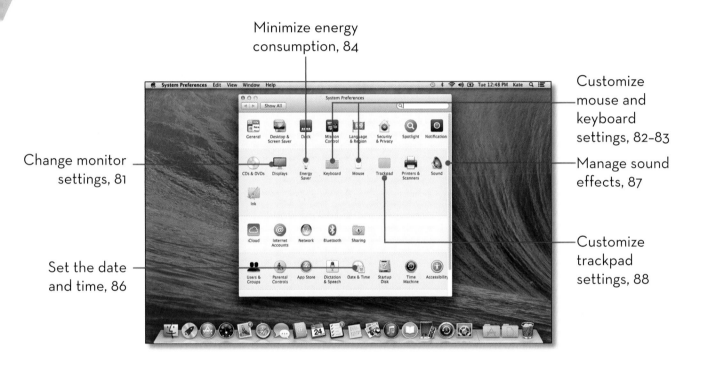

Customize
trackpad
settings, 88

Set the date
and time, 86

SETTING SYSTEM PREFERENCES

In a flashback to the days of the Mac's System 6, Mac OS X stores all its preferences in a central window called System Preferences. It's accessible via the Apple menu, so you can reach it from any program. You can find preference panes for non-Apple programs and utilities in System Preferences, in the Other section at the bottom of the window.

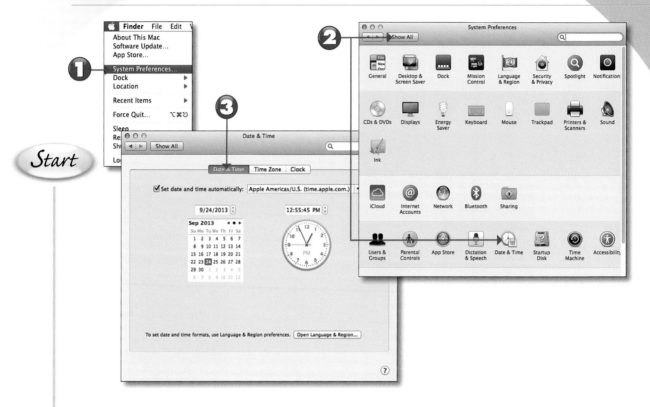

Start

① Choose **Apple menu**, **System Preferences** to display the System Preferences window.

② Click **Show All** to see all the buttons; then click the button for the preferences you want to change.

③ Click buttons across the top of the preference pane to access various groups of settings.

Continued

TIP

Haven't I Been Here Before? To return to a preference pane you've just visited, click the left arrow at the top of the System Preferences window. The left and right arrows take you forward and back through the preference screens. ∎

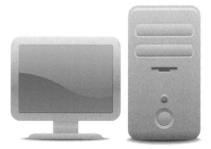

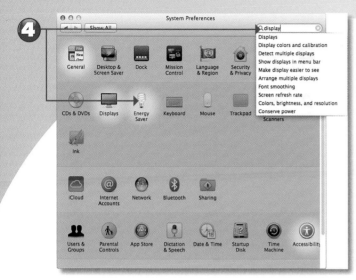

 Type a word or two into the search field to locate a preference panel you can't find.

5 Choose **View**, **Customize** to add and remove preference panes you don't use often.

 Uncheck the box next to any preference button to remove it; you'll still be able to access those preferences in the View menu.

End

TIP

Down by the Dock If you make many trips to the System Preferences, the Dock can be a quicker way to get there than the Apple menu. If it's not in the Dock, open your Applications folder, find System Preferences, and drag it to the left side of the Dock. ■

TIP

Now You Know Your ABCs If the System Preference categories don't make sense to you, choose **View**, **Organize Alphabetically**. This command reorders the buttons in good old alphabetical order, instead of dividing them by category. ■

CHANGING YOUR ALERT SOUND

The alert sound is that annoying beep you hear when you do something your Mac doesn't like or when you tell it to do something it can't do. The nice part about this is that you can change the sound that's played, as well as adjust its volume independently of the system's overall volume level.

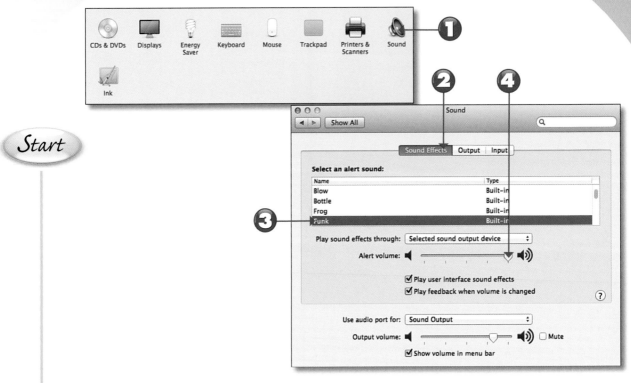

Start

① Click the **Sound** button in the System Preferences window to display the sound preferences.

② Click the **Sound Effects** button to see your choices.

③ Click a sound in the pick list to hear it.

④ Click and drag the **Alert volume** slider to set the volume level for alert sounds.

End

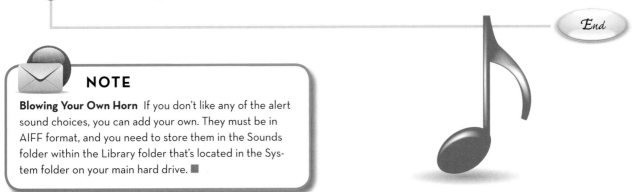

NOTE

Blowing Your Own Horn If you don't like any of the alert sound choices, you can add your own. They must be in AIFF format, and you need to store them in the Sounds folder within the Library folder that's located in the System folder on your main hard drive. ■

CHANGING DISPLAY SETTINGS

Your monitor's display resolution is the number of pixels it displays horizontally and vertically. You can change the resolution of most monitors. With a lower resolution, everything on the screen is bigger and you can't see as many windows at one time, and with a higher resolution everything is smaller, but you can fit more.

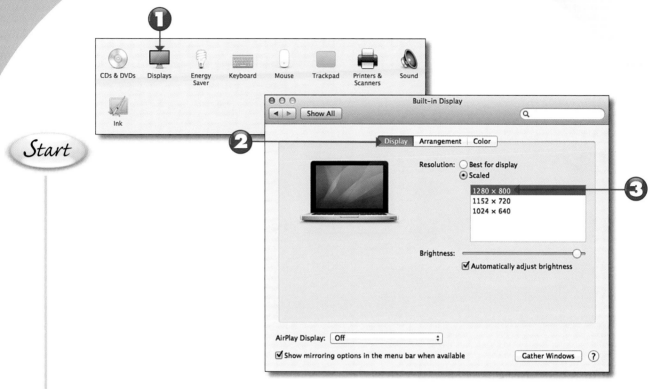

Click the **Displays** button in the System Preferences window to display monitor preferences.

Click the **Display** button to see your choices.

Click **Scaled** and then choose a setting in the **Resolutions** pick list to determine the scale of the Images on your monitor. If the setting you choose doesn't look right, wait 15 seconds for the previous setting to be restored, and then click another.

End

NOTE

The More, the Merrier Expert users generally choose the highest resolution that still allows them to read text onscreen. It makes onscreen objects seem small at first, but you get used to that quickly. You can fit more windows onscreen at higher resolutions. ■

CHANGING THE MOUSE SPEED

When you're in a hurry, there are few things more annoying than a slow mouse, or one that's so fast you can't keep track of it. Whether your mouse moves too slowly or too quickly for your taste, you can adjust its setting until it's just where you like it. You can also change the speed at which you must click for two clicks to register as an official double-click.

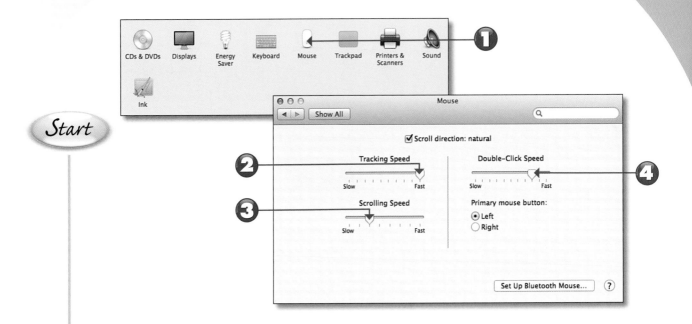

 Start

① Click the **Mouse** button in the System Preferences window to display mouse preferences.

② Drag the **Tracking Speed** slider to change how quickly the mouse moves across the screen.

③ Drag the **Scrolling Speed** slider to change how fast windows scroll when you use a mouse with a scroll wheel.

④ Drag the **Double-Click Speed** slider to change the speed at which you must click in order for your Mac to recognize two clicks as a double-click.

End

NOTE

Scrolling Naturally One of the most confusing settings of all time is found at the top of the Mouse pane in System Preferences: **Scroll direction: natural**. The confusion arises from a difference of opinion between Apple and the rest of the world about what's really "natural." Without taking sides, I'll just explain here that the "natural" setting results in your moving to the top of a window when pulling a scroll wheel toward yourself. If you find it more natural to go the other direction, by all means change this setting by unchecking the box.

CHANGING KEYBOARD SETTINGS

Most aspects of the way a keyboard works are determined by the hardware—in other words, the keyboard itself. However, there are a couple of keyboard settings you can adjust, having to do with how quickly your Mac repeats keys when you hold down a key.

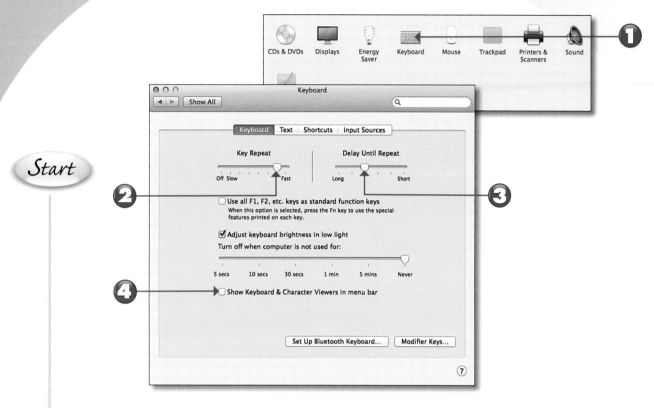

Start

1. Click the **Keyboard** button in the System Preferences window to display keyboard preferences.

2. Drag the **Key Repeat** slider to control how quickly keys repeat when you hold them down.

3. Drag the **Delay Until Repeat** slider to control how long the Mac waits before starting to repeat keys when you hold them down.

4. Click the **Show Keyboard & Character Viewers in menu bar** box to add a quick access menu for the Character and Keyboard Viewers, which help you type special characters.

End

NOTE

Taking a Shortcut You can use the Shortcuts tab of the Keyboard preferences to choose custom keyboard shortcuts for several Mac OS X system functions: taking screen shots; navigating the Finder using the keyboard; using the Dock, Mission Control, and Dashboard; invoking Spotlight; and more. ■

SETTING ENERGY SAVER OPTIONS

You might not think your quiet little computer, sitting over there in the corner not even moving, could eat up that much electricity—but think again. That's why the Energy Saver settings are important; they enable you to reduce your Mac's power consumption during times when you're not using it. Be sure to take as much advantage of Energy Saver as possible.

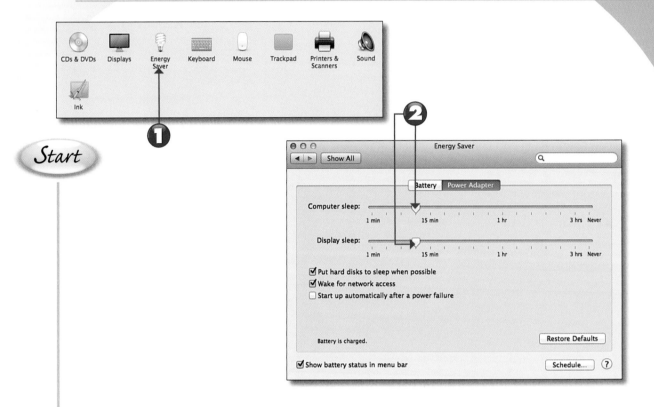

Start

Click the **Energy Saver** button in the System Preferences window to display energy preferences.

Drag the top slider to choose when your Mac will sleep and the bottom slider to set a separate time for when your monitor will sleep.

Continued

NOTE

Seeing Double? You've probably noticed that there are two tabs in the Energy Saver preference pane shown here. That's because these screen shots were taken on a MacBook Pro. If you have a desktop Mac, you'll only see one set of preferences, but laptop users can set different preferences for when their Macs are plugged in and when they're running on battery power. ■

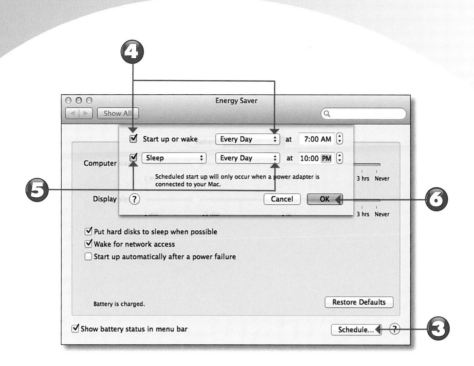

3 Click the **Schedule** button to display scheduled startup and shutdown options.

4 Check the box and choose when to start up the Mac automatically.

5 Check the box and choose when to shut down the Mac automatically.

6 Click **OK**.

End

TIP

Are You Getting Sleepy? Sleep is a state between powered up and powered down. A sleeping computer consumes much less power, but it's not completely turned off. Of course, it wakes up more quickly than it boots up from a powered-down state. ■

NOTE

Quick Start In step 5, you can also set your Mac to sleep at a particular time instead of shutting down. This is a good choice if you keep programs running all the time that you don't want to have to start up again every day. ■

SETTING THE TIME AND DATE

If you opt to set the date and time yourself, you can do it by clicking a calendar and dragging clock hands—no messy typing needed! If you have a constant or frequent online connection, you can choose instead to have your Mac's clock set automatically over the Internet.

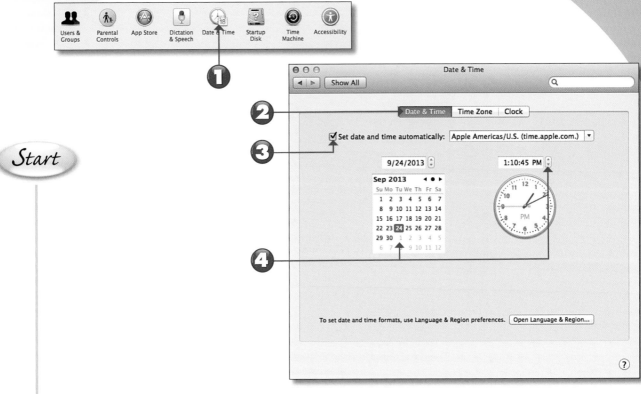

Start

Click the **Date & Time** button in the System Preferences window to display time and date preferences.

Click the **Date & Time** button to see your choices.

If the **Set date & time automatically** box is checked, click to remove the check mark.

Click a day on the calendar to set the date, or type in the date; drag the hands on the clock to set the time, or type in the time.

End

NOTE

Do You Have the Correct Time? If you use a timeserver to set your Mac's clock automatically over the Internet, be sure you've chosen the correct time zone in the Time Zone tab of the Date & Time preferences. ■

TIP

A Clockwork Preference The third button in the Date & Time preferences pane opens the Clock tab, where you'll find settings for the menu bar clock. You can even choose an analog clock with hands instead of the regular digital display. ■

ADJUSTING THE SYSTEM VOLUME

A small thing such as the volume of the sounds your Mac plays can have a significant impact on your experience while using the computer. You can always increase the volume when you're working in the next room or when you want to turn up the radio and sing along, or lower it when you don't want to wake the baby.

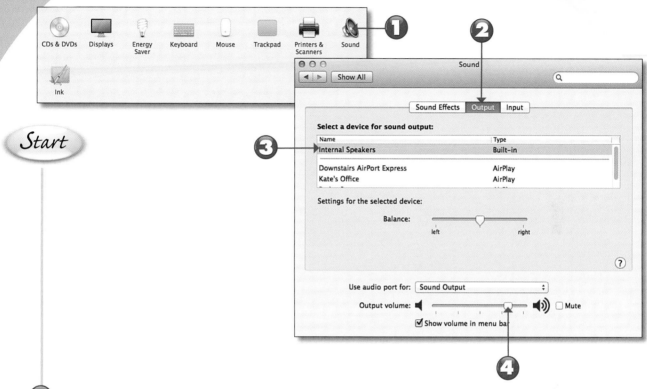

Start

1 Click the **Sound** button in the System Preferences window to display sound preferences.

2 Click the **Output** button to see your choices.

3 If you have more than one output device (internal speaker and external speakers), choose the device you want to use from the pick list.

4 Drag the **Output volume** slider to change the volume for all sounds produced by your Mac.

End

TIP

Muting for Discretion's Sake Click the **Mute** check box next to the Output volume slider if you want to turn the volume all the way down. ■

TIP

Getting Louder (or Softer) Faster Click the **Show volume in menu bar** check box to put an extra menu in your menu bar that's simply a volume slider. To use it, click its icon, release the mouse button, and click and drag the slider. Also, many keyboards now have volume controls at the top of the numeric keypad. ■

SETTING TRACKPAD PREFERENCES

Trackpads—those snazzy touch-sensitive pads laptops use instead of trackballs these days—are funny creatures. Because they don't feel the same as a mouse, you might want to use different speed and double-clicking settings than you would for a mouse. You'll need to experiment until you're comfortable with the settings.

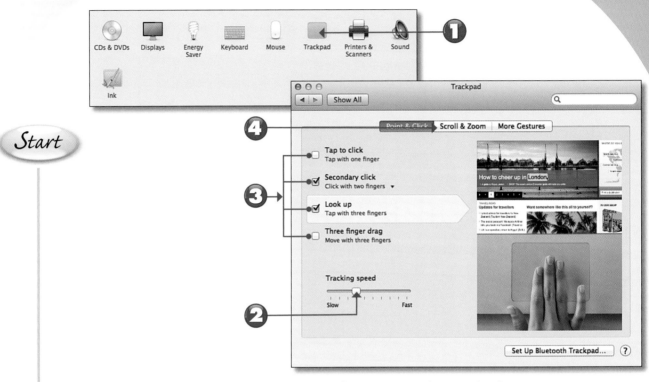

Start

Click the **Trackpad** button in the System Preferences window to display mouse preferences.

Drag the **Tracking Speed** slider to set how fast the trackpad cursor moves.

Modify the settings to control your Mac with multi-finger gestures.

Click the **Scroll and Zoom** button to change how you use your trackpad to scroll through windows and pages and how you zoom in and out.

End

TIP

A Thoughtful Gesture If any of the built-in trackpad gestures don't work for you—sometimes my fingers just don't want to go that way—feel free to try the alternative gestures Apple has provided. Just click the triangle next to the gesture's description to see a list of choices. ■

NOTE

A Trackpad but No Laptop If you love trackpads but don't use a MacBook, you can still satisfy your craving. Apple's Magic Trackpad costs $69 and connects to any Mac with Bluetooth. ■

MONITORING BATTERY USE

If you're a laptop user, you know how important it is to keep track of the charge in your MacBook's battery. Running out of power at a crucial moment could be a disaster—you'll definitely want to keep an eye on the Battery menu to make sure you don't lose unsaved data when your Mac shuts down suddenly.

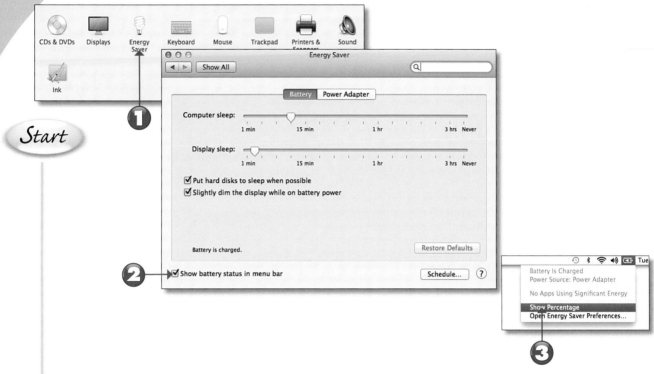

Start

1. Click the **Energy Saver** button in the System Preferences window to display energy preferences.

2. Click the check box to display a battery menu in your menu bar.

3. Click the battery status menu to change the way it displays how much battery charge is left.

End

NOTE

Saving More Power Look at the Energy Saver functions in the System Preferences—you can save a lot of power by setting the right preferences. See the task "Setting Energy Saver Options" earlier in this chapter to learn more about Energy Saver settings. ■

Chapter 5

CUSTOMIZING YOUR MAC

It's your Mac—why not have some fun with it? You can make your Mac your own in myriad ways, from changing its desktop picture, its screen saver, and even your own login icon to changing the way the Finder works and responds to you. You can even change the Finder's language to any of a couple dozen alternatives, including Asian languages.

Your custom settings are associated with your login name, so they're automatically put into effect each time you log in. When other users log in, their own settings are activated. That means a single Mac can offer each user a custom experience. Your custom settings can include useful preferences such as network locations and more fun preferences such as your desktop wallpaper.

In this chapter, you'll learn how to customize the Finder, the Dock, the desktop, your screen saver, and your security preferences. You'll also learn how to make your own Dashboard widgets—tiny custom programs that you can build from pieces of your favorite websites.

TAKING ADVANTAGE OF CUSTOM SETTINGS

Choose your desktop wallpaper, 96

Secure your files, 105

Choose a screen saver, 97

Set up multiple displays, 100-101

Build custom widgets for Dashboard, 107

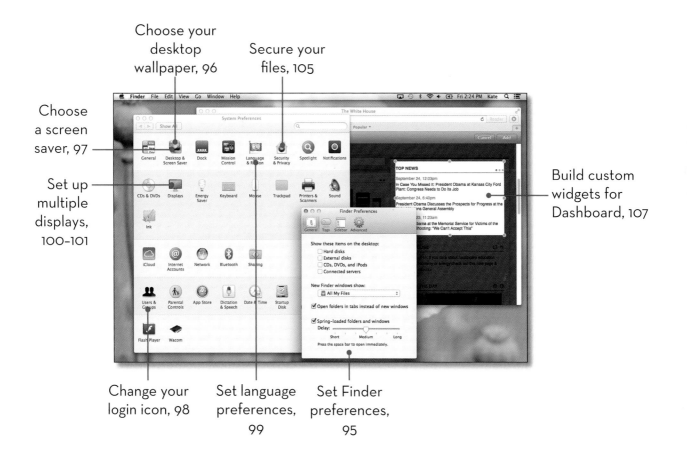

Change your login icon, 98

Set language preferences, 99

Set Finder preferences, 95

MOVING THE DOCK AROUND

Although the Dock normally lives at the bottom of your screen, it doesn't have to stay there. If you prefer, you can put it on the left or right side of the screen instead. No matter which edge of the screen it's on, the Dock works the same way and you can set its preferences to suit your tastes.

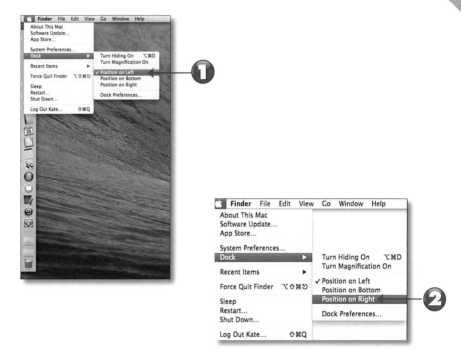

Start

Choose **Apple menu**, **Dock**, **Position on Left** to move the Dock to the left edge of the screen.

Choose **Apple menu**, **Dock**, **Position on Right** to move the Dock to the right edge of the screen.

End

TIP

Hide and Go Dock To hide the Dock, choose **Apple menu**, **Dock**, **Turn Hiding On**; now the Dock sinks off the edge of the screen whenever you're not using it. Move your mouse back to that edge, and the Dock pops back out. ■

NOTE

Dock Substitutes The Dock can get pretty crowded. Some users use the Dock strictly as an application switcher, with inactive programs and documents stored in a third-party Dock substitute such as DragThing (www.dragthing.com). ■

CHANGING THE DOCK'S SIZE

The more stuff you stash in the Dock, the more room it takes up on your screen. If it gets too full, you can shrink it to give you more room onscreen—or, if you prefer, you can make it larger so it's easier to see what it contains.

Start

 Click the line between the two halves of the Dock and drag upward to enlarge the Dock.

2 Drag downward to reduce the Dock's size.

End

TIP

There's Always Another Way You can also use the Dock Size slider in the Dock preferences (choose **Apple menu**, **Dock**, **Dock Preferences**) if you happen to be going there to change other preferences as well. ■

CUSTOMIZING THE DOCK'S BEHAVIOR

As if moving the Dock around and changing its size weren't enough, there's yet more you can do to make the Dock work just the way you want it to. The Dock preferences enable you to control the way the Dock moves—or, more precisely, the way its icons move and change size and the way windows enter the Dock.

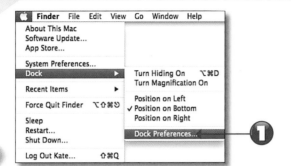

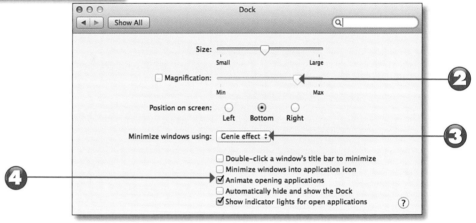

Start

1 Choose **Apple menu**, **Dock**, **Dock Preferences**.

2 Check the box marked **Magnification** and then click and drag the **Magnification** slider toward Max if you want Dock icons to be enlarged as you pass the mouse cursor over them.

3 Choose an option from the **Minimize windows using** pop-up menu.

4 Click the **Animate opening applications** check box to make Dock icons bounce as their programs start up.

End

TIP

Dock Behavior in Another Context You can control Dock Preferences by **Control-clicking** the dividing line between the halves of the Dock. The contextual menu has controls for magnification, hiding, position, and the minimization effect, as well as a Dock Preferences command. ■

CHANGING THE WAY THE FINDER WORKS

The Finder—the program that generates the desktop and enables you to explore your hard drive and network drives visually via windows—is where you'll spend a lot of time while using your Mac. You have several choices about the way it operates; here's how to set up the Finder to suit your tastes.

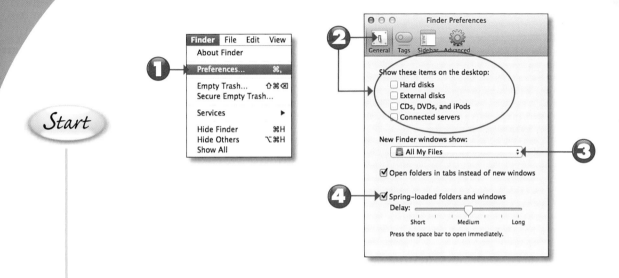

Start

1 In the Finder, choose **Finder**, **Preferences**.

2 Click the **General** button to see basic Finder preferences, and then click check boxes to set the kinds of disks to appear on the desktop.

3 Choose an option from the **New Finder windows show** pop-up menu to determine which folder or disk location appears in new Finder windows.

4 Click the check box to set whether each folder opens in a new tab instead of a new window.

End

TIP

Finding Files with the Finder The Finder got its name for its capability to find files. To find files in the Finder, choose **File**, **Find** or press ⌘-**F** and type in the information for which you want to search. ■

NOTE

Keeping Tabs on Things The Finder preferences can also control whether new Finder windows open as tabs in the current window, or as windows all by themselves. To learn more about tabbed windows in Finder, turn to "Using Tabbed Windows" in Chapter 2. ■

CHANGING YOUR DESKTOP PICTURE

Every time you sit down in front of your Mac, you're looking at your desktop—or, more specifically, at the picture displayed on it. Why not have some fun with it? You can change the desktop picture any time you like, using any photo, cartoon, or other graphic that catches your fancy.

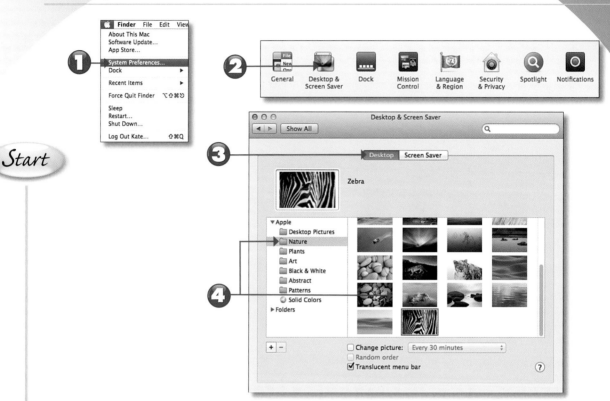

Start

1 Choose **Apple menu**, **System Preferences**.

2 Click the **Desktop & Screen Saver** button to see your choices.

3 Click the **Desktop** button.

4 Click a folder and an image from within the folder to apply that image to the desktop.

End

TIP

Surprise Me If you want your desktop picture to change automatically, click the + button in the Desktop tab and pick a folder full of your favorite images. Then check **Change picture** at the bottom of the Desktop tab and choose a time interval. ■

NOTE

The Mother Lode Looking for more desktop pictures to relieve your boredom? You can download hundreds of high-quality desktop images at MacDesktops (www.macdesktops.com). ■

CHANGING YOUR SCREEN SAVER

Originally invented to stop the kind of screen burn-in that you see on automatic teller machines, screen savers are actually little more than pretty entertainment these days. But that shouldn't prevent you from using them; screen savers provide some privacy, shielding your screen from casual observers, as well as being fun to look at.

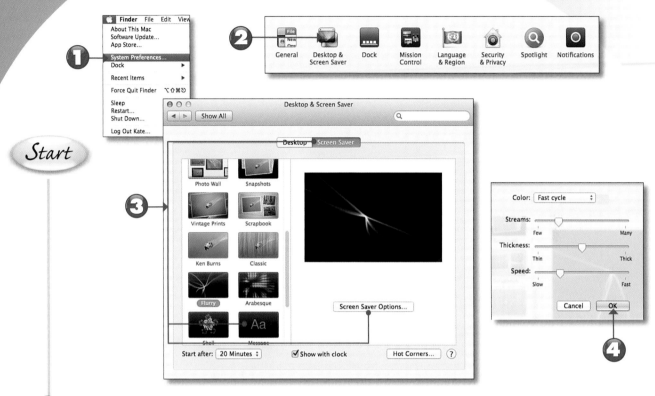

1. Choose **Apple menu**, **System Preferences**.

2. Click the **Desktop & Screen Saver** button to see your choices.

3. Click the **Screen Saver** button, and then click a screen saver in the list to select it. Click the **Screen Saver Options** button.

4. Use the settings in this dialog box to change settings specific to each screen saver. Click **OK** when finished.

End

TIP

Got Savers? If you're not satisfied with the built-in selection of screen savers—or if you've run through them all and are desperately in need of new ones—check out www.macscreensavers.com. ∎

TIP

A Screen Saver All Your Own For a custom screen saver, put your favorite photos in a folder and click a slideshow style; then choose the folder from the **Source** pop-up menu. ∎

CHANGING YOUR LOGIN ICON

Your login icon represents your face within the world of your Mac. It's used as your buddy icon for online messaging in iChat, it appears next to your personal information in the Address Book, and you see it every time you log in. You can use one of the built-in pictures, or you can add any picture you like—your photo or anything else.

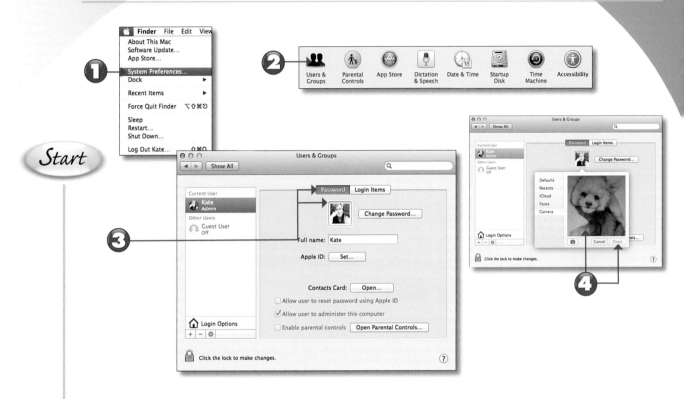

1 Choose **Apple menu**, **System Preferences**.

2 Click the **Users & Groups** button to see your choices.

3 Click the **Password** button; then click your picture and choose **Edit Picture** (the notepad icon) in the pop-up menu.

4 Drag or paste an image file into the Images window, drag the image and the scaling slider until the square shows the area you want for the icon, and then click **Done** to make it your login picture.

End

TIP
Using Your Own Picture If you're concerned about privacy, it might not be wise to use your own photo as a login icon. If people you don't know will see the photo—as an iChat icon, for instance—you might want to substitute a personal logo of some kind. ■

TIP
I'm Ready for My Close-Up, Mr. Jobs If you have an iSight camera, either standalone or built in to your Mac, you can use it to take a picture right from the Edit Picture dialog and turn that photo into an icon on the spot. ■

CHANGING YOUR MAC'S LANGUAGE

You might have thought that you would need to buy a special version of Mac OS X if you want your Mac's interface to use a language other than English. Actually, Mac OS X ships with the capability to display menus, dialog boxes, and other interface elements in a couple dozen languages, including those with non-Roman alphabets.

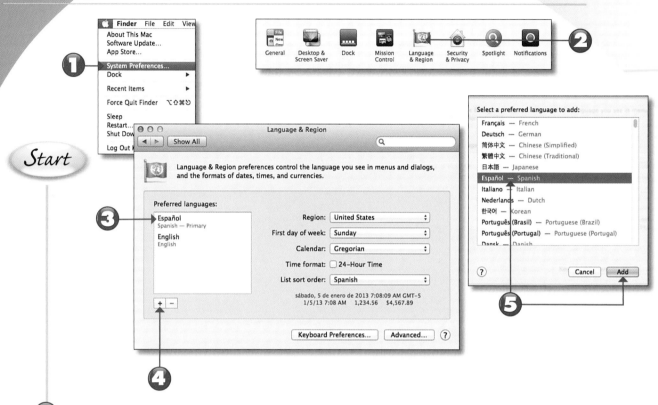

1 Choose **Apple menu**, **System Preferences**.

2 Click the **Language & Region** button to see your choices.

3 Drag and drop the languages listed to set your preferred priority.

4 Click **+** to add more languages.

5 Choose a language and click **Add**.

End

TIP

Making a Menu When you switch languages, you should also switch keyboard layouts to activate each language's special characters. In the Keyboard preferences' Keyboard tab, you can click the **Show Keyboard & Character Viewers** box so you can access special characters quickly. ■

USING MULTIPLE DISPLAYS

When one screen just isn't enough to hold all the stuff you're doing with your Mac, it's time to add more. Your Mac can support multiple displays that can be used side-by-side or for mirroring—displaying the same image on more than one screen, for easier viewing by everyone. You'll find that working with multiple displays increases your efficiency tremendously.

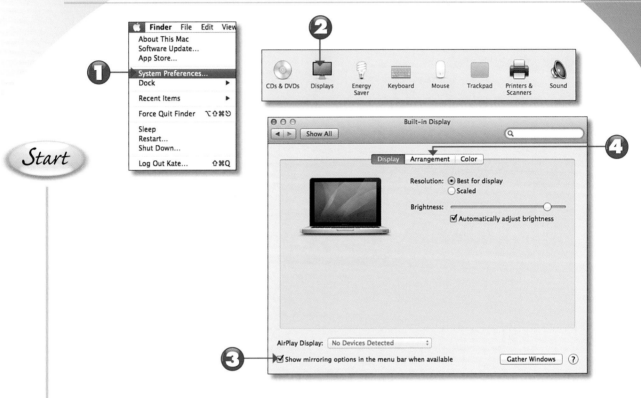

Start

Continued

1. Choose **Apple menu, System Preferences**.

2. Click the **Displays** button to see your choices.

3. Check the box marked **Show mirroring options in the menu bar when available**.

4. Click the **Arrangement** tab.

NOTE

How Many Is Multiple? If you're wondering exactly how many monitors you can actually hook up to your Mac, well—I've seen as many as six connected to a Mac Pro. Most people find two or three sufficient, though. ■

NOTE

Making the Most of It You may need to experiment and find out what workflow changes suit you best. Some users place different app windows on each monitor, while others prefer to save a second display for palettes, toolbars, and status windows. I like to keep my main work on one and put my email, messaging apps, and iTunes on the other. ■

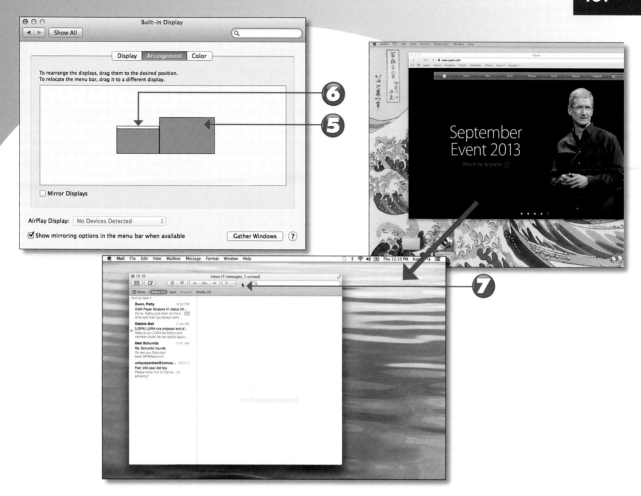

5 Drag the **blue display proxies** to arrange them as you prefer.

6 Drag the **menu bar proxy** to the display proxy you want to be your primary display.

7 When you're using multiple displays, click a window or the desktop on the display you're not using to switch the menu bar to that display.

End

TIP

Hide and Seek To make the Dock follow your cursor from display to display, turn on Dock Hiding by choosing **Apple menu**, **Dock**, **Turn Hiding On**. ■

NOTE

Getting a Straight Line If your monitors are different sizes, a window or other object spanning both displays won't line up properly. If this bothers you, click the Display tab in Display preferences and set both monitors to the same resolution. ■

SENDING VIDEO TO APPLE TV

When you have an Apple TV installed on your network, you can use AirPlay to choose what video gets sent to what device—your connected monitors or an HDTV. This means you can use your TV as a second or third monitor, or just send music and video to the big screen for optimal viewing. AirPlay isn't new with Mavericks, but before Mavericks you could only mirror whatever was showing on your primary display. Now you can play video on TV while still using your Mac normally.

Start

1. To play videos in iTunes, open iTunes.

2. Click the **AirPlay** menu in the iTunes menu and choose **Apple TV**.

3. Choose the content you want to view on your HDTV and click Play.

4. Control playback with your Mac's mouse or using the Apple Remote that came with your Apple TV.

Continued

TIP

First Things First If you're having trouble connecting to your Apple TV, first make sure that the Apple TV is connected to your network and to your television and that the TV has the correct input setting. The next thing to check is software—do you have the latest version of iTunes, and is your Apple TV's software up to date? If so, try restarting both your computer and your Apple TV. ■

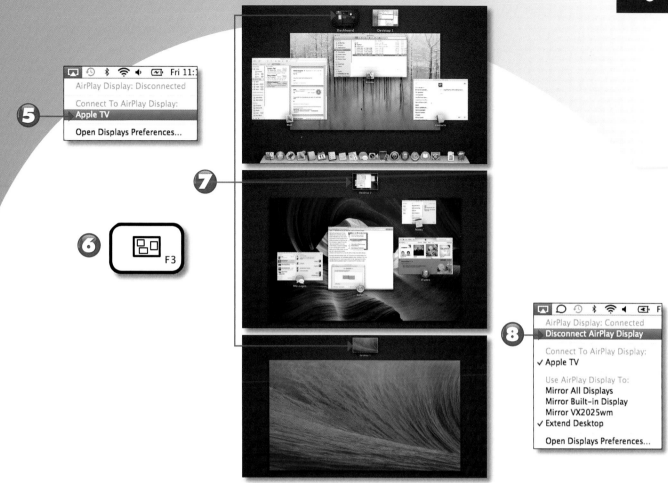

 To use your HDTV as an additional display, choose **Apple TV** from the AirPlay menu in your menu bar.

To get a bird's-eye view of what's on your computer screen and what's on your TV screen, press the **Mission Control** button or **F9**.

Switch windows from one screen to another by dragging them to the thumbnail of your choice at the top of the screen.

Turn off AirPlay by choosing **Disconnect AirPlay Display** in the AirPlay menu.

End

NOTE

You've Been Here Before AirPlay is the same as what used to be called AirTunes—back when the feature only worked to send audio to speakers connected to an Airport Express. Now that it can handle video, it gets a shiny new name, both on your Mac and on your iOS devices. ■

TIP

AirPlay or AirPlay? Confused about which AirPlay menu to use when? Remember it this way. When you want to show your computer screen on the TV, use one in the menu bar. If you want to play video or audio, use the one in iTunes. ■

ADDING LOGIN ITEMS

If, like many, you're a creature of habit, you'll love this feature. By designating login items for your user account, you can make any documents and apps you like open up automatically any time you log in to your Mac. You might want to start up your email and calendar programs every time you log in, for example.

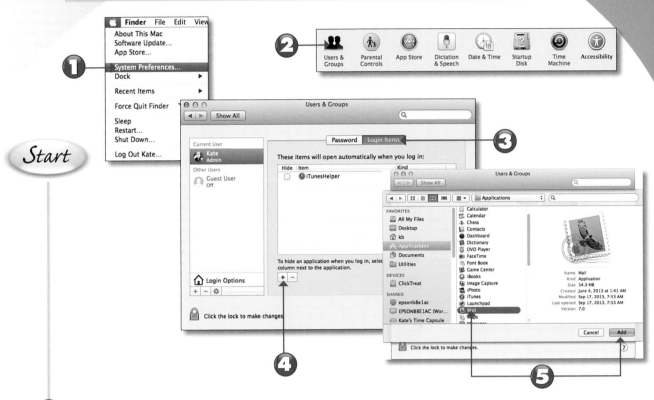

Start

End

1. Choose **Apple menu**, **System Preferences**.

2. Click **Users & Groups** in the System Preferences window.

3. Click **Login Items**.

4. Click **Add**.

5. Navigate to the application or file you want to open automatically; then click **Add**.

NOTE

Login Versus Startup Don't get confused: Login items are things that start up automatically when you log in to your account on the Mac; startup items are those that start up automatically when you turn on the Mac. ■

TIP

Quick Login If you're in a hurry and don't need the programs you've specified as login items, you can disable them at login time by pressing Shift from the time you press Enter in the login window until you see your desktop picture appear. ■

INCREASING YOUR MAC'S SECURITY

Whether these settings are important to you depends on how vulnerable your Mac is to snoopy intruders. If your computer is in a dorm room or an open office, or if it's a laptop, you'll probably want to put at least some of these measures in place to ensure that un-authorized people can't use it.

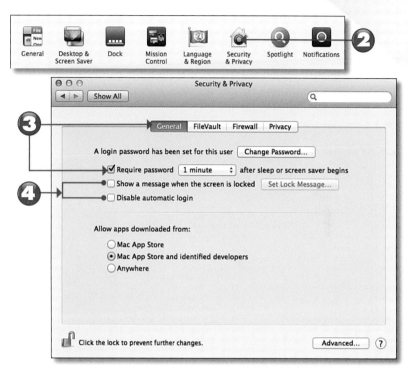

 Start

 Choose **Apple menu**, **System Preferences**.

2 Click the **Security & Privacy** button to see your choices.

3 Click the **General** button, and then click the **Require password** check box to make sure that only you can wake up the computer when it's sleeping.

4 Click the check boxes next to the other options to turn them on or off.

End

NOTE

Learning to Live Together To learn about ways to get along when you share your Mac with other users, turn to Chapter 11, "Sharing Your Mac with Multiple Users." ■

NOTE

The GateKeeper A group of settings on the General Tab in the Security & Privacy preferences enables you to control where your applications come from. You can choose to allow only programs from the Mac App Store, those from the App Store and from Apple's certified developers, or any program at all. This way you don't have to worry about damage caused by incompatible or malicious programs. ■

ADDING NEW DASHBOARD WIDGETS

The first time you open Dashboard—which you may do by pressing the Dashboard key on your keyboard, by clicking the Dashboard icon in Mission Control, or by switching Spaces until you get to the Dashboard—you'll see a default set of widgets. But the fun starts when you customize Dashboard by adding the widgets that are most useful to *you*.

Start

① In Dashboard, click the **+** to open the widget organizer.

② In the organizer, click a widget's icon to add it to your Dashboard.

③ Back in Dashboard, move the widget to the position you want it to occupy.

End

NOTE

Widget Options Customize your widgets further by holding your mouse cursor over the widget and clicking the **i** button that appears. (If you don't see an **i** button, that widget has no settings.) This enables you to, for example, set your location for weather forecasts and movie times. ■

MAKING YOUR OWN WIDGETS

Dashboard is great—if you haven't tried it, click its Dock icon and take a look at the cool widgets you can add. And you can even make your own widgets; it's very simple to turn your favorite web pages into Dashboard widgets, and you do it right from Safari.

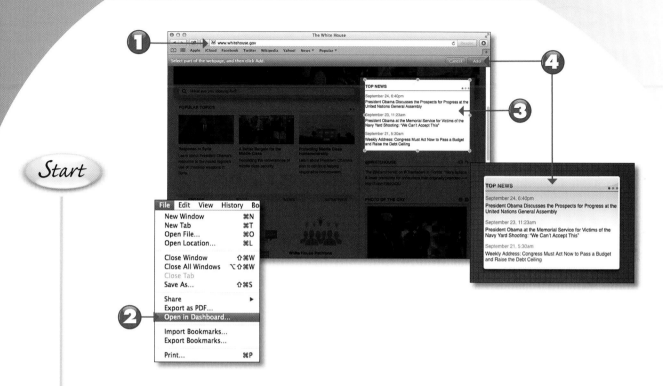

Start

1 In Safari, type the URL of the web page you want to turn into a widget.

2 Choose **File**, **Open in Dashboard**.

3 Select the area on the web page that you want to include in your widget.

4 Click **Add**; the new widget opens in Dashboard.

End

TIP

Make It Your Very Own To customize the appearance of your widget, click the **i** button in its lower-right corner. The widget flips neatly over and presents you with a choice of visual themes. Click the one you want to use. ∎

TIP

The Widget Underground Want to be just a little bit subversive? Use this feature to avoid ads on web pages by turning the pages into widgets—and cropping out all the area occupied by ads. ∎

ORGANIZING YOUR LIFE

Mac OS X includes several programs that work together to keep you organized: Contacts, Reminders, and Calendar. Contacts is a contact manager where you can store your friends', family members', and colleagues' names, addresses, and phone numbers along with their instant messaging IDs, websites, email addresses, and more. Reminders help you track events and a to-do list in your Calendar. Calendar keeps track of your appointments and a to-do list, and it can both publish and subscribe to online calendars so you can share them with others. And all the data in Contacts and Calendar is available to your iPad, iPhone, or other devices so you're never without it.

In this chapter you'll learn how to create and organize contacts in Contacts and how to view a map of a contact's address. Calendar Tasks show how to create appointments and how to invite contacts to events; how to search calendars; and how to publish, subscribe to, and print calendars.

WORKING WITH CONTACTS AND SCHEDULES

Set reminders that appear on all your devices, 117

View days, weeks, or entire months, 119

Organize your schedule, 119

Search your calendar, 127

Maintain multiple calendars, 119

Track notes, 118

Keep track of contacts, 110

ADDING CONTACTS

Mac OS X's Contacts is accessible systemwide, meaning its information can be used by other programs such as Messages, Mail, and even Microsoft Word. Adding contacts and sorting them into groups is easy, and Contacts has an up-to-date selection of information fields, including places to stash online messaging IDs.

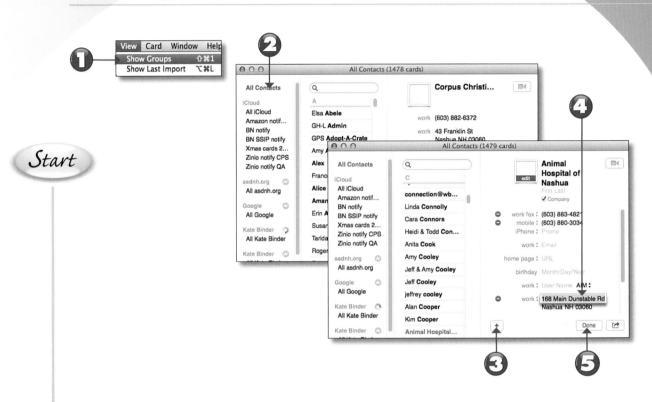

Start

1 Choose **View**, **Show Groups**.

2 Click the group name to which you want to add the contact, or **All Contacts** if you don't have a group in mind.

3 Click the **+** button.

4 Type the person or company's name and other information.

5 Click **Done** to complete the contact.

End

CREATING GROUPS OF CONTACTS

You can use Contacts' groups many ways. For example, you can create a group of people working on a current project so you can email them all at once. Or you can create a group of addresses for holiday cards so you can print address labels. Each contact can be in as many groups as you want to put it in; deleting it from a group doesn't delete it from Contacts.

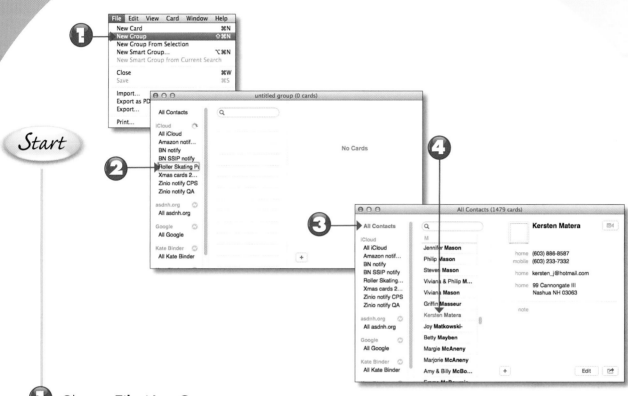

Start

1. Choose **File**, **New Group**.

2. Give the new group a name.

3. Click **All Contacts** or a group that contains the contacts you want to add to the new group.

4. Drag the contacts into the new group.

End

TIP

A Two-Way Street Creating a new group can work backward, too. First, ⌘-**click** to select the contacts you want to put in the group; then choose **File**, **New Group from Selection**. ▪

TIP

Edit This The **Edit** button is also where you should head (or, more precisely, click) when you want to make changes to an existing Contacts entry. To apply your changes, click **Done**, or you can just click another contact or group instead. ▪

CREATING A SMART CONTACT GROUP

You create smart groups in Contacts, but your Mac maintains them. After you determine the criteria for a contact's inclusion in a smart group, the Mac makes sure that the right contacts are sorted into that group at all times, even after you've changed contact information or added new contacts.

Start

Continued

1. Choose **File**, **New Smart Group**.

2. Type a name for the group.

3. Choose criteria for the group's members.

4. Click **+** to add criteria.

NOTE

Going Negative Don't forget that you can set most smart group criteria to negative values—meaning you can choose to include everyone in Contacts who *doesn't* match a particular criterion. ■

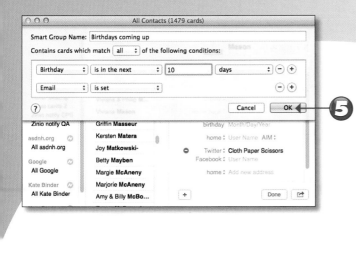

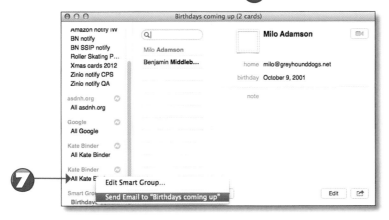

5 Click **OK** to create the group.

6 Click the group's name to see its members in the Name column.

7 Control-click the group's name to email its members or export their contact data.

End

NOTE

Setting Conditions You're not limited to just one criterion when creating a smart group. You can set as many conditions for inclusion as you like, and you can choose whether group members must satisfy all the conditions, or just some of them. ■

NOTE

What's It Good For? Use smart groups to track contacts' birthdays, anniversaries, or other important dates; collect all contacts from a particular company into a single group; or look up which friends and family members live near your next vacation spot. ■

EXPORTING CONTACTS AS VCARDS

Apple has chosen the vCard as its standard method of exchanging contact information among Contacts users as well as between Contacts and other programs. vCards are very small files that you can attach to email messages. Most contact management programs can read them, so they're a good way to send contact information to just about anyone, including Windows users.

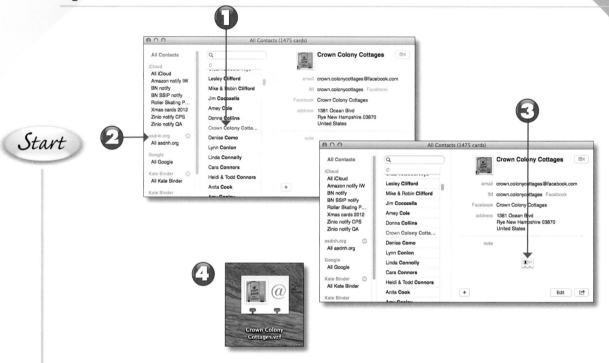

Start

Crown Colony Cottages.vcf

① Click a name in the contacts column to select a single person, or ⌘-**click** to select more than one person.

② To create a vCard for an entire group, click the group's name in the first column.

③ Drag the group, contact, or contacts onto the desktop to create the vCard file.

④ The vCard appears on the desktop and can now be attached and sent via email.

End

NOTE

The Express Route You can find contacts quickly by clicking the **All Contacts** group and typing a name, city, or other information into the Search entry field at the top of the window. ■

IMPORTING A VCARD

Getting vCards into Contacts is just as easy as getting them out of Contacts. When you receive a vCard attached to an email as a sort of electronic business card, you need to locate the file in your attachments folder—you'll recognize it because of its .vcf filename extension and its address card icon.

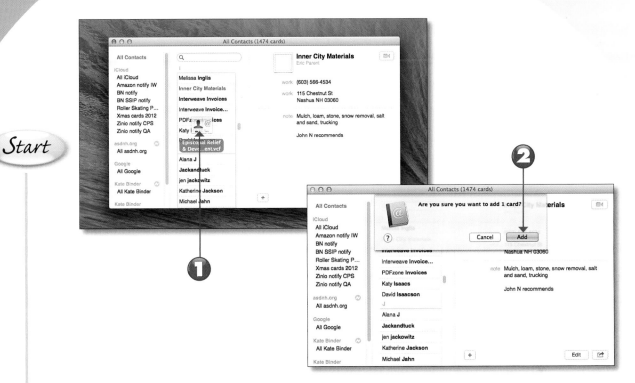

Start

1 Drag the vCard file from the desktop into the Contacts window.

2 Click **Add** in the confirmation dialog box.

End

NOTE

The Case of the Missing Attachment vCard files typically end up in your email attachments folder—the location and name can vary depending on which email program you use. To get at these files easily, try clicking their names or icons in the email window and dragging them onto the desktop, or even directly into the Contacts window. ∎

MAPPING A CONTACT'S ADDRESS

If you have an instant-on or constant Internet connection, you're going to love this Contacts feature. You can view a map (and from there, driving directions) for an address in your contact list. It all starts with a simple click to a pop-up menu. Just remember, it won't work if you're not online.

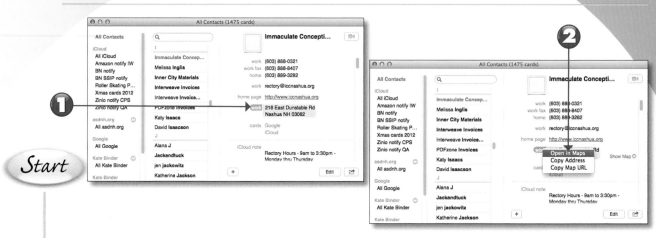

Start

1 Click the address label next to the address to display a pop-up menu.

2 Click **Open in Maps**.

3 The map is displayed in Maps.

End

NOTE

Just the URL, Please If you want to pass a map along to a friend, rather than just use it yourself, take advantage of another choice in the address pop-up menu: **Copy Map URL**. After you choose this command, click in any text document or email window and press ⌘-**V** to paste the map's URL so the reader can click it to see the map. ■

ADDING REMINDERS

Using a calendar to keep track of events is very important (turn to the next task to see how this works in Calendar), but for many people, tracking a to-do list is an even more vital function. With Reminders, you can assign each to-do item to a specific list, so you can distinguish among work, home, and hobby- or club-related tasks.

Start

1 Start up **Reminders** (in the Applications folder).

2 Click the name of the list you want to add the reminder to.

3 Click in the blank space and enter the reminder text.

4 Click the **i** button to assign a time or place to the reminder.

End

TIP

It's All My Default If you use multiple lists of reminders but you usually keep reminders on one list, choose **Reminders**, **Default List** and pick a list for new reminders to be added to. For example, you might find most of your reminders have to do with things you need to buy, so you could choose **Errands** as a default list. ■

TIP

It's a Date To link a to-do item to a particular date, click the **Calendar** button at the bottom of the Reminders window to display a calendar, and then click a date to assign the reminder to that day. ■

MAKING NOTES

Writing yourself a note should be simple, and with the new Notes app, it is. Notes comes to OS X from iOS, where it works like a charm for millions of iPad and iPhone users. Whether you need to compose a grocery list, drag in a photo, or scribble the first sentence of your new novel before you forget it, Notes will store your data safely—and searchably.

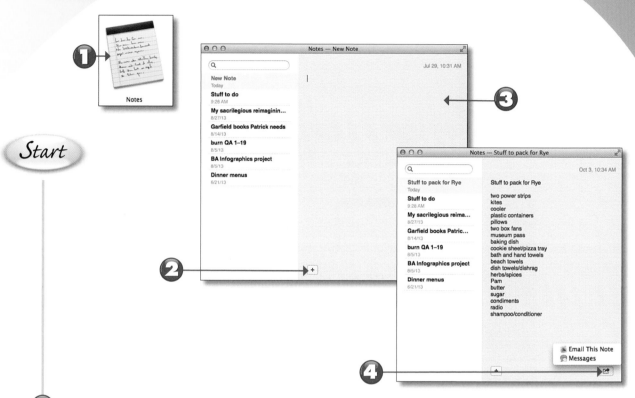

Start

End

1 Start up **Notes** (in the Applications folder).

2 Click + to create a new note, or click the name of an existing note.

3 Enter note text.

4 Click **Share** to send the note's contents as an email or chat message.

NOTE

Finding It To search Notes, click in the search field at the top of the list of notes and type your search terms. Notes shows you all the notes that contain those terms. ■

TIP

What Works? Notes can store a lot more than just text. Try copying and pasting content from a web page, for example, or dragging an image file onto a note page. ■

ADDING AN APPOINTMENT TO YOUR CALENDAR

Calendar is compact and easy to use, but don't underestimate it. This little calendar program has a surprising amount of power. Its primary purpose, of course, is keeping track of your appointments. Adding new ones couldn't be simpler, and reading Calendar's neatly color-coded calendar is as easy as it gets.

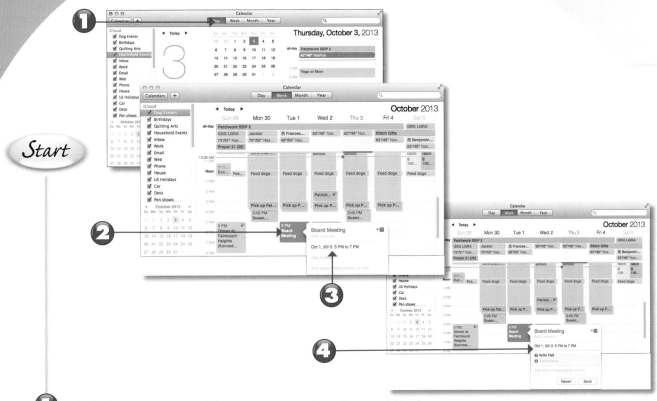

Start

1. Click the **Day** or **Week** button to switch to Day or Week view.

2. Click and drag on the hour grid for the day of the appointment to define the time span for the appointment.

3. Type in the appointment text.

4. Add more information (such as the event's location) and assign a calendar.

End

TIP

Filling in the Details To refine your appointment entry, double-click the appointment and then click the section of information you need to change. Enter a location, add an alarm notification, set the appointment to repeat regularly, and more. You can also change the event's calendar here. ■

MODIFYING AN EVENT IN YOUR CALENDAR

The more things change, well, the more confused you get. Unless you have Calendar, that is—it's easy to make changes to events you've scheduled previously. You can, of course, change an event's day and time by simply dragging it to another place on your calendar. Here you'll learn how to make other changes.

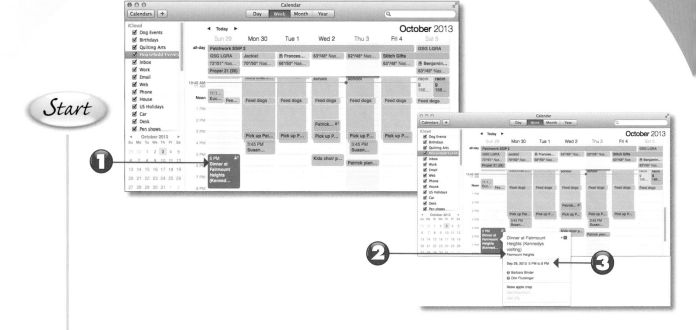

1 Double-click the event you want to change.

2 Click the section of information you want to change.

3 Make changes to the event's time or other attributes.

End

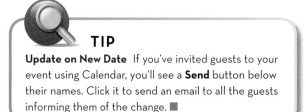

TIP

Update on New Date If you've invited guests to your event using Calendar, you'll see a **Send** button below their names. Click it to send an email to all the guests informing them of the change. ■

SHARING CALENDARS WITH ICLOUD

If you've ever held those seemingly endless negotiations to find a time when you and your friends are all free, consider sharing your calendar with those people. They won't be able to change anything, but everyone will be able to see what times you're free—and when you're busy. Since Calendar supports multiple calendars, you can keep private info on private calendars while still sharing your schedule with those who need to see it.

Start

1 Click **Calendars** to see a list of your calendars, then choose a calendar from the list.

2 Choose **Edit**, **Share Calendar**.

3 Check the box marked **Public Calendar** if you want to make the calendar viewable by anyone who has the link.

4 Enter email addresses (or names, if the people are already in your Contacts) of the people with whom you want to share the calendar, then click **Done**.

End

TIP

Share or Don't Share You can change calendar sharing settings at any time. Choose **Edit**, **Sharing Settings** to see your settings. Or choose **Edit**, **Stop Sharing** to turn off sharing for that calendar. ■

TIP

Letting People Know Click the **Share** button in the Sharing Settings window to send an email or a message with the link to the calendar, or to post it on Facebook. ■

SETTING UP AN EVENT ALERT

If you want to be reminded before an appointment, you can set up an alert that will get your attention to let you know the appointment is coming up. Calendar alerts take several forms: displaying a dialog box, displaying a dialog box and playing a sound, sending an email, or opening a specified file.

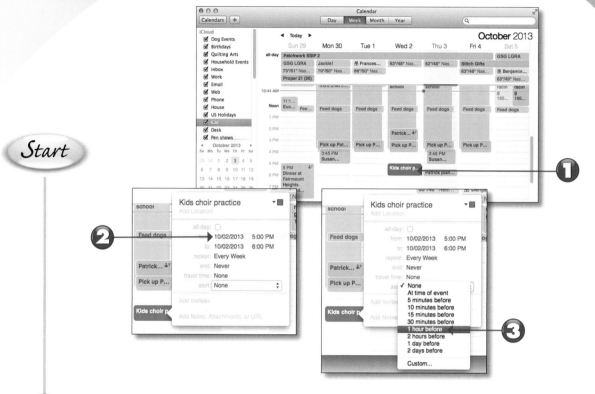

1. Double-click the appointment to which you want to add an alert.

2. Click in the date and time section.

3. Click the **alert** pop-up menu and set the time for the alert to appear.

End

TIP

Hitting the Snooze Button Calendar alerts do have a snooze button—click **Snooze** to clear the reminder and have it pop back in 15 minutes. ■

RESPONDING TO NOTIFICATIONS

Notifications pop up to let you know of newly arrived emails, FaceTime calls, and messages from your friends. Now, with OS X Mavericks, you can reply to those messages right in the Notification window, with no need to switch to Mail, Messages, or whatever other program is alerting you to what's happening.

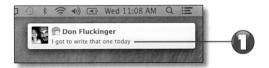

 Start

1 When a message notification appears, click it to focus on it.

2 Click **Reply** if you want to respond immediately.

3 If you change your mind about your response, click **Cancel**.

4 When you're done typing your response, press **Enter** to send it.

End

NOTE

On the Record Messages you send directly from a Notification window also show up in Messages and Mail, so you don't have to worry about not having a record of what you've said. ■

TIP

If You Miss It If you don't get to a notification right away and it disappears before you can see what it said, no worries—just click **Notification Center** in the menu bar to see all your current notifications. ■

ADDING CUSTOM NOTIFICATIONS

Another new feature of notifications in OS X Mavericks is the ability to receive notifications from your favorite websites. This has to be implemented at the site itself—it's not something you can set up yourself. If a site offers push notifications—which appear even when Safari's not running—you'll be asked if you want to receive them, and you can change how they should appear in System Preferences.

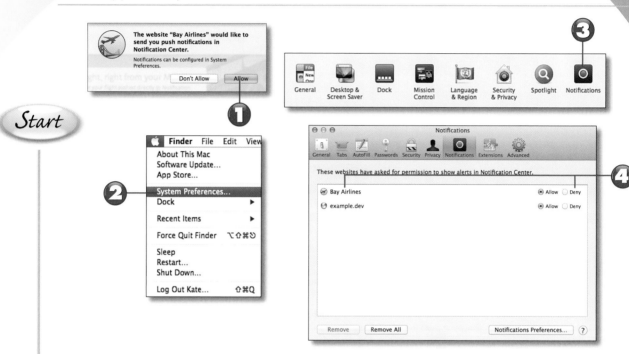

1. When you're asked if you want to see push notifications, click **Don't Allow** or **Allow**.

2. To change the format of notifications, choose **Apple menu**, **System Preferences**.

3. Click **Notifications**.

4. Click the site whose notifications you want to modify in the list and click the alert style you prefer.

End

NOTE

Why It's a Good Thing Because website notifications are funneled through Apple's servers, Apple can keep unscrupulous developers from spamming you with notifications you don't want. And Apple requires that websites let you choose which notifications you want to receive from their sites. ■

TIP

I've Changed My Mind If you want to revoke permission for push notifications, choose **Safari**, **Preferences** and click **Notifications**. Choose the site you want to banish from Notification Center in the list and click **Remove**. ■

INVITING CONTACTS TO EVENTS IN CALENDAR

If you use Apple's Mail as your email program, you can invite people to scheduled events right from Calendar, and even update information about the event as it gets closer. You'll just need to know the email addresses of the people you want to invite to your event.

1 Double-click the appointment to which you want to invite others.

2 Click **Add Invitees**.

3 Enter the names or email addresses of the people you want to invite; Calendar inserts email addresses for names that are in Contacts.

4 Click **Send** to send email invitations.

End

NOTE

Separate Names To invite more than one person to an event, type a comma after each name before you type the next name. Otherwise, Calendar isn't sure where one name ends and the next begins. ■

TIP

Getting People in the Door Another way to add people to the attendees list for an event is to choose **Window**, **Address Panel** and drag names from the list to the event's listing in the calendar. ■

PUTTING CONTACTS, BOOKMARKS, AND CALENDARS ONLINE

If you have an iCloud membership, you can sync your contact information, web bookmarks, calendars, and other information between two computers—or more. You can also access this information from the Web when you're using a computer that's not synced up, such as a public terminal or a friend's PC.

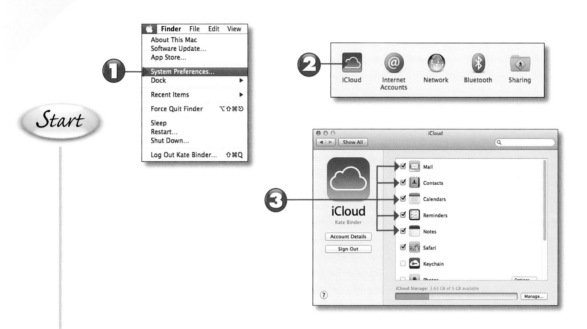

Start

1 Choose **Apple menu**, **System Preferences**.

2 In System Preferences, click **iCloud**.

3 Check the boxes for the items you want to sync.

End

TIP

In Touch Anywhere To see your information using a web browser on any computer, go to www. iCloud. com and log in using your iCloud name and password. Then click one of the links on the left side of the page, such as **Contacts**. ■

NOTE

Making Room for It All You get 5GB of space for free to store your info on iCloud. If you need more room for your stuff, you can buy more space—up to 50GB on top of the 5GB you already have. ■

SEARCHING CALENDARS

You know you put Aunt Kathleen's birthday in Calendar, but you can't even remember the month, much less the day. Never fear: Calendar will find the date for you. Just search for "Kathleen," and your trusty calendar will offer you a list of every event containing her name, including that elusive birthday.

Start

1 Click **Calendars**, then click the check boxes next to the calendars you want to search.

2 Type the text you want to search for in the **search** field.

3 Click an event or to-do in the **Search Result** list to go to it.

4 To clear the search field and get rid of the Search Result list, click the **X**.

End

GETTING DIRECTIONS IN MAPS

Once upon a time, maps were made of paper, and they were renowned for never folding back the way they started. These days, maps are electronic, and your Mac has them built-in—as long as you have an Internet connection—and can show you how to get anywhere you want to go.

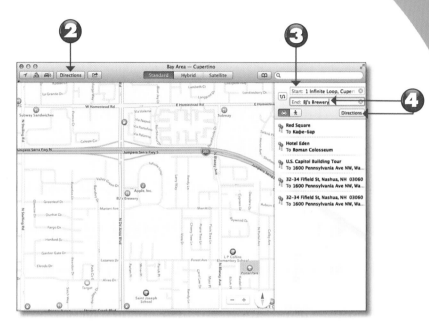

Start

 Open **Maps**.

 Click **Directions**.

3 Enter your starting address in the **Start** field.

4 Enter the address of the place you want to go in the **End** field and click **Directions**.

Continued

NOTE

No Matter Where You Go The closer in you zoom on a map, the more detail you'll see. So if you already know where you're going and you want to know what's nearby, just keep zooming in—you'll see parking facilities, restaurants, shops, schools, and more all neatly labeled on the map. ■

TIP

In Search Of You can search for a location in Maps by typing keywords into the search field in the upper right-hand corner of the app window. Maps offers you suggested addresses and nearby businesses that match your search terms, as well as similar search terms used by others that may match your needs better. ■

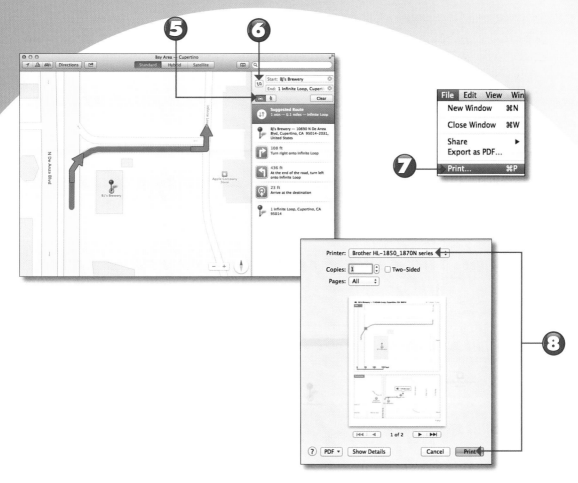

5 Click **Car** to display driving directions or **Walk** to display walking directions.

6 To reverse directions so you can see your route home, click the **Swap** button.

7 To print directions, choose **File**, **Print**.

8 Choose a printer and click **Print**.

End

TIP

You Can Choose You don't have to stick with Maps' first choice of route. Typically you're offered multiple routes to choose from; to view an alternative route, just click its time bubble in the map. To avoid confusion, Maps tells you which alternative number you're looking at as well as the main road it uses. ■

USING DIFFERENT VIEWS IN MAPS

Like the mapping websites you're probably used to using, Maps can display the terrain in different ways, depending on what you need to see. And you can customize that view by spinning the map around, changing its perspective, and even dropping pins in it to mark spots that you want to find again.

Start

1 Open **Maps**.

2 Click **Standard** to see a regular map view showing only streets and major geographical features.

3 Click **Satellite** to see a birds-eye photo of the same area.

4 Click **Hybrid** to see streets and geographical features superimposed on a satellite photo.

Continued

NOTE

Where Am I? No matter which Maps view you're using, you can always click the **Current Location** button at the top left-hand corner of the Maps window to zoom straight to wherever you are now. If this doesn't work, you'll need to grant Maps access to Location Services in the Security & Privacy pane of System Preferences. ■

TIP

Making It Easy You want to send directions to your grandpa, and he's okay with email, but the whole Web thing is a bit too much for him? No problem. Just export your directions as a PDF that he can print out before his trip. ■

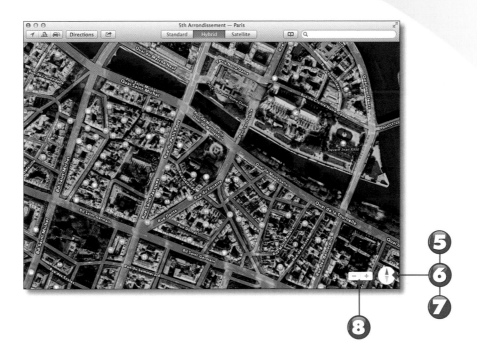

5 Click the **compass** to toggle between a 3D view and a flat overhead view.

6 Click and drag the **compass** to rotate the map.

7 Double-click the **compass** to spin the map around so north is at the top of the window.

8 Click **+** or **–** to zoom in or out of the map.

End

TIP

Remember That Place? You can teach your Mac what places Maps should remember for you. Just Ctrl-click/right-click any point on the map to drop a pin there. Then you can give that location a name (such as "incredible candy store!!") and add it to your bookmarks so you'll be able to find it again even without knowing its name or address. ∎

SENDING DIRECTIONS TO YOUR IPHONE

Of course, your Mac doesn't go everywhere you go. But your iPhone does, if you're lucky enough to have one. Once you've mapped out a route using Maps on your Mac, you can send that route to your iPhone, where it'll appear in the Maps app, all ready for you to take along on your walk or car ride.

Click on the route you want to use.

2 Click **Share**.

3 Choose **Send to [your iPhone]**.

End

NOTE

You Have Choices In Step 3 you can also choose to send the directions to a number of other places in other ways, including as an email or by posting on Facebook. Use the AirDrop option to send directions to a nearby device that's not otherwise connected with your user account, such as your friend's iPhone. ■

TIP

You've Got Directions! When you send directions to your iOS device (this works with iPads and iPod Touches, too!), you'll receive a notification on that device that the directions have arrived. Tap the notification to open the directions right in the Maps app. ■

BOOKMARKING LOCATIONS IN MAPS

When you want to remember what page you're reading in your current book, you put in a bookmark. And you bookmark websites so you can get back to them in the future. Now you can bookmark locations on a map and use those bookmarks to return to the map locations any time you want.

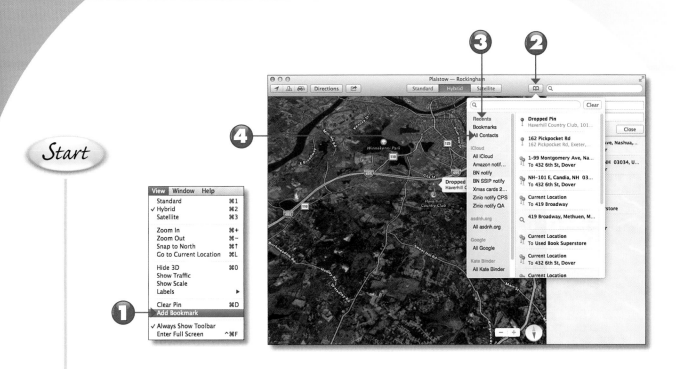

1. To add a bookmark for a location you're currently viewing, choose **View**, **Add Bookmark**.

2. To view your bookmarks, click the **Bookmarks** button.

3. Click **Recents** to see a list of the places you've mapped recently or **Bookmarks** to see places you've bookmarked.

4. Click **All Contacts** or a contact group and choose a contact to zoom in on that address.

End

NOTE

Bookmark Me Remember that Maps doesn't bookmark specific sets of directions, it bookmarks locations. So it makes sense to add bookmarks for places you already know how to get to, such as your home, so that you can easily send directions to other people. ■

NOTE

In The Cloud Bookmarks in Maps are synced to all devices linked to your iCloud account, so anything you bookmark on your Mac will be easy to find on your iPad on iPhone. To learn more about iCloud, which is free for all Mac or iOS users, turn to the tasks in Chapter 9, "Living Online." ■

PRINTING, FAXING, AND SCANNING

Mac OS X makes it easy to use your printer, fax modem, and scanner. All three functions are built in to the system, so you don't need to worry about buggy, incompatible software that slows you down when you're trying to get things done. You have lots of options for printing, faxing, and scanning that enable you to get the most from your devices, but if you're in a hurry, each function can be accomplished with just a few clicks.

Faxing happens the same way and in the same place as printing—the Print dialog box—so if you have a modem, you can fax any document you can print. And a small, simple, but powerful program called Image Capture is responsible for scanning duties.

Meanwhile, Mac OS X helps you install and organize your fonts with just a click or two. You can even group related fonts—those for a specific project, for instance—into collections so that it's always easy to find just the typeface you have in mind.

USING PRINTERS, FAX MODEMS, SCANNERS, AND FONTS

Set up
printers, 136

Switch
printers, 138

Install and or-
ganize fonts,
144–145

Scan documents
and pictures, 142

Print and
fax, 139–141

SETTING UP A PRINTER

First, you need to know at least one thing about your printer: how it's connected. It might be a USB printer plugged in to the Mac itself, or it could be a network printer. When you get that figured out, the Mac can go out and find the printer for itself.

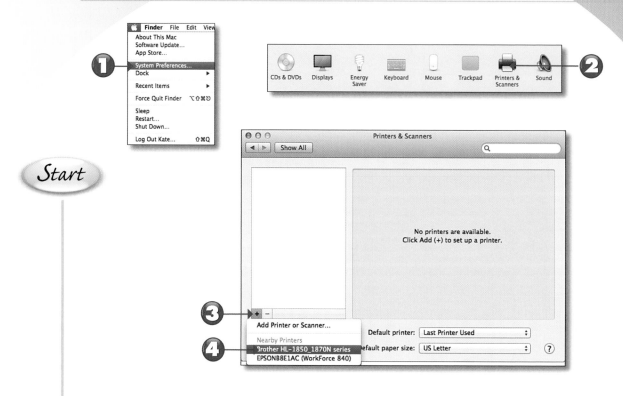

Start

1 Choose **Apple menu**, **System Preferences**.

2 Click the **Printers & Scanners** button to see your choices.

3 Click the **Add** button below the **Printers** list.

4 Choose a printer from the pop-up menu.

Continued

TIP

Missing Pieces To work with your printer, the Mac has to have access to the printer drivers (the software) that came with the printer. Your Mac can automatically download many printers' drivers, but if it doesn't find them, you'll need to dig out the disc that came with the printer or visit the manufacturer's website to download the latest drivers. ■

If you have multiple printers but use one of them most of the time, choose it from the **Default Printer** pop-up menu.

Click **Options & Supplies** to change settings for the printer's features.

Choose options for your printer.

Click **OK** when you're done.

End

NOTE

Close Enough If you don't have the correct printer driver for your printer, you can usually get away with using one that's similar. Just choose the closest model available. ■

TIP

Two for One If your printer doesn't have its model name and number on the front, check the manual that came with it. Sometimes multiple similar models share a driver, and in that case, all the similar models should be listed in the manual. ■

SWITCHING PRINTERS

If you have more than one printer, you want to make sure you send each document to the right printer. You can choose a printer each time you print, or you can change the default printer to ensure that the next time you click **Print**, the desired printer will be chosen. Start by choosing **File**, **Print** in any program and then follow these steps.

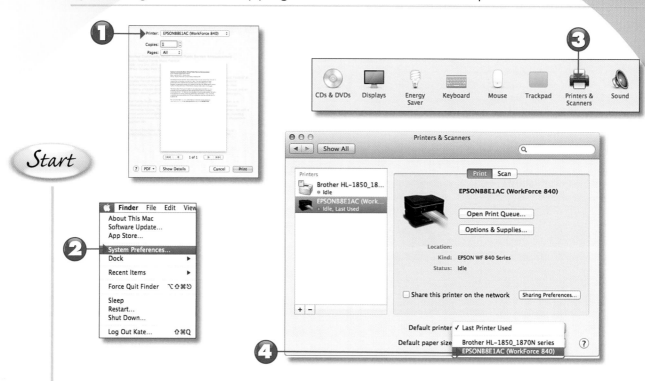

To change printers on-the-fly as you prepare to print, choose a different printer from the **Printer** pop-up menu at the top of the Print dialog box.

To change default printers ahead of time, choose **Apple menu**, **System Preferences**.

Click the **Printers & Scanners** button to see your choices.

Choose a printer from the **Default Printer** pop-up menu.

TIP

Who's Who? If you're not a fan of printer names like "SuperPrint PhotoJet XL67825 Pro v8.5.1c," click your printer in the Printers & Scanners preferences, and then click **Options & Supplies** to change its name to whatever you like. ■

TIP

Printing Success If a friend or family member will be using your computer and you're not confident of that person's ability to select the right printer on-the-fly, set the default printer ahead of time so the right printer is preselected in the Print dialog. ■

PRINTING A DOCUMENT

For all practical purposes, the actual process of sending a document to the printer works the same in Mac OS X as it has in previous generations of the Mac OS. You can exert greater control if you want by inspecting each pane of the Print dialog box and adjusting the settings you find there, or you can just click **Print** and go.

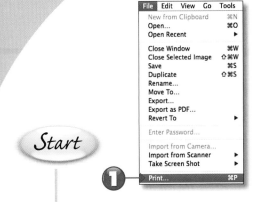

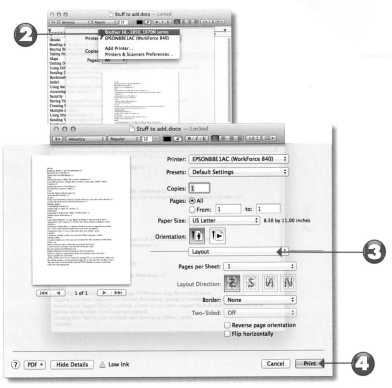

Start

End

1 Choose **File**, **Print** (or press ⌘-**P**) to display the Print dialog box.

2 Choose a printer from the **Printer** pop-up menu and then click **Show Details** to reveal more settings menus.

3 Check the settings in each pane of the Print dialog box using the pop-up menu and make changes as needed.

4 Click **Print**.

TIP

The Print Dialog Box The Print dialog box's panes vary according to the printer, but they always include Layout (how many pages to print on each sheet of paper), Paper Handling (which paper tray the printer should use), and one for program-specific features. ■

SENDING A FAX

If you have a fax modem, you've probably spent some time wrestling with third-party fax software, which never seems to work right with either the system software or all the programs from which you want to fax. Those days are over; fax sending capability is built in to Mac OS X, and it's as close as the Print command.

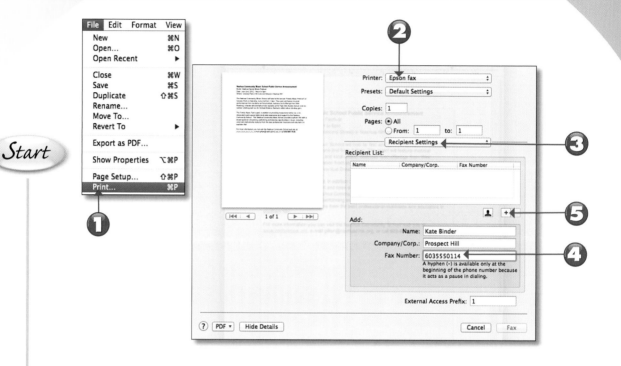

Start

1 Open the document and choose **File**, **Print**.

2 Choose your fax modem from the **Printer** pop-up menu.

3 Choose **Recipient Settings** from the pop-up menu.

4 Type the name and fax number of the person you want to fax. If the fax recipient's name is in the Address Book, the fax number is filled in automatically and won't show.

5 Click the + button to add your recipient.

Continued

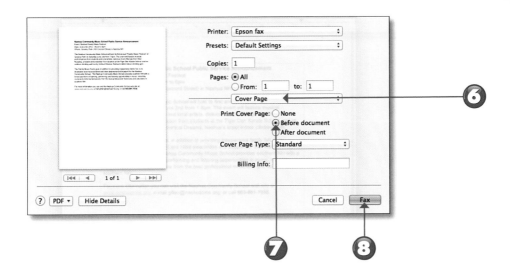

6 Choose **Cover Page** from the pop-up menu.

7 Choose a location for the cover page.

8 Click **Fax**.

End

TIP

What Goes Out Can Come In, Too To receive faxes on your Mac, choose **Apple menu**, **System Preferences** and then click **Printers & Scanners**. Choose your fax modem from the pick list and click **Receive Options**. Click the check box labeled **Receive faxes on this computer**. Then set options for what your Mac is to do when a fax is received. ■

USING A SCANNER

Your scanner is the way to get pictures inside your Mac, whether you need to copy a document, email a photo, or produce a web-ready image of a flat item you're selling online. First, install the scanner and its software according to the instructions that came with it. Then you're ready to get scanning.

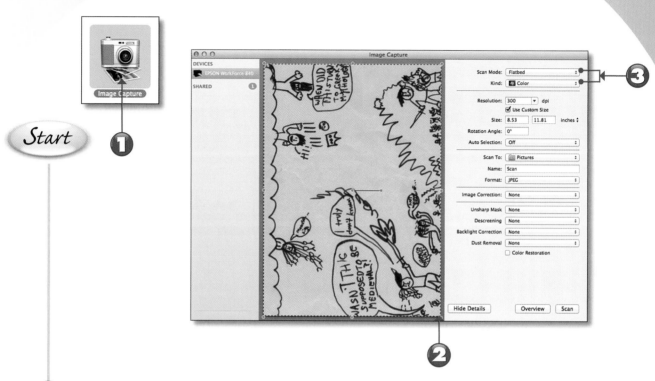

Start

1 Double-click **Image Capture** in the Applications folder.

2 Click and drag in the window to select the portion of the image you want to scan. (If you don't see a preview scan of the image, click **Show Details**.)

3 Choose a source type from the **Scan Mode** pop-up menu, and select a document type from the **Kind** pop-up menu.

Continued

NOTE

Sticking to the Safe Side You should be conservative in selecting the scan area. If you scan a larger area than you need, you can easily trim it when you edit the image in Preview, Adobe Photoshop, or another program. If you don't scan enough, you'll have to rescan the whole image. ■

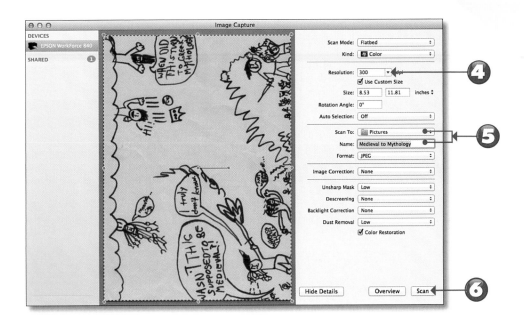

4 Set the **Resolution**.

5 Choose a location for the image file and give it a name.

6 Click **Scan**. The image is saved in the selected folder.

End

TIP

Making It Better If you don't plan to edit your scanned image in an image editor such as Photoshop, you can adjust it using the controls located at the bottom of the dialog box, directly over the **Scan** button. These options can improve the quality of your scans. **Unsharp Mask** can sharpen an out-of-focus image, and **Descreening** removes the pattern you get when you scan printed images from books or magazines. **Backlight Correction** compensates for bright light behind a photo's subject, and **Dust Removal** attempts to remove small specks in the image. ■

ADDING FONTS

There's no such thing as a font collection that's too big. Don't take that the wrong way—using all the fonts you have in one document is usually a very bad move, design-wise. But having a lot of fonts to choose from when you're creating graphics or printed documents is a luxury that's available to anyone with a Mac. Here's how to install a new font.

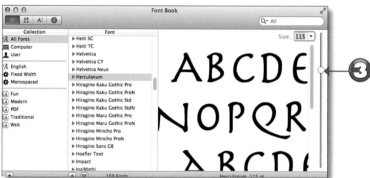

Start

1 Double-click the font's icon. Font Book starts up and displays the font.

2 Click **Install Font**. The font is installed in your home folder's Library folder.

3 Drag the **Size** slider in the Font Book window to preview the font at different sizes.

End

TIP

Shopping Time Where do fonts come from? My favorite font store is myfonts.com, run by the pioneering digital type foundry Bitstream. Not only can you shop from thousands of fonts, ranging from classic to bizarre, you can upload an image of an unidentified font to the site's WhatTheFont area for an automatic identification. ■

ORGANIZING FONTS

If your font collection has been growing, you'll love the capability to group the installed fonts into collections. Collections keep your fonts organized so you can quickly apply the fonts you're using for a given project. Mac OS X comes with a few predefined collections, but feel free to create as many collections as you want.

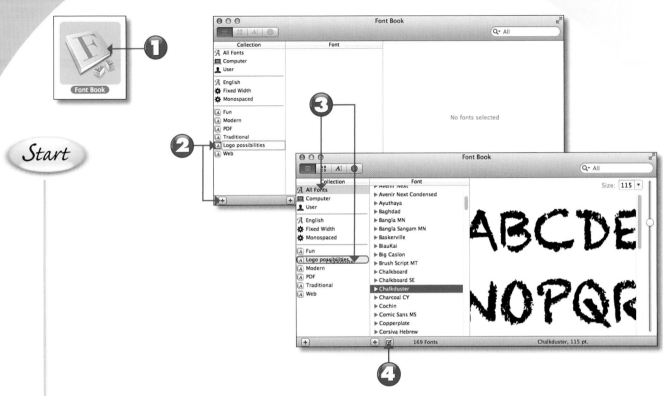

Double-click **Font Book** in the Applications folder.

Click the + button below the Collection column to create a new collection and then type in a name.

Click **All Fonts** in the Collection column and drag a font from the Font column into the new collection.

Click a collection name or a font name and click **Disable** to remove that font from the Font panel. If you see a confirmation dialog box, click **Disable** again.

TIP

Putting Fonts Back on the Menu Disabling a font doesn't delete it—you can always return to Font Book, select the font from the **All Fonts** collection, and click the same button to make the font available again. ■

KEEPING IN TOUCH

Before you can do anything online, you have to actually get online. Fortunately, with Mac OS X, getting online couldn't be easier. In fact, your Mac might have completed some of these tasks for you already based on the information you gave it when you first started up Mac OS X. If not, don't worry—nothing here will take you more than a couple of minutes to complete, and then you'll be ready to go.

In this chapter, you learn how to set up Mail accounts and use them to send and receive email. And you'll learn ways to keep your email spam-free, organized, and easy to deal with—no matter how much email you receive each day. You can even automate some organizational tasks so Mail takes care of them for you, such as filing your email in the proper mailboxes according to sender, recipient, or subject; this chapter shows you how.

Other tasks in this chapter show you how to send and receive chat messages and make audio and video calls online with Messages. You can even apply special video effects in real-time when you're in a video chat, and you can give presentations online as well.

USING EMAIL AND CHAT

Set up multiple email accounts, 148

Get rid of spam, 158

Send and receive email, 150–151

Make video calls, 160

Sort and filter email messages, 154–157

Chat with your friends online, 166

SETTING UP EMAIL ACCOUNTS

Setting up new email accounts works the same way whether you're using Mail for the first time or adding an umpteenth different email address for yourself. You'll go through a series of dialog boxes that ask you for your username, password, server names, and other information.

 Start

1 In Mail, choose **Mail**, **Add Account**. (If you're starting Mail for the first time, you may be taken directly to this series of dialogs.)

2 Choose the type of account you want to add and click **Continue**.

3 Enter your name, email address, and password and click **Create**. If you chose any of the first five options in Step 2, Mail will skip some of the dialogs in the following steps because it already has most of the information it needs.

4 If you see "Account must be manually configured," click **Next**.

Continued

NOTE

More Fun with Mail Accounts You can set up as many Mail accounts as you have email addresses. Mail automatically filters your incoming email into a separate mailbox for each address, so you can keep your messages organized. ■

NOTE

Hit the Ground Running If you've already set up your iCloud account (see page 188) and set your preferences to use it for Mail, then Mail sets up that account automatically. ■

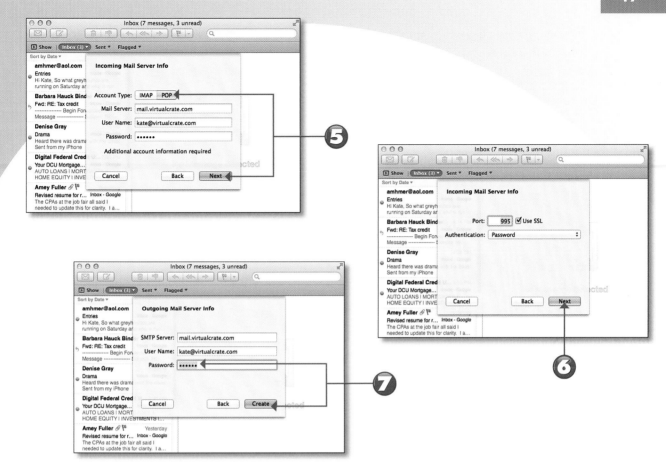

5 Choose the type of account you have (see the Note below for guidance), fill in your server address and other info for incoming email, and click **Next**.

6 If your ISP has asked you to use a particular port for incoming email, enter it; otherwise, accept the default and then click **Next**.

7 Enter the server address and other info for outgoing email and click **Create**.

End

NOTE

Pop Goes the Email! POP and IMAP, the two Account Type choices that you are most likely to use, refer to the way your email is handled on the server, the computer that receives your email over the Internet and forwards it to your Mac. Most commercial ISPs use POP, but university systems, for example, often use IMAP, and so do iCloud and Gmail. If you're not sure which account type your email uses, check with your network administrator or technical support department. ∎

SENDING EMAIL WITH MAIL

The steps given here assume that you're composing a new message. If you click a received message in one of your mailboxes, you'll see toolbar buttons for replying and forwarding; just click the appropriate button and then add your message text and an email address if you're forwarding the message.

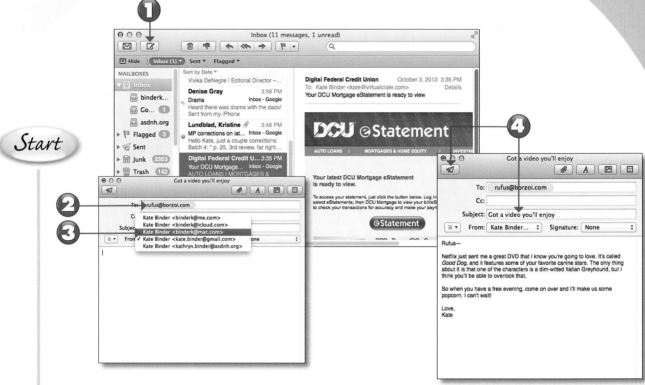

Start

1 Click the **Compose New Message** button in the toolbar.

2 Type the name of the person you want to email. If the email address doesn't appear automatically, it's not in your Contacts, and you'll need to type in the email address.

3 If you've set up multiple email accounts, choose the one from which you want to send in the **From** pop-up menu.

4 Type a subject in the **Subject** line and your message in the message area. Click **Send**.

End

TIP

Jazzing Up Your Emails To attach a file, click the **Attach** button in the message window's toolbar and navigate to the file you want to attach. To make your email text colored, click the **Show Format Bar** button and choose a color in the Colors panel. ■

RECEIVING EMAIL WITH MAIL

There's nothing quite like that friendly chime (or beep, or other sound) from your computer indicating that you, yes you, have email. By default, Mail drops all of your new, unread email into your Inbox each time you check for new messages.

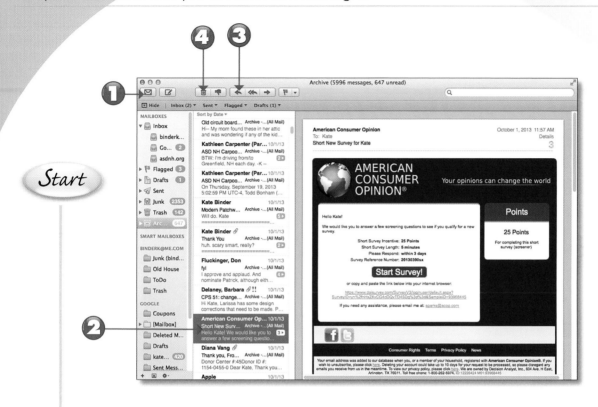

 Start

 End

1. Click **Get Mail**.

2. Click a message listing in the Inbox to see the message's contents.

3. Click **Reply** to answer the current message.

4. Click **Delete** if you want to send the message to the Trash.

TIP
I've Got Mail? Mail can retrieve your email messages automatically on a schedule you determine. Choose **Mail**, **Preferences** and click **General**. Choose a time interval from the **Check for New Mail** pop-up menu. ■

TIP
More Ways to Reply To answer an email message, click **Reply** to send your answer to just the original sender. Click **Reply All** to send it to everyone who originally received the email. Click **Forward** to send it to another recipient. ■

ORGANIZING MAILBOXES

If you get a lot of email, you'll quickly find your Inbox filling up. Creating a system of mailboxes in which you can file all that email will save you time in the long run because it makes finding what you want when you need it easier. You can nest mailboxes within other mailboxes to set up as complex a system as you need.

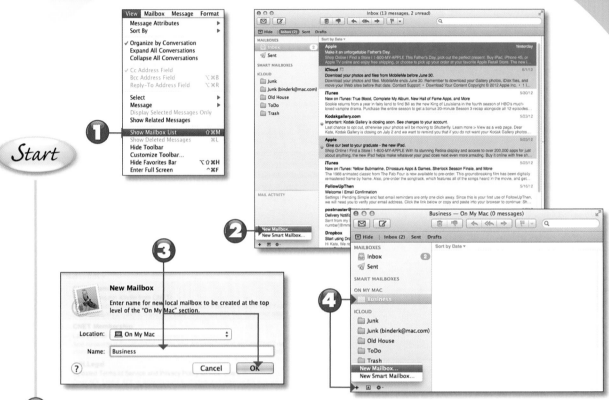

Start

1. In Mail, select **View**, **Show Mailbox List** if mailboxes are not visible.

2. Click the + button at the bottom-left corner of the window and choose **New Mailbox** to create a new mailbox.

3. Enter a name for the mailbox and click **OK**.

4. To create a mailbox inside another mailbox, click a mailbox name and then click the + button.

Continued

TIP

Like Parent, Like Child If a mailbox is selected when you click the + button, the new mailbox is created as a child of the selected mailbox—in other words, it is within the selected one. ■

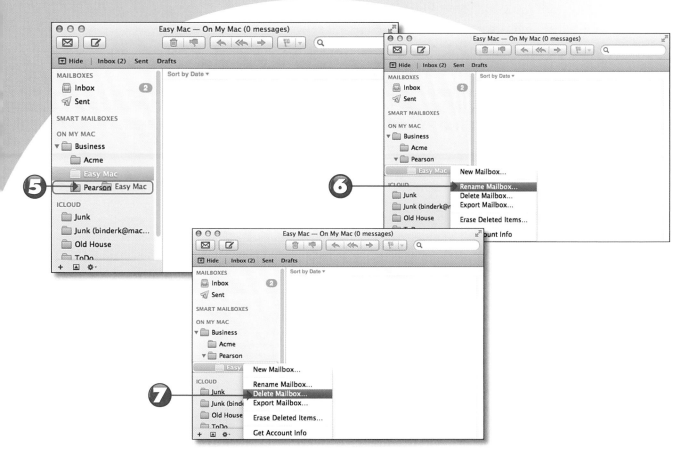

5 To move a mailbox inside another mailbox, drag and drop it into position.

6 Control-click a mailbox and choose **Rename Mailbox** from the contextual menu to change its name.

7 Control-click a mailbox and choose **Delete Mailbox** from the contextual menu to remove it.

End

NOTE

You Can't Go There You can't add mailboxes inside the default mailboxes (In, Out, Drafts, and Sent). However, Mail automatically creates mailboxes within your Inbox to segregate mail received at different email addresses. ■

TIP

Another Way to Get There The same commands you see in the contextual menu are available in the Action menu at the bottom of the **Mailbox** drawer—click the gear button to see the menu. ■

CREATING A SMART MAILBOX

Like smart groups in Contacts, smart mailboxes in Mail are maintained by your Mac. After you determine the criteria for a message's inclusion in a smart mailbox, the Mac takes over to sort messages into that mailbox as you receive new mail. Because messages can exist in both a regular mailbox and a smart mailbox, smart mailboxes don't interfere with your usual filing scheme.

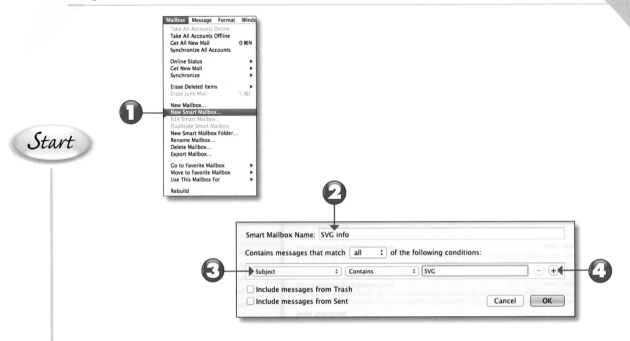

Start

1 Choose **Mailbox, New Smart Mailbox**.

2 Type a name for the mailbox.

3 Choose criteria for which messages should be sorted into the mailbox.

4 Click + to add more criteria.

Continued

NOTE

What's It Good For? Use smart mailboxes to track messages related to a particular project or from people who share a company or ISP. For example, you can have Mail sort all messages about your upcoming Flamingo Party into a smart mailbox. ■

 Select **any** or **all** from the pop-up menu to determine whether messages must meet all the criteria or any single criterion.

Click the box labeled **Include messages from Trash** to file messages that are in the Trash folder.

Click the box labeled **Include messages from Sent** to file messages you send along with ones you receive.

Click **OK** to create the smart mailbox.

End

TIP

Any or All Use **any** to collect messages that fulfill one criterion or another (if the subject contains "Paris" or "Grand Canyon," file it under Vacation Plans). Use **all** to collect messages that fulfill both criteria (if the message sender's name is "Claus" and the email address contains "northpole.com," file it under Christmas). ■

FILTERING EMAIL IN MAIL

The more email you get, the more you'll appreciate having Mail help you with the filing. Mail can analyze each message you receive based on who sent it, where it was addressed, what it says, or several other criteria, and it can file that message in the appropriate mailbox. Mailboxes with unread messages are shown in bold type.

Start

1 In Mail, choose **Mail**, **Preferences**.

2 Click the **Rules** button to see the filtering options.

3 Click **Add Rule**.

4 Give the rule a name in the **Description** field.

Continued

TIP

Excluding Messages from Rules You can make a set of rules that acts on all email messages except those in a particular group. First, create a rule that filters the group you don't want to act on into the Trash or a mailbox. Then create another rule to apply your action to Every Message; this rule acts on all the messages remaining after the first rule is executed. ■

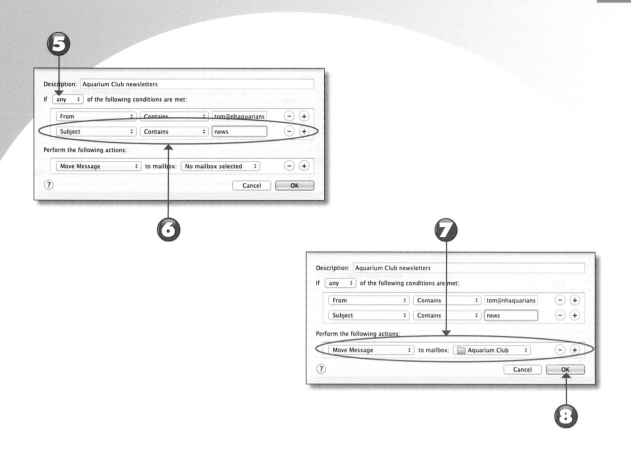

 Choose **any** or **all** from the pop-up menu; with any, the rule is activated if one or more condition is met, and with all, it's activated only if they're all met.

 Set up the condition you want to filter on; click the ✦ button to add more conditions.

 Set up the action to be invoked if the conditions are met; click the ✦ button to add more actions.

 Click **OK**.

End

 TIP

Explore Your Options There are many ways to select messages for special treatment. You can tag all messages sent to a particular address with a red-colored label, for example, or you can put messages from anyone in a Contacts group into a specific mailbox. ■

 TIP

Watching for Rule Interactions The last action step in most rules should be *Stop evaluating rules*. That way, a message properly filed according to one rule won't be refiled by another. You can also drag and drop rules to change the order they're executed in. ■

INTERCEPTING SPAM IN MAIL

Spam (or junk mail or unsolicited commercial email) is everywhere, and it's increasing by the moment. Email users are constantly looking for new ways to deal with the deluge, and Apple has done its part by including a built-in, smart junk mail filter in Mail. With your help, the filter learns to better recognize spam day by day.

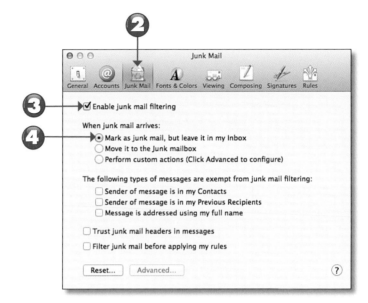

Start

1 In Mail, choose **Mail**, **Preferences**.

2 Click the **Junk Mail** button to see the spam options.

3 Click the **Enable junk mail filtering** check box.

4 Click a radio button to tell Mail what to do with junk mail it receives.

Continued

NOTE

How Does It Work? Mail recognizes junk mail using what Apple calls "latent adaptive semantic analysis." The program scans email messages for certain word patterns—not typical spam keywords such as "make money," but speech patterns that spammers tend to use. ■

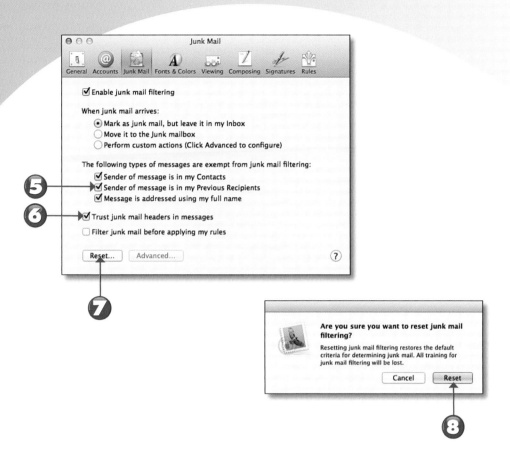

5 Click the check boxes to indicate which types of email shouldn't be considered spam.

6 Click the check box to take advantage of junk mail prefiltering done by your ISP.

7 If you want to make Mail forget the list of known junk mail senders and subjects it has compiled, click **Reset**.

8 Click **Reset** again to confirm that you want Mail to forget its list of junk mail senders and subjects.

End

TIP

Teaching Mail More About Spam Mail marks junk mail with a brown label. If a message is brown but isn't spam, click it and choose **Message, Mark As Not Junk Mail**. If you get spam that's not labeled brown, choose **Message, Mark As Junk Mail**. ■

TIP

Where to Put Spam To put all your junk mail in a special mailbox, choose **Mail, Preferences** and click **Junk Mail**. Click **Move it to the Junk mailbox**. You can get rid of all the spam you've received by choosing **Mailbox, Erase Junk Mail**. ■

MAKING VIDEO CALLS WITH FACETIME

FaceTime, Apple's video chat program, uses video technology that provides better quality with lower bandwidth and at full-screen resolution. And FaceTime works with any Mac or Apple device with FaceTime installed, so you can use it to call your friends on their Macs, iPad 2s, iPod touch 4gs, or iPhone 4s. Move over, Dick Tracy—real-life video calling has finally outdone your wristwatch phone.

Start

1 Start up FaceTime—it's in your Applications folder, and you may have a FaceTime icon in your Dock.

2 Enter your Apple ID and password and click **Sign In**. (If you don't have an Apple ID, click **Create New Account** and follow the prompts to get your very own Apple ID.)

3 Click a contact group to see a list of contacts.

4 Click the name of the person you want to call.

Continued

NOTE

Who's Calling, Please? When you get a FaceTime call, FaceTime starts up automatically and shows you who's calling. You can click **Accept** to take the call or **Decline** to ignore it. When you click **Decline**, FaceTime tells the caller you're not available. ■

NOTE

You Can Get with This, or You Can Get with That FaceTime only works with other Macs and Apple devices using FaceTime. So, if you want to chat with someone using a Windows computer, or with more than one person at a time, try Messages instead. Turn to page 166 later in this chapter to learn more. ■

5 Click the phone number or email address you want to use for the call.

6 Click the double arrow to switch to full-screen mode.

7 Click the **Mute** button to mute your microphone.

8 Click **End** to hang up on the call.

End

NOTE

New Friends FaceTime picks up contact information from Contacts and Exchange, so if you don't see someone you want to call in your FaceTime contacts, that person either isn't in your Contacts or the entry for the person doesn't have a phone number or email address. Create a Contacts entry for your new friend, and he or she will show up in your FaceTime contacts. ■

TIP

How It Gets There FaceTime uses email addresses to call Macs, iPods, and iPads—devices that don't have phone capabilities—and phone numbers to call iPhones, If you have both an email address and a phone number for a person, you can use either to place the call. No matter which method you use to call someone, the call rings through on all of their FaceTime devices. ■

GETTING AN APPLE ID FOR CHATTING

Messages works primarily with your Apple ID, though it can also connect to Yahoo!, AIM, and Gmail accounts. If you buy stuff through iTunes, you already have an Apple ID, and it's the same deal if you have an iCloud membership. If not, getting an Apple ID is easy and free. The following steps walk you through getting your ID and then entering your account info in Messages so you can get online and start chatting.

Start

1 In Safari, go to **appleid.apple.com**.

2 Click **Create an Apple ID**.

3 Enter your email address, a password, and the other information requested.

4 At the bottom of the page, click **Create Apple ID**. You'll get a confirmation email. Follow the steps given to verify that this email address is really yours, then go on to Step 5.

Continued

TIP

Chat This Messages isn't just for chatting—you can use Messages to transfer files as well. Click a person in your buddy list and choose **Buddies**, **Send File** to open a dialog box where you can choose the file. ◼

NOTE

What's in a Name? When choosing a screen name for a messaging service, think about how you want to appear. If you'll be using iChat with clients and colleagues, you probably don't want to choose "FluffyBunny." And if you'll be chatting mainly with friends, "AcmeInc" isn't the best choice. ◼

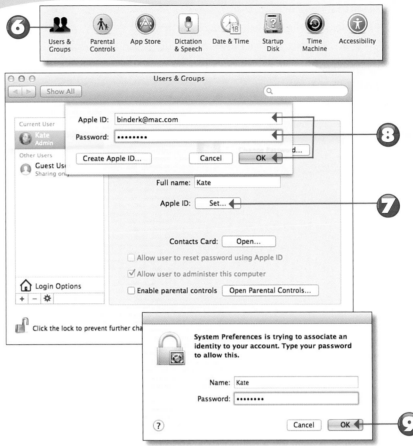

5 Choose **Apple menu**, **System Preferences**.

6 Click the **Users & Groups** button to see Users and Groups preferences.

7 Click **Set**. You may have to click the padlock button and enter your password to unlock the preferences first.

8 Enter your new Apple ID and password and click **OK**.

9 Click **OK** in the confirmation dialog. Messages automatically adds your new account in the next few minutes.

End

TIP

Chatting on the Menu Choose **Messages**, **Preferences** and click the **General** button to enter global Messages settings. The most useful one is *Show status in menu bar*, which enables you to start a chat with an online member of your buddy list without even starting up Messages first. ◼

NOTE

First Time for Everything When you start Messages for the first time on your Mac, you'll see a series of dialog boxes in which you can enter your screen name and password. ◼

USING MESSAGES WITH OTHER SERVICES

Naturally, Messages works with your Apple ID, whether you obtained it through iTunes, an old MobileMe account, or some other way. And Messages also works with your AIM account. But did you know that you can also configure Messages to log into your Jabber, Google, and Yahoo! accounts?

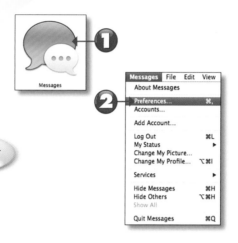

① Double-click the Messages icon in your Applications folder (or click the Messages icon in your Dock, if it's there).

② Choose **Messages**, **Preferences**.

③ Click the **Accounts** button, and then click the **Add** button.

Continued

TIP

Where's My Messages Dock Icon? If you've made changes to your Dock, the Messages icon may no longer be there. No worries! Just open your Applications folder and drag Messages right to the Dock to put it back. ∎

4 Choose the type of account and click **Continue**.

5 Choose an account type. If you choose Google, AOL, or Yahoo! in Step 4, you won't see this menu.

6 Enter your user name and password.

7 Click **Create**.

End

NOTE

What's That You Say? There are scads of free messaging services around, and I find it's convenient to set up accounts with a bunch of them so I can keep in touch with my friends no matter which service they prefer. To set up a Jabber account, go to register.jabber.org. To set up a Google account, go to www.google.com/accounts/SignUp. And to set up a free Yahoo! account, go to edit.yahoo.com/registration. ■

SENDING CHAT MESSAGES

Chatting with Messages requires two things: You must sign on to one of the messaging services it supports and you must know the screen name of the person you want to reach. Conveniently enough, your buddy list is stored online with your account info, so it follows you around—you'll always see your own buddy list even if you log in on a computer other than your own.

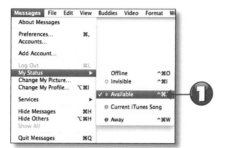

Start

1 Open Messages from the Applications folder and (if not already logged in) choose **Messages**, **My Status**, **Available**.

2 Choose **Window**, **Buddies** if your buddy list isn't visible.

3 Double-click the name or screen name of the person to whom you want to send an instant message.

4 Type your message at the bottom of the message window and press **Return** to send the message.

End

NOTE

On the Record You can save transcripts of your chat conversations: Choose **Messages, Preferences** and click the **Messages** button. Click **Save chat transcripts to**; then choose a folder from the pop-up menu. ■

TIP

A Two-Way Street Note that you can use an AOL screen name with AOL Instant Messenger and with Messages, but you can't use an Apple ID name with AIM. ■

MAKING VOICE CALLS

With Messages and a microphone, you can enjoy voice conversations over the Net with anyone similarly equipped. All MacBooks have built-in microphones, and mics for other Macs are very inexpensive—so it's time to say hello to Messages and goodbye to your long-distance phone bill.

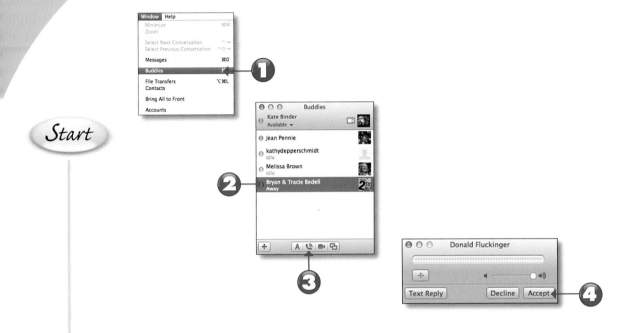

Start

1. In Messages, choose **Window**, **Buddies** if your buddy list isn't visible.

2. Click the name or screen name of the person to whom you want to talk; a phone icon tells you that person has audio capabilities, and a movie camera icon indicates someone who has both audio and video capabilities.

3. Click the **Start Audio Chat** button at the bottom of the Buddies window.

4. If you receive an audio chat invitation, click **Accept** to begin the conversation.

End

 NOTE

Going One Way If the person you want to talk to has Messages but no microphone, you can still have one-way audio along with two-way text. This feature is great for calling up your microphone-less friends via Messages and singing "Happy Birthday" to them. ■

 NOTE

One-Way Street What if you have a camera and your friend doesn't, or vice versa? Well, you can still do video chat with Messages—just one-way. Hey, it's better than nothing! ■

HOLDING A VIDEOCONFERENCE

Who needs a videophone? You don't—you have your Mac. If you also have a high-speed Internet connection and a webcam, you're good to go. First, make sure your camera is plugged in to your Mac and working correctly. Then check your Messages preferences to ensure that Messages realizes the camera is there.

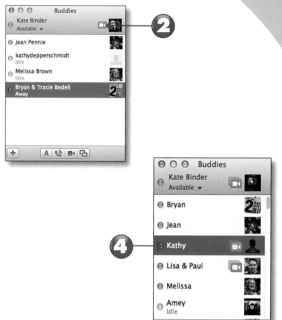

Start

1 In Messages, choose **Window**, **Buddies** if your buddy list isn't visible.

2 Click the **camera** button next to your own icon.

3 Looking at the preview window, adjust your camera angle and height until you're happy with your appearance.

4 Click the name of the person to whom you want to talk.

Continued

TIP

In a Rush? A quicker way to begin a videoconference is to click the camera button next to the name of the person with whom you want to chat. You can start an audio chat session quickly by clicking the microphone button next to a buddy's name. ■

TIP

Let's Have a Party To conference with multiple people, ⌘+**click** to select their names in the Buddies window; then click the **Start Video Chat** button. To add a participant during a chat, click the + button in the chat window. ■

 Click the **Start Video Chat** button at the bottom of the Buddies window.

6 The video window opens and you can see yourself; when your buddy answers, you can see both your buddy and yourself in the window.

7 Click the **Full Screen** button to expand the window to fill your screen.

8 Click the **Mute** button to freeze the video and mute the audio of yourself.

End

TIP

Knock Knock If someone initiates a video or audio chat with you, you see a dialog box telling you so. As soon as you've combed your hair, you can click **Accept** to begin chatting. ■

NOTE

No Webcam? No Worries If you haven't got a webcam but you do have a digital camcorder, you can use that instead. You'll find a small tripod helpful in positioning the camera so it can "see" your face; try looking for one at the dollar store. ■

APPLYING SPECIAL VIDEO EFFECTS

This isn't your grandma's chat application, that's for sure. These days, video chats can make use of some of the same special effects found in Photo Booth (turn to "Applying Fun Photo Effects" in Chapter 10, "Getting an iLife," to learn more). As long as you and the people you're chatting with are all using at least Mac OS X Leopard, you can go to town with these cool effects.

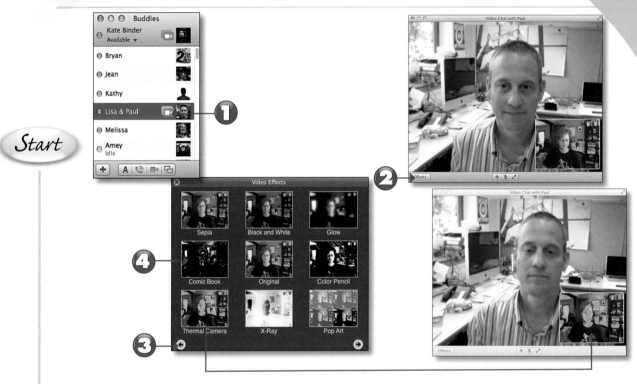

Start

1 In your Buddies list, click the **camera** button next to a buddy's name to begin a video chat.

2 Click **Effects** to open the Video Effects window.

3 Click the arrows to scroll through the different effects that you can use.

4 Click the thumbnail of an effect to apply it to your video image.

Continued

TIP

Don't Overdo It Using special effects takes a lot of processing power, and even more when more than one chat participant is using effects. If your video gets slow and jerky, or parts of the picture are dropping out, try removing the effects for better performance. ■

 5 Click the **Original** thumbnail to remove the video effect from your image.

End

NOTE

In the Background When using background effects in Messages, watch the screen to set them up properly. Messages will tell you to step out of the screen for a short time so that it can see what the background looks like without you. ■

LIVING ONLINE

So much of modern life happens online. Despite some people's complaints that a sense of community is disappearing from our society, community is thriving on the Internet. That's what the Internet is all about—a network of people sharing a network of information—and your Mac is your passport to that network.

In this chapter, you learn about surfing the Web with Apple's very own web browser, Safari—a fast, compact browser that you'll quickly learn to love. You'll learn how to create bookmarks and use the History so you can return to your favorite sites, as well as how to keep those bookmarks organized and accessible. And you'll enable Safari to fill in your online passwords and even, if you like, your credit card info for you to save time when navigating the Web and shopping.

You'll also learn about ways of connecting with your friends that you'll find throughout Mac OS X—instantly sharing what interests you on Twitter or comparing high scores in your favorite games through Game Center. Finally, you'll learn how to use iCloud to make sure your personal data and documents are available to you anytime, anywhere, on any Apple device.

HANGING OUT ON THE NET

Control kids'
computer use, 196

Use tabbed
browsing, 180

Surf the Web
with Safari, 174

SURFING IN SAFARI

For many years, Mac web surfers had a simple choice of web browsers: Netscape or Internet Explorer. Then Apple trumped everyone with its very own, Mac-only browser, Safari. It's fast, it's smooth, and—best of all—it's designed from the ground up to work the way a Mac should.

Start

1. Start up Safari (in the Applications folder).

2. Click a link on your home page to go to another page.

3. Choose **View**, **Show Toolbar** if the toolbar isn't already visible.

4. Type the URL in the address field on the toolbar for the site you want to visit.

Continued

TIP

Two for the Price of One If you want to view a new web page without getting rid of the one you're looking at now, press ⌘-**N** or choose **File, New Window** to begin surfing in a new window while leaving the current window open in the background. ■

TIP

Finding Your Way Back If you want to remember a page so you can return to it at another time, create a bookmark in the Bookmarks menu for it by pressing ⌘-**D**, or drag its URL to the Bookmarks bar at the top of the window to place a bookmark there. ■

5 Click the **Previous Page** and **Next Page** buttons to go back and forward through the web pages you've visited.

6 Click the Top Sites button to see a selection of the web pages you've visited most often lately.

7 Type search terms in the **Safari Search** field and press **Return** to go to the Google site and initiate the search. If one of the search terms Safari suggests is correct, just click it to perform the search.

End

TIP

Checking Your Status Safari's Status bar shows you when it's contacting a web server, and it shows you the address behind any link you hold the mouse cursor over. To see the Status bar, choose **View, Show Status Bar**. ■

ORGANIZING BOOKMARKS

Some people never bookmark anything. Others are sensible enough to bookmark only sites they know they'll need again. And still others—naming no names here—bookmark just about everything. If you're in that third group, chances are you could stand to spend some time organizing your bookmarks.

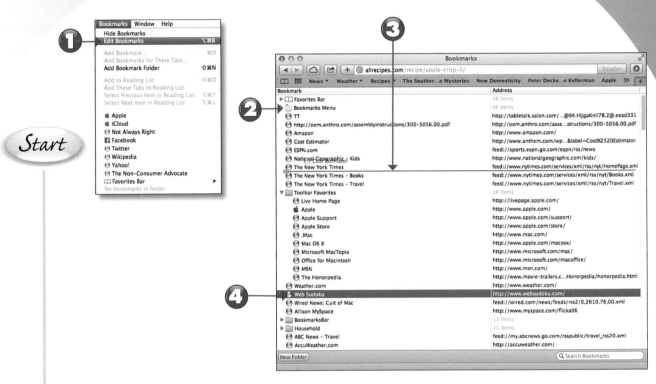

Start

1 Choose **Bookmarks**, **Edit Bookmarks**.

2 Click a disclosure triangle next to the name of a collection in the **Bookmarks** column to see the bookmarks it contains.

3 Drag bookmarks up or down to change their order.

4 Click a bookmark and press **Delete** to remove it.

Continued

NOTE

More Bookmarks You can fit a lot more bookmarks in the Bookmarks bar by using submenus. Create a folder for each bookmark category, and then drop your bookmarks inside. Back in the main window, click a category name to see the submenu of bookmarks. ■

5 To add a bookmark to the Favorites bar, drag it into the **Favorites Bar** collection.

6 To add a bookmark to the Bookmarks menu, drag it into the **Bookmarks Menu** collection.

7 To add a submenu to the Bookmarks menu or the Favorites bar, add a folder by clicking the **New Folder** button, give it a name, and then drag bookmarks into the folder.

8 To change the name of a bookmark or folder, click it again, type the new name, and press **Return**.

End

TIP

More Address Book Integration If you keep your contacts' website URLs in the Address Book, you can add them to the Bookmarks bar or menu automatically. Choose **Safari, Preferences** and click the **Bookmarks** button; then click the appropriate check box to add Address Book items. ■

ACCESSING YOUR TOP SITES

Whenever you open a new window or tab in Safari, you'll see a selection of Top Sites arranged in a neat grid. These are web pages you've visited frequently in the recent past, which means they represent Safari's best guess at what your own personal top sites actually are. Fortunately you can adjust your Top Sites to reflect the web locations you *really* want to visit most often.

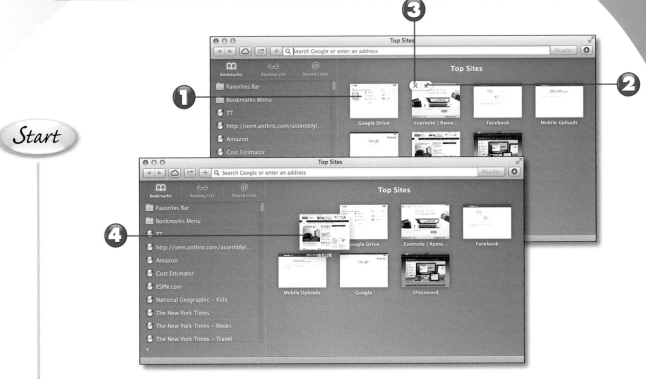

Start

Click a page thumbnail to visit that site.

Hold the cursor over a thumbnail and then click the pin icon to make sure that site stays in your Top Sites.

To banish a page from your Top Sites, hold the cursor over its thumbnail and then click X.

Drag the thumbnails into your preferred order to ensure that your most important sites are always at the top of your Top Sites.

End

TIP

You're the Top If you want to add a new site to your Top Sites, regardless of whether you've visited it lately, drag its bookmark from the sidebar into the Top Sites grid and drop it where you want the thumbnail to go. ■

NOTE

Top That! If you don't find Top Sites useful and would rather get rid of its visual clutter, you can choose whether new pages and tabs open with Top Sites, your home page, or an empty page in the **General** tab of Safari's preferences. ■

USING THE HISTORY IN SAFARI

Safari's History listing is just what you need when you need to go back to a website you visited recently but forgot to bookmark. It keeps track of the last several days of your surfing exploits, neatly listing the websites you visited in folders labeled by date.

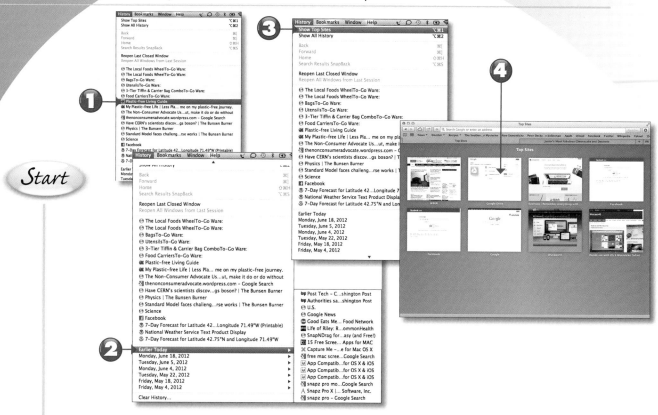

Start

End

① To return to one of the pages you've visited recently, click the **History** menu in Safari and choose the page's name.

② To go back to an earlier page, click the **History** menu and choose the appropriate submenu; then choose the page's name.

③ Choose **History, Show Top Sites** to see thumbnails of the sites you visit most often.

④ Click a thumbnail to visit that site.

TIP

A Fresh Start for History If you've been surfing a lot and you're finding the History list a bit too crowded to let you find what you want, choose **History, Clear History** to start over with a blank History. ■

TIP

Automatic SnapBack When you use Safari's Google search field, search results are automatically marked for SnapBack. After clicking to view a page in the results, choose **History, Search Results** to return to that page. ■

USING TABBED BROWSER WINDOWS

Neatniks will love this feature. If you like to flip from one web page to another and back again, here's how you can keep from cluttering up your screen with a zillion Safari windows: tabs. Keep all your pages open in one window, and move from one to another by just clicking the tab at the top of the window.

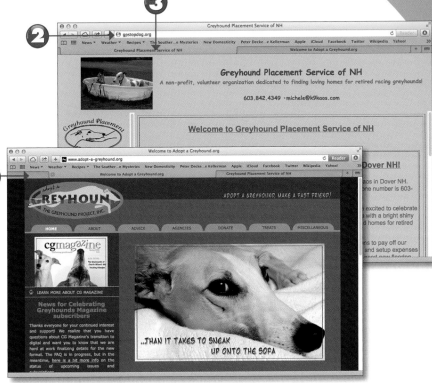

Start

1 To create a new tab in the current window, choose **File, New Tab**.

2 Enter the address for the new page or choose a bookmark.

3 Click a tab to view the page it contains.

4 To change the order of the tabs in a window, click a tab's handle and drag it to its new location.

Continued

TIP

Don't Stop Now If you're in a hurry, you'll appreciate knowing the quickest way to open a web page in a separate tab: Press ⌘ while you click the **Back** or **Forward** arrows or as you click a link. ■

NOTE

Not the Only One Cool as it is, tabbed browsing isn't unique to Safari. Apple uses the concept elsewhere, such as in iChat (it's great for managing multiple conversations), and other web browsers, including Firefox, Opera, and Camino, support it as well. ■

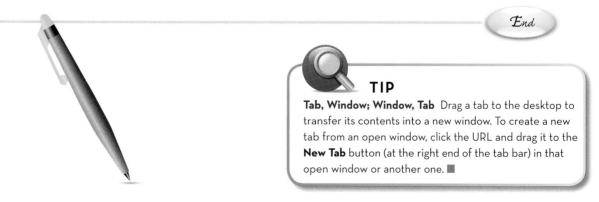

5 To turn multiple open windows into tabs in a single window, choose **Window, Merge All Windows**.

6 Choose **Bookmarks, Add Bookmarks for These Tabs** to add a bookmark set that contains a bookmark for each tab in a window.

7 Move the mouse cursor over a tab's name and click the **X** to close that tab.

8 Click the **Close** button at the top of the window to close the window and all its tabs.

End

TIP

Tab, Window; Window, Tab Drag a tab to the desktop to transfer its contents into a new window. To create a new tab from an open window, click the URL and drag it to the **New Tab** button (at the right end of the tab bar) in that open window or another one. ■

SAVING YOUR PASSWORDS TO ICLOUD

Passwords these days are supposed to be "strong" so they can't be hacked, which makes them practically impossible to remember, and you're supposed to have a different password for *everything*. Well, iCloud Keychain can help you with with that by saving your web passwords to iCloud, so they'll be remembered for you on all your Apple devices.

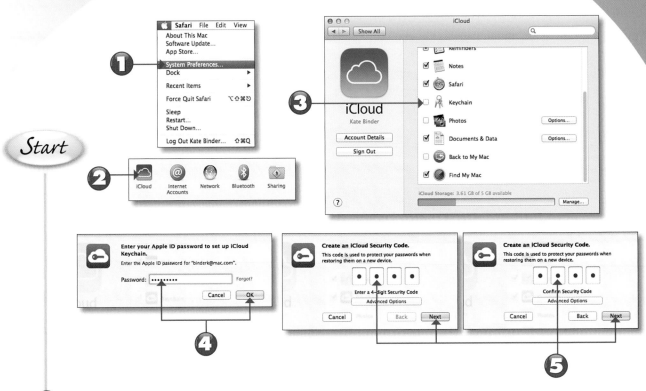

Start

1 Choose **Apple menu**, **System Preferences**.

2 Click the **iCloud** button to see your options.

3 Check the box marked **Keychain** in iCloud's System Preferences pane.

4 Enter your iCloud password and click **OK**.

5 Enter a security code and click **Next**; on the next screen enter the code again and click **Next** one more time to finish.

End

NOTE

What It Does After you've turned on iCloud Keychain, it will automatically enter your passwords for you when you need to log in to a web account. It will even keep track of the passwords for multiple accounts with the same service—just enter your email address, and iCloud Keychain does the rest. ■

TIP

When Not on Safari iCloud Keychain works only with Safari, so if you prefer to use a different web browser such as Google Chrome you'll want to look into a third-party service such as 1Password (agilebits.com/onepassword), which does the same thing using any browser. ■

CREATING STRONG PASSWORDS

When you're using iCloud Keychain, you'll find that Safari suggests lovely, secure passwords for you any time you sign up for a new account online. These randomly generated passwords are much harder for any password-cracking program to guess, and since you don't have to remember them yourself—which would be near impossible for most of us—using them is a great idea.

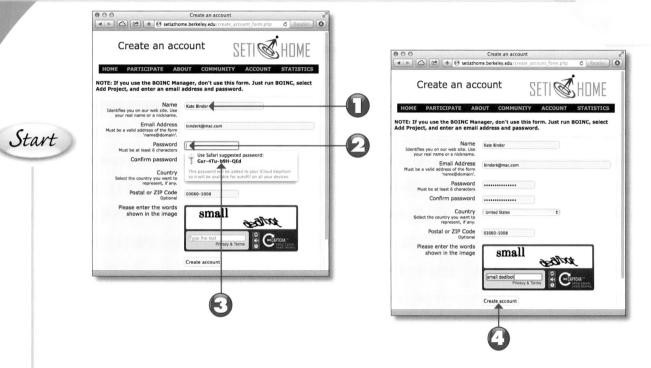

Start

 When creating a new web account, enter your name and/or a username for the site.

 Click in the password field to see Safari's suggested password.

 Click the password to accept it.

 Complete the rest of the required info and click **Create Account** (or the equivalent).

End

NOTE

Encrypted and Safe Apple uses 256-bit AES encryption to keep your iCloud Keychain data private—that's the same encryption method that the U.S. government uses to protect its own top-secret data. ■

NOTE

Give the Keychain Some Credit iCloud Keychain can also store your credit card numbers. These are protected using the same strong encryption that's used for your passwords, so you can feel confident that they're secure. To make absolutely sure your credit card data is safe, iCloud does not store your cards' security codes—the three-digit CVV number on the back of each card. ■

SEARCHING WITHIN A WEB PAGE

Sure, Spotlight finds anything on your computer, and Google finds anything on the Web (and pretty much anywhere else), but sometimes you've gotten to the right web page and you *still* can't find what you want. That's when it comes in handy to be able to search through the text on the page itself.

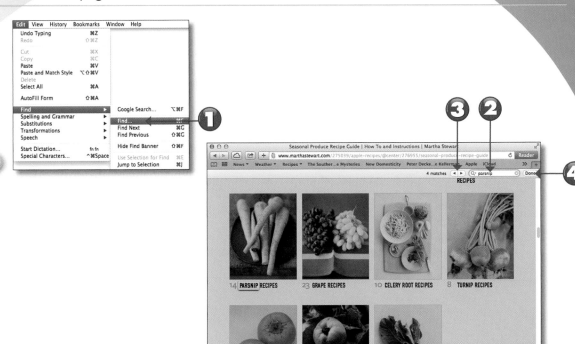

 Start

① Choose **Edit**, **Find**, **Find**, or press ⌘-**F**.

② Type the word for which you want to search.

③ Click the arrow buttons to highlight each instance of the search term.

④ Click **Done** to hide the Find banner.

End

NOTE

It Counts! Note that when it finds your search terms on the page, Safari also tells you how many matches it found. This is a great way to get a quick count of, for example, the number of employees named "Paula" in a company directory. ■

VIEWING WEB PAGES IN READER MODE

Safari's Reader mode, introduced after more than one similar third-party add-on saw wild success in the marketplace, enables you to strip away all the clutter from web pages so that you can concentrate on the content. Ads, navigation links, and extraneous design elements are all removed, and text is reset in easy-to-read, widely spaced type on a plain background—which you can customize to suit your very own tired eyes.

Start

1. Navigate to the web page you want to read.

2. Click the **Reader** button in the URL bar. (If you don't see it, that means that Safari isn't able to display the current page in Reader mode.)

3. Click the **Zoom In** or **Zoom Out** buttons to change the text size.

4. Click **Reader** again to leave Reader mode.

End

TIP

Reading List in Reader Mode for the Readers   You can also use Reader view on articles you've saved to your Reading List (see "Saving Web Pages to Your Reading List" on the next page). As you click through the list, Safari stays in Reader mode until you choose to leave it. ■

NOTE

Seeing It in Print   If you choose **File**, **Print** while in Reader mode, the resulting printout will look like the Reader mode version of the web page. Even when you don't need Reader mode to read on-screen, it's a great way to get a nice, clean printout for sharing. ■

SAVING WEB PAGES TO YOUR READING LIST

Have you ever kept a tab in your web browser sitting open for hours or even days because you want to read its contents, don't have time now, and worry that you'll forget all about it if you close the window? Now Safari offers a simple way to make sure that you don't forget what you want to read, so that when you do have the time, the articles and blog posts that caught your interest will be right there waiting for you.

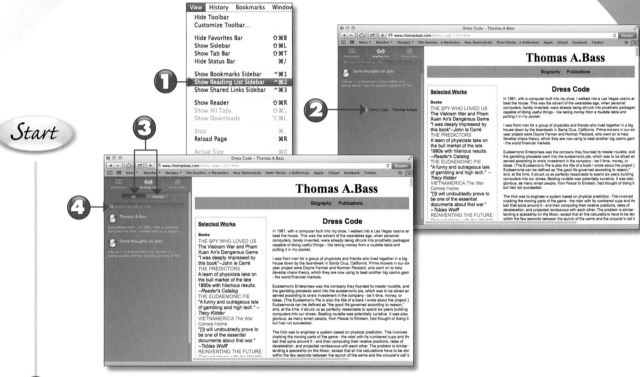

Start

1 Choose **View**, **Show Reading List Sidebar**.

2 To add the current page to your list, drag its URL into the Reading List.

3 To switch between viewing all your articles and only the ones you haven't read, scroll to the top of the Reading List and click **All** or **Unread**.

4 Enter search terms in the **Search** field to look for a particular article.

End

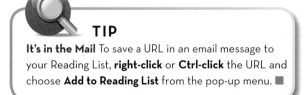

TIP

It's in the Mail To save a URL in an email message to your Reading List, **right-click** or **Ctrl-click** the URL and choose **Add to Reading List** from the pop-up menu. ■

TIP

In a Hurry? Press ⌘-**Shift-L** to open the Reading List quickly. ■

BROWSING SECURELY

Not a week goes by that we don't hear about another frightening case of identity theft or data theft in the news. One way to protect yourself is to make sure that no one else can see where you've been on the Web and what you did there. To accomplish this feat, Safari features Private Browsing.

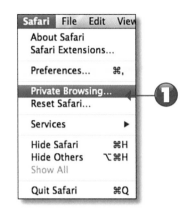

1 Choose **Safari**, **Private Browsing**.

2 Click **OK** to turn on Private Browsing.

End

TIP

Keeping It Really Safe If you're concerned about online safety, you can take more precautions. Choose **Safari, Preferences** and click **Security** to see a range of options for disabling features like JavaScript, managing cookies, and turning on high-end encryption so that if intercepted, your personal information still can't be deciphered. Of course, some websites won't work if you turn on the strongest security options—life is all about trade-offs. ■

SHARING WEB PAGES WITH YOUR FRIENDS

Increasingly, information on the Web is crowd-sourced. People share photos, videos, drawings, essays, poetry, whatever comes to mind—and the people they share with pass all this on to the global audience. To make sharing easier for Mac users, Apple has added a Share button to many of the places where you might run across things you want to share while using your Mac. Here's how it works.

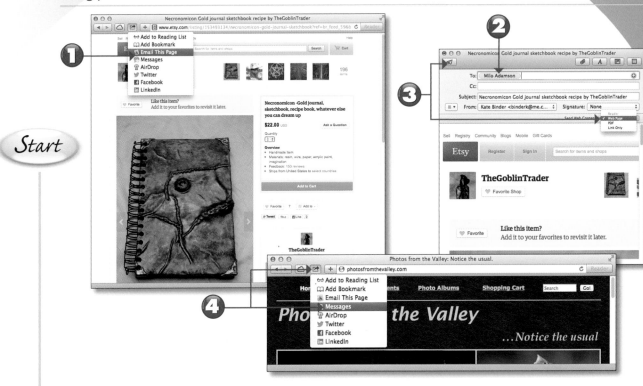

Start

1 Click the **Share** button and choose **Email this page** to share the web page via email.

2 In the new Mail message that Safari creates, enter email addresses in the To field.

3 Choose an option for how the page appears in the email message, such as **Web Page**; then click **Send**.

4 Click the **Share** button and choose **Messages** to share the web page via Messenger.

Continued

NOTE

Laying the Groundwork If you haven't entered your usernames and passwords for the sharing services you want to use in the Mail, Contacts & Calendars pane of System Preferences, you'll be directed there the first time you use each service under the Share button. ∎

NOTE

More to Come Other options may show up in your Share menus from time to time, as Apple adds new connections with services such as Facebook. ∎

5 Type a buddy's name or click the **+** button to choose from your contacts, then click **Log In and Send**.

6 Click the **Share** button and choose **Twitter** or **Facebook** to tweet the web page or share it on Facebook.

7 Add your own message and click **Send** or **Post**.

End

NOTE

It's Everywhere The Share button appears throughout OS X, in places such as Quick Look preview windows and within apps. See the next task to learn more. ▪

SHARING FROM ANYWHERE

Keep your eyes open—your Mac has suddenly gotten very interested in sharing via social media. You'll find Share buttons and commands throughout OS X, enabling you to pop pictures, text, videos, and more right out to your favorite social media sites with just a click or two. Here are a couple of examples of how this works to get you started.

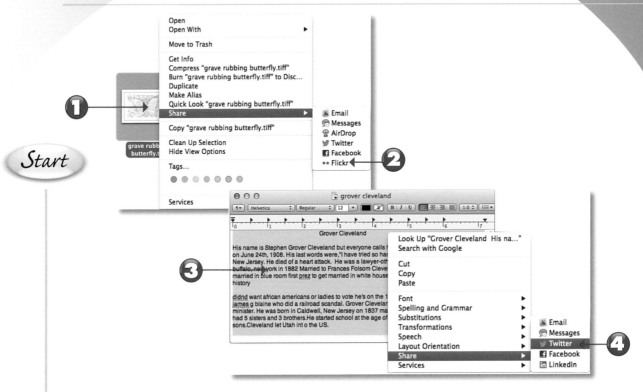

Start

End

1. Right-click or Ctrl-click an image file in the Finder.

2. Choose an option from the **Share** submenu, such as **Flickr**.

3. Select text in TextEdit, Mail, or another app that knows how to share, and right-click or Ctrl-click.

4. Choose an option from the **Share** submenu, such as **Twitter**.

TIP

All in One After you've entered your Facebook and Twitter info in System Preferences, you can receive notifications in the Notification Center when someone sends you a message or tweets about you. ■

NOTE

Which Apps? Apps with Share buttons include Notes, Photo Booth, Preview, and iPhoto. Third-party apps—those produced by companies other than Apple—can also include Share buttons if the developers want to enable the feature. ■

CONNECTING WITH GAME CENTER

iOS users have been having fun with Game Center for quite some time now, but now it's Mac users' turn to get in on the game. With Game Center you can connect with friends to match up your game scores against each other as well as learn about new games people you know are recommending. You can even jump directly from Game Center to the App Store to download games.

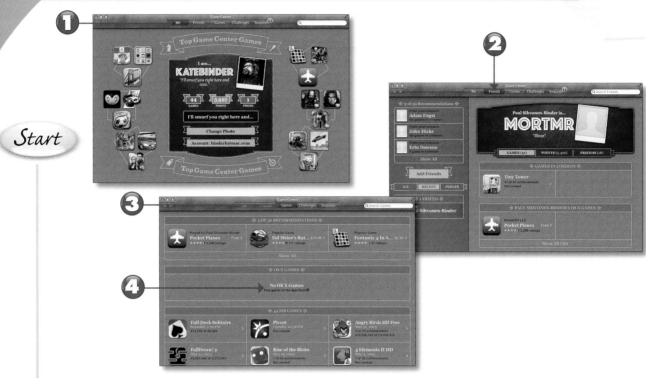

Start

1. In Game Center (you'll find it in your Applications folder), click **Me** to see and modify your status and account settings.

2. Click **Friends** and click a friend's name on the left side of the window to see the games your friends play and their standings.

3. Click **Games** to see the Game Center–friendly games you have installed.

4. Click **Find games on the App Store** to open the App Store and shop for new games.

End

TIP

Ready to Play On the Me screen, you can sign in and out of your account as well as set your status message, which all your friends can see. In the mood for an Angry Birds smackdown? Here's where you let your friends know! ∎

NOTE

Compatible or Not? Game Center shows both your Mac games and your iOS games, but sadly that doesn't mean you can play iOS games on Mac or vice versa. ∎

STORING PERSONAL DATA IN ICLOUD

What's iCloud good for, you may ask? Here's your answer—iCloud does other things, but this is its most important function: Your calendar and contacts will look the same on all your devices, and it'll be available wherever you go, as long as you have Web access.

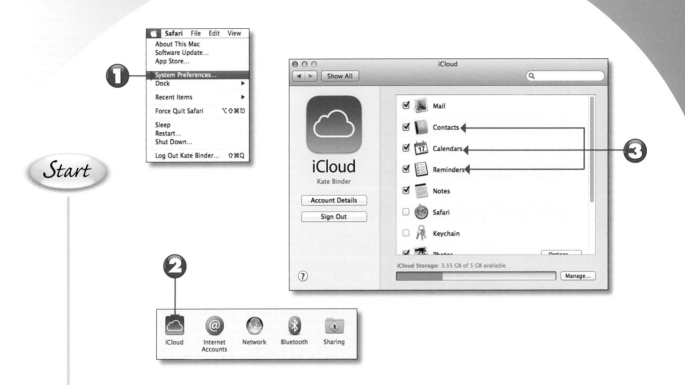

Start

1. Choose **Apple menu**, **System Preferences**.

2. Click **iCloud** in System Preferences.

3. Click the checkboxes next to **Contacts** and **Calendars & Reminders** to share your contact data and the data from your calendar.

Continued

NOTE

Sign In If the checkboxes are grayed out, it's because you're not signed into iCloud. If you need an account, go to **www.icloud.com** to get one, then return here and click **Sign In** after step 2, then enter your Apple ID and password. ■

NOTE

Doing Even More In step 3, you can check several other boxes to sync various kinds of info via iCloud: Mail, Notes, even your photos using Photo Stream. ■

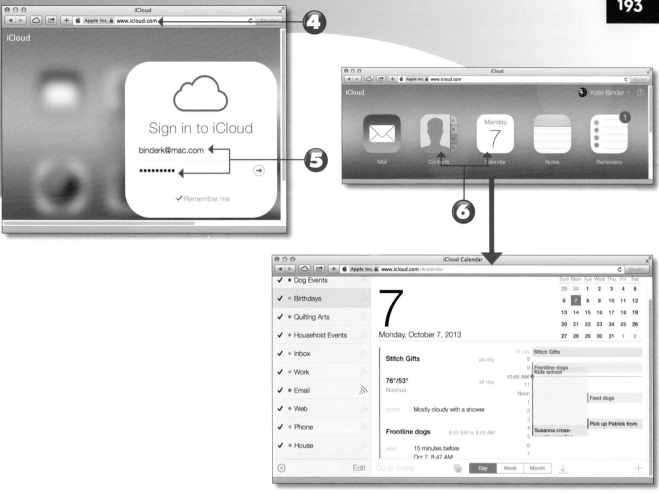

4 To see your calendar or contacts on the Web, go to **www.icloud.com**.

5 Enter your Apple ID and password and press **Enter**.

6 Click **Contacts** to see your contact info or **Calendar** to see your calendar.

End

TIP

How Much Is Too Much? iCloud gives you 5GB of space to store iOS device backups, email, contacts, calendars, documents, and data needed by your apps. Apps, music, movies, and shows that you buy don't occupy that space, and neither does your Photo Stream. ■

KEEPING YOUR DOCUMENTS IN ICLOUD

So you can take your virtual address book and date book with you anywhere using iCloud—but what about all the actual work you're supposed to be doing? Yes, in fact, you can take that with you, too. If you use any of Apple's iWork applications (Keynote for presentations, Pages for writing and page layout, or Numbers for spreadsheets), and you have an iCloud account, you can sync those documents across your Macs and iOS devices so you'll never have an excuse to take the day off.

Start

1. Go to **www.icloud.com** in your web browser.

2. Enter your Apple ID and password and press **Enter**.

3. Click the iWork application you want to work with.

Continued

NOTE

Windows Too Don't think your Windows computer has to be left out—iCloud can talk to Windows Vista or Windows 7 using a control panel that you can download here: **www.icloud.com/icloudcontrolpanel**. ■

TIP

DIY iWork documents on your iOS devices are automatically synced with iCloud; to sync iWork documents that originate on your Mac, you'll need to follow these steps. ■

④ Drag documents into the window from the Finder to load them to iCloud.

⑤ Ctrl-click/right-click and choose a command to download, duplicate, or delete a document.

⑥ Double-click a document thumbnail to open it and work on it directly in your browser.

End

NOTE

Dealing with Conflicts When you make edits to your data on one device and then make changes to the same file on another device before your first changes are integrated, the app asks which version you'd like to save. Save both, or save one by choosing one version and tapping or clicking **Keep**. ■

CONTROLLING KIDS' COMPUTER USE

Learning how to work with computers is important—in fact, for today's kids, it's pretty much unavoidable—but no parent wants kids sitting in front of the computer all day and all night. Mac OS X's Parental Controls enable you, as an admin user, to set limits on how much your kids use your Mac and what they can use it to do.

Start

1 Choose **Apple menu**, **System Preferences**.

2 Click **Parental Controls**.

3 Click the unlock button, and then enter an administrator account's username and your password and click **Unlock**.

4 Click the name of the user for whom you want to set controls.

Continued

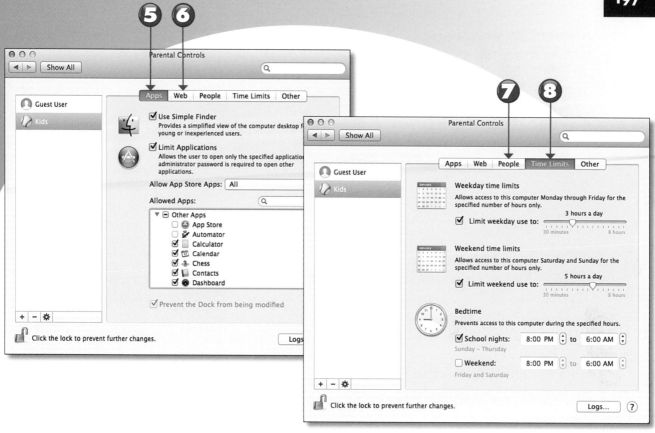

5 Click the **Apps** tab and set restrictions on access to the Finder, the programs installed on your Mac, and hardware configuration.

6 Click the **Web** tab to hide adult content in the Mac OS X Dictionary and on the Web.

7 Click the **People** tab to limit use of email and instant messaging to specified users.

8 Click the **Time Limits** tab to set time limits for computer use.

End

NOTE

More Than the Internet Parental Controls aren't just about the Internet. Check out the settings on the Other tab: You can control whether a user can burn discs, administer printers, and change his or her password. ■

TIP

Mother, May I? To receive automatic notice that a restricted user is attempting to contact someone who's not on your approved list, go to the **People** tab, check **Send permission requests to**, and enter your email address. ■

GETTING AN ILIFE

iLife is Apple's name for its collection of "digital hub" programs, which includes iPhoto and iMovie. Along with iTunes and iBooks, this software represents the company's effort to empower Mac users to create and control their own entertainment media. With these programs you can manage, edit, and share your digital photos; acquire and mix music; produce digital movies; and enjoy all the media-rich book titles that have been released for iBooks.

In this chapter, you'll learn how to get your pictures into iPhoto and organize them into albums. When you have albums, you can print your photos and share them on the Web. You'll also learn how to import music from your CD collection into iTunes, create custom mixes called *playlists*, and burn your own CDs. With a visit to the iTunes Music Store, you'll pick and choose from the latest tunes on the market—at about a buck a pop.

With iMovie, you'll learn how to import video from your camera or phone and turn it into your own professional-looking home movies. Finally, you'll be introduced to iBooks; with this program, you can buy and read books right on your Mac as well as take notes and highlight important passages.

MANAGING PHOTOS, VIDEO, AND MUSIC

Share photos
online, 204

Turn playlists
into CDs, 211

Rip CDs to your
hard drive, 208

Organize
photos in
albums, 201

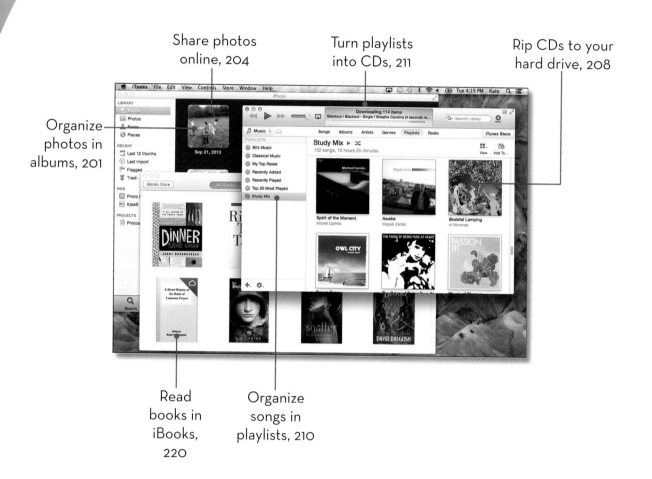

Read
books in
iBooks,
220

Organize
songs in
playlists, 210

IMPORTING PHOTOS INTO IPHOTO

iPhoto can do a lot of things, but its most important function is simply providing a place to keep all your digital photos. Think of it as a super-duper photo album, or maybe a filing cabinet for your photos (if you take a lot of them). So, the first step in doing anything with iPhoto is getting your photos into its database.

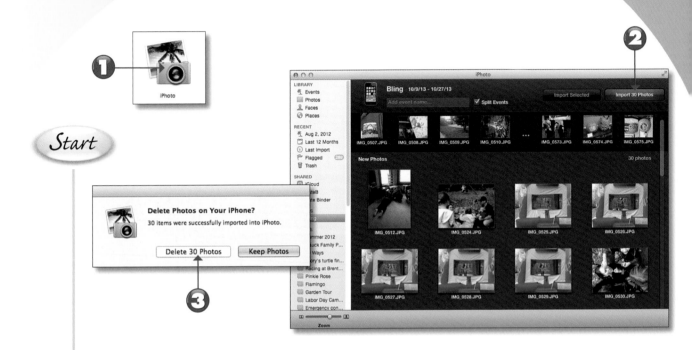

Start

End

1. Plug your camera or phone into your Mac's USB port, turn it on, and start up iPhoto (in the Applications folder).

2. Click **Import Photos**.

3. Click **Delete Photos** if you want to clear the original images off the device; otherwise, click **Keep Photos**.

TIP

You Can Get There from Here To import image files from your hard drive, a removable disk, or camera media you've mounted on the desktop, drag and drop the files directly onto the Library entry in iPhoto's sidebar. ■

NOTE

Found, Not Lost If you can't find the latest photos you brought into iPhoto, check out the Last Import album under the **Recent** heading in the sidebar. That's where the most recent group of images you imported is always stored. ■

CREATING IPHOTO ALBUMS

Rather than being exactly parallel to a real-world photo album, an iPhoto album is really just a way to group photos together so iPhoto knows which photos you want to print, display, or export. Albums are the way you organize your photos so you can find the ones you want. Creating an album is also the first step in creating a book or web page.

Start

① In iPhoto, select the first photo you want to include in the album, click the **Share** button, and choose **Album** from the Create section of the pop-up menu.

② Type a name for the new album and press **Enter**.

③ Click **Photos** or the name of another album in the sidebar.

④ Add photos to the new album by dragging and dropping them from the preview area to the album's name.

⑤ Click the album's name, and then drag and drop the album's photos in the preview area to change their order.

End

TIP

Information Please You can add descriptive information to the photos in your albums. Click the **Show Info** (i) button in the lower right-hand corner of the iPhoto window to display useful information about each photo, including Title and Comments fields that you can fill out. ∎

PRINTING PHOTOS

It's not a paperless world yet, so you're bound to want to print your photos at some point. iPhoto offers several printing layouts so you can create standard prints, picture packages like the ones photo studios offer, or just plain printouts in your choice of size and number.

Start

1. ⌘-**click** in the preview area to select individual photos.

2. Choose **File**, **Print**.

3. Choose a printer from the **Printer** pop-up menu.

4. If available, choose an option from the **Presets** pop-up menu to set the output type.

Continued

TIP

Fine-Tuning Print Settings Although your printer driver probably includes presets for photo and plain paper, you might need to fine-tune the settings for your printer. Click **Show Details** in the final iPhoto Print dialog box to get to a Print dialog box with the usual options, including color and media. ■

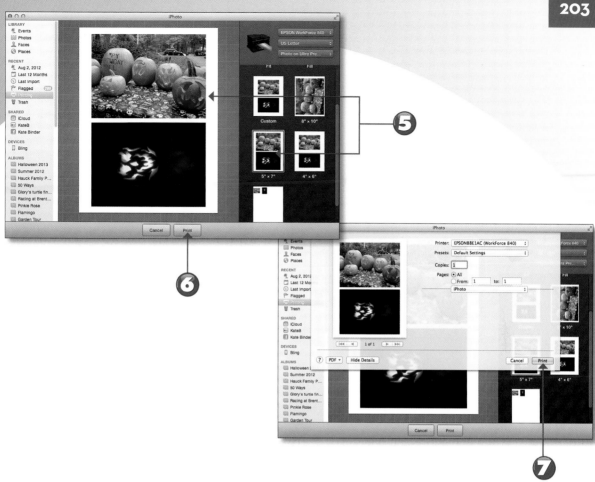

5 Choose a **Print Size** option and make sure the Paper Size setting is correct for your printer.

6 Click **Print**.

7 Click **Print** again.

End

NOTE

Proxy Preview The preview area in iPhoto's Print dialog box shows you how your printouts will look with the selected printer's paper size. The preview updates on-the-fly as you change the settings for the selected style. ■

TIP

Custom for the Customers If you want to change the settings for a print size, such as the order in which the photos print or their size on the page, choose the **Custom** size option. ■

SHARING PHOTOS ONLINE

The best way to share your photos with friends and family all over the country or the world is to put them on the Web. iPhoto makes getting your photos online easy, whether you want to upload to Flickr or share via another service such as Facebook. Here you see how the process works with Flickr, but it's similar with other services.

Start

Continued

1 Click the album you want to share on a web page.

2 Click **Share**, and then choose a photo-sharing service, such as **Flickr**, from the pop-up menu.

3 Click **New Set**.

4 Choose options for the web gallery and then click **Publish**.

NOTE

First Time for Everything If you haven't shared photos via Flickr before, you'll first be asked to enter your username and password and then to authorize Flickr to talk to iPhoto. ■

NOTE

What's in a Name? iPhoto inserts the album's name in the Title field, but you can change that page title to anything you want. ■

 Click the arrow next to the album name at the top of the window to see your album online.

End

 NOTE

Big and Little iPhoto creates all the full-size and thumbnail images your web album needs, but you must specify sizes. Thumbnail images are small versions of the photos on which viewers can click to see the full-size versions. ■

NOTE

Don't Stop Now You can also order prints or email photos directly from iPhoto, so even if you're not much of a Web person, don't let that stop you from spreading the photo love. ■

APPLYING FUN PHOTO EFFECTS

Ever spent time in one of those mall photo booths, messing around to produce a strip of funny photos? Now there's no trip to the mall needed; just use Photo Booth to take pictures of yourself using your webcam. You can also add cool special effects and even change the background so it looks as though you're sitting in, say, the mall.

Start

1 Start up **Photo Booth** (you'll find it in the Applications folder).

2 Adjust your position within the photo frame and click the **Effects** button.

3 Use the arrow buttons to scroll through the available effects.

4 Double-click on the thumbnail image for the effect you want to use.

Continued

NOTE

Wait! There's More Photo Booth's Effects include lens effects—such as fisheye—and backdrops that you can put behind your image. You can even add your own backdrops: Just drag a photo into one of the blank spaces in the Effects pane of the Photo Booth window. ■

NOTE

Beyond the Basics If you're ready for your close-up already, you can skip the countdown by Option-clicking the **camera** button. And if you're finding your photos a bit too washed-out, disable Photo Booth's flash by Shift-clicking the button. Finally, if you decide partway through a countdown that you don't want to take the photo after all, press **Esc** to cancel. ■

5 Click the **camera** button when you're ready to shoot a picture. Photo Booth counts down and then takes the photo.

6 Click one of the photos shown at the bottom of the window to use it.

7 Click a button to indicate what you want to do with the photo: email it, send it to iPhoto, use it as your login picture, or use it as your buddy icon in iChat.

End

TIP

More in Store When you feel that you've exhausted Photo Booth's possibilities, hold your horses. You can also take quick bursts of four pictures (which are then displayed four-up, rather than singly), and you can take videos as well. Click the **Burst** button in the lower-left corner of the Photo Booth window to shoot a burst, and click the **Video** button to shoot a movie. ■

TIP

It's Curtains for You Be sure you try out Photo Booth in full-screen mode for a special visual treat! ■

RIPPING SONGS FROM A CD

You'll be amazed at how much more use you get from your CD collection after you get the music off CDs and into iTunes. The songs on CDs are already digital files; *ripping* them consists of transferring them to your hard drive and resaving them in MP3 format.

Start

 Insert the CD.

2 If iTunes doesn't start up automatically, open the Applications folder and double-click to start up **iTunes**.

3 Click **Import CD**.

4 Click **OK**.

End

TIP

The Sounds of Silence iTunes plays songs while it's importing them, but if you don't want to listen to them, you can click **Pause** to stop the playback. iTunes continues importing the songs. ■

TIP

Import Settings You can control the quality and size of the song files you import by changing the setting in the Import Using pop-up menu during Step 4. **Apple Lossless Encoder** creates great-sounding but large files, and **MP3 Encoder** is a good option if you need smaller files. ■

USING ITUNES MATCH

Want to put your music collection in the cloud without all that pesky uploading? iTunes Match is for you. This Apple service inventories your music library and adds high-quality versions of each song you already have to iCloud for you, while uploading anything from your Mac that isn't found in the iTunes store. So you get a portable music library that also serves as a cheap ($25/year) and easy music backup solution.

Start

End

1 In iTunes, click **iTunes Store**.

2 Click **Sign In**.

3 Enter your Apple ID and password and click **Sign In**.

4 Click the **Match** button.

5 Click **Subscribe**.

TIP

It's Just There In addition to storing your tunes in the cloud, iTunes Match also synchronizes your music library to all your devices automatically. Anything you add on one device gets added to all your devices with no need for you to even think about it. ■

TIP

In Case of Emergency If you're missing songs that you think should be in your library, or you run into any other issues with iTunes Match, choose Store, Update iTunes Match. This command forces iTunes to check its database against your iCloud database and download anything that's missing. ■

MAKING A NEW PLAYLIST

Playlists are simply groups of songs, containing just one song or hundreds. You can use them to create party mixes, plan mix CDs, or categorize your music by genre or any other criterion. Building playlists is a simple drag-and-drop operation.

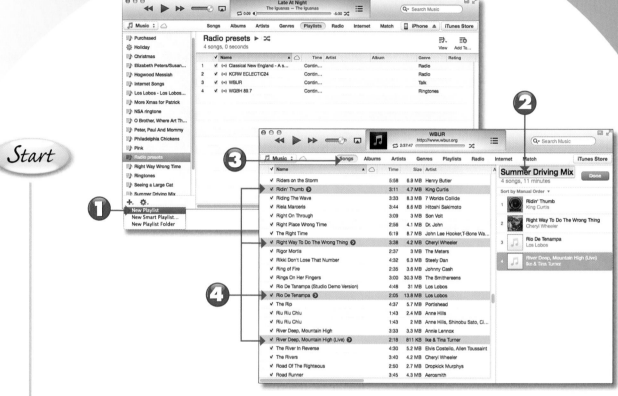

 Start

1 In iTunes, click the **Create Playlists** button and choose **New Playlist**.

2 Type a name for the playlist.

3 Click the **Songs** button to see all your songs, or click the name of another playlist.

4 Drag songs from the **Name** column and drop them into the new playlist.

End

TIP

Finding What You Want To locate a specific song in the Library or in a playlist, click in the **Search** field and type part of the song name. As you type, the list of songs shortens to include only the songs that match your search term. ■

TIP

Changing Your Mind To remove a song from a playlist (but not from your Library), click to select it and press **Delete**. ■

BURNING A MUSIC CD

You can take your music with you in the form of custom mix CDs for parties, for gifts, or just to use in the car. Before you burn a CD, you need to create a playlist containing the songs you want to use on the disc. And, of course, you need to have a CD drive that can write CDs as well as play them.

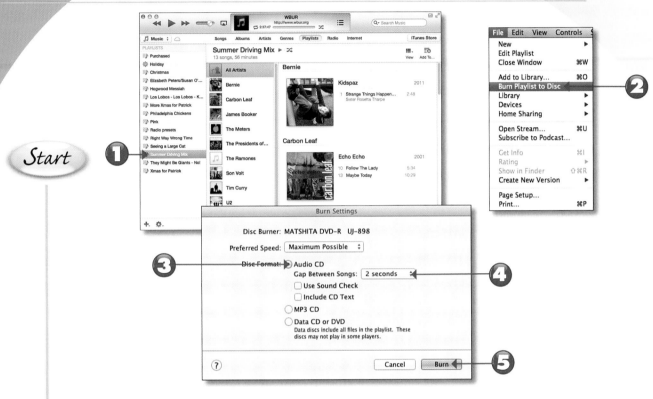

1. Click to select the playlist you want to make into a CD.

2. Choose **File, Burn Playlist to Disc**.

3. Click **Audio CD**.

4. Choose a time from the **Gap Between Songs** pop-up menu.

5. Insert a blank CD-R disc and click **Burn**; iTunes burns your playlist onto the disc.

TIP
The Right Media Make sure you use CD-R media, rather than CD-RW media, if you plan to play your CD in a regular CD player (meaning, on your stereo) rather than in a computer CD drive. ∎

BUYING SONGS THROUGH ITUNES

The iTunes Store offers thousands of tunes in all genres at very reasonable prices. You can download entire albums or one song at a time. Your purchases are charged to your credit card, and the songs are downloaded directly into iTunes, where you can play them on your computer, transfer to them to an iPod, or burn them to a CD.

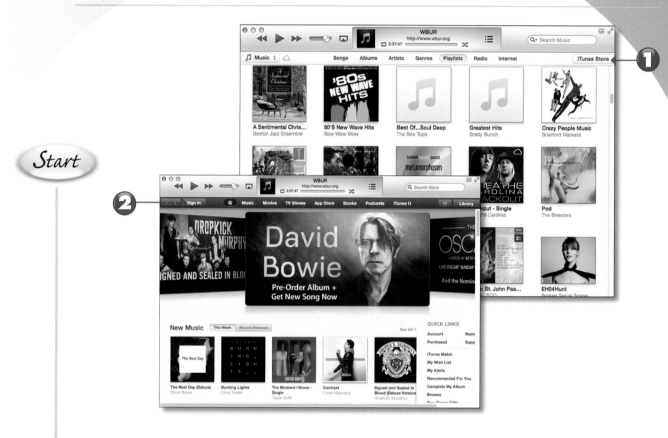

Start

1 In iTunes, click the **iTunes Store** button.

2 Click **Sign In**.

Continued

TIP
Picture This Any song you buy from the iTunes Store comes with cover artwork. When you burn a compilation, iTunes creates a custom mosaic of the songs' cover art and drops that into a template to create an insert for the CD case. ■

TIP
Stop Right There To stop the CD burner after you click **Burn Disc**, click the **X** next to the progress bar. You can use your CD drive again immediately, but the CD you canceled is no longer usable. ■

3 Type your Apple ID and password and click **Sign In**.

4 If you haven't made a purchase before, a dialog box tells you that this ID hasn't been used with the iTunes Store; click **Review**.

5 Click **Continue**.

Continued

TIP

Getting an iTunes Account If you already have an Apple ID, you're all set—just enter that username and password to sign in to the iTunes Store. If you have a subscription to iCloud, use that username and password for the iTunes Store. If you don't have either, follow the Store's prompts to create a new ID and supply your credit card information for purchases. ■

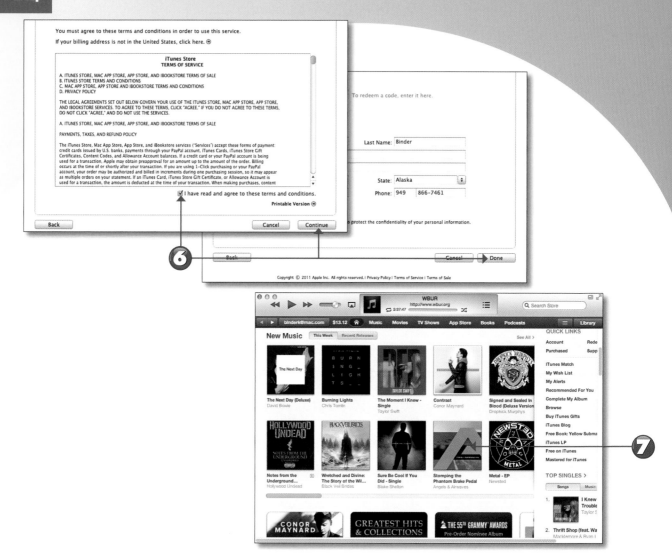

6 Read the Terms and Conditions and click the checkbox and **Continue**; then click **Done**.

7 Click a song or album title to see more information about it.

Continued

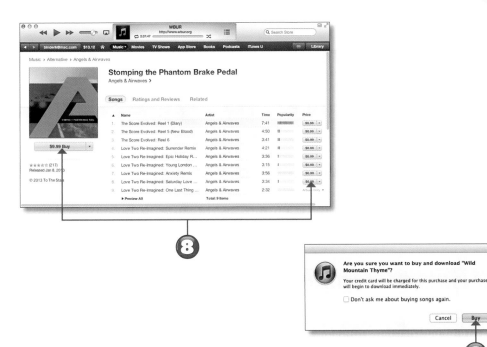

 Click **Buy** to purchase music.

Click **Buy**. The song downloads into iTunes and appears in a new playlist called Purchased.

End

TIP

Quick and Clean Searching You can search the iTunes Store quickly for any text by entering the search text in the regular iTunes search field at the top of the iTunes window. Type the song or artist name you want to look for and press **Return**. ■

TIP

Just a Taste When you're browsing the iTunes Store, click iTunes' **Play** button to hear a high-quality, 30-second snippet of a selected song. ■

RENTING MOVIES AND TV SHOWS

You say you're a couch potato? iTunes has you covered. Any time you want something to watch, you have only to start up iTunes and peruse a wide selection of movies and TV series episodes available both for purchase and for rental. Movies and TV shows download right into iTunes so you can watch them on your Mac, stream them to your Apple TV, or move them to another Apple device to watch them on the go.

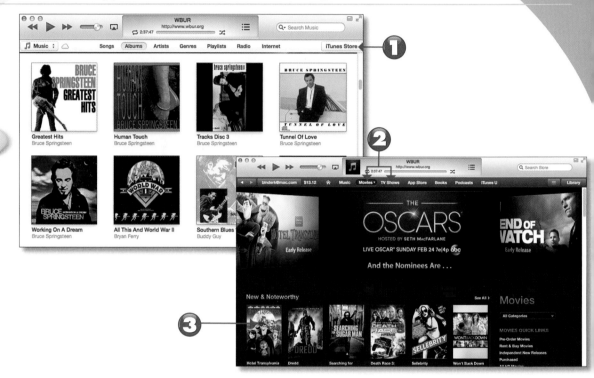

Start

1 In iTunes, click the **iTunes Store** button.

2 Click **Movies** or **TV Shows** at the top of the iTunes window.

3 Find the movie or TV show you want to rent and click its thumbnail.

Continued

TIP

Seek and Ye Shall Find If you have a particular movie or TV show in mind, you can enter its name in the iTunes search field while you're in the store and search for it. Choose the item you have in mind from the list of search results and proceed with step 4. ■

NOTE

To Rent or To Buy? For many video offerings in the iTunes store, you have a choice of renting or buying. Rentals expire 24 hours after you start watching them, but content you buy sticks around forever. Be sure to back up your iTunes library periodically by choosing **File**, **Library**, **Back Up to Disc**, so that you never have to worry about losing your purchased content. ■

 **4** Click **Rent**.

 5 Enter your Apple ID and password and click **Rent**.

End

NOTE

All This and More The iTunes Store also enables you to sign up for a season pass and have each episode of your favorite series delivered automatically. ■

TIP

Taking It on the Road To transfer your rental to your iPad, iPhone, or other device to watch it, first connect the device to your Mac; then choose your device (below Devices in the sidebar) and click the **Movies** or **TV Shows** tab. Choose the video you rented and click **Move**. ■

SUBSCRIBING TO AUDIO AND VIDEO PODCASTS

More and more, we don't have to turn on the TV or the radio to catch up with the latest multimedia news or entertainment. The podcasts available to you in iTunes range from recordings of your local minister's latest sermons to slickly produced, high-end news and interview shows. And they're all free!

Start

1. In the iTunes Store, click **Podcasts** at the top of the window.

2. At the bottom of the window, choose a podcast category to go to the iTunes Store's listing of podcasts on that topic.

3. Click a podcast icon to see more information about it, including a list of episodes.

Continued

NOTE

What's the Difference? Audio and video podcasts are essentially the same thing, except that, of course, video podcasts come with video instead of just recorded audio. You should be aware, though, that this means video podcasts take up a lot more space on your hard drive. Oddly, however, the iTunes Store doesn't indicate on a podcast's page whether it's video or audio-only—you just have to try an episode and find out. If you want to stick to downloading only audio podcasts, however, you can click the Audio button at the top of the iTunes Store's Podcasts main page. ■

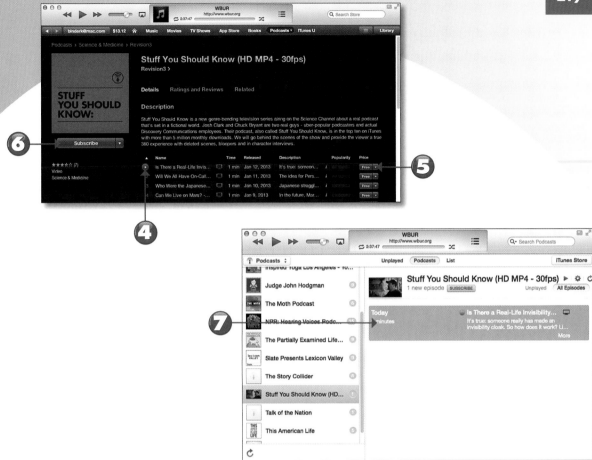

4 Click **Play** to hear or see a snippet of a podcast.

5 Click **FREE** or the price to download an episode.

6 Click **Subscribe** to subscribe to the podcast.

7 Double-click the name of an episode in your podcast listing to play it.

End

TIP

Just Like New If you haven't listened to any episodes of a subscribed podcast for a while, iTunes will stop downloading new episodes. If you want it to start updating your subscription regularly again, click Refresh at the bottom of the iTunes window. ■

READING IN IBOOKS

No matter how hard you cling to your paper books, with their lovely lignin scent and their retro aesthetic, there will come a time when you want or need to read a book on your computer. With the introduction of OS X Mavericks, Apple's ebook reading program—iBooks— finally makes its way to the Mac. Here's how you can get started reading.

1 In iBooks, choose **Store**, **Sign In**. After you sign in, if you've bought any books from the iTunes Store previously, they automatically appear in your Library.

2 If you don't see your library of books, click **Library**.

3 To open a book, double-click its thumbnail.

4 Turn pages by pressing the arrow keys on your keyboard.

Continued

NOTE

Getting Started When you first open iBooks, the program walks you through the set-up process, so you won't see the first few dialogs shown here. You'll need to follow the instructions here, however, if you aren't the first one to use iBooks on your Mac. ∎

TIP

It's There, Trust Me To see the iBooks toolbar, you have to move your mouse to the top of the iBooks window. It's normally hidden, so as to make your reading experience more book-like. ∎

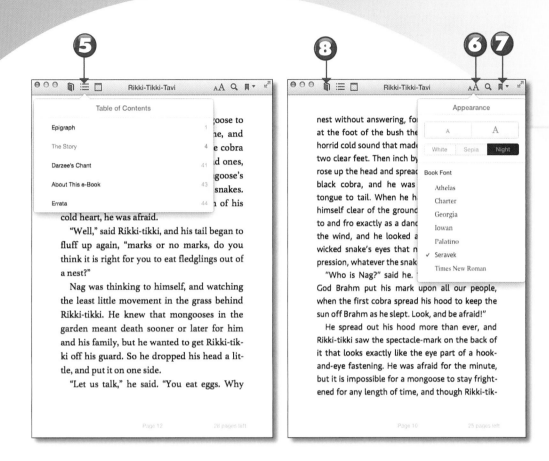

5 Click the **Table of Contents** button to view a table of contents for the current book.

6 Click the **Appearance** button to change the size or typeface of the book's text or to switch page colors.

7 Click the **Bookmark** button to add a bookmark; click the triangle next to the Bookmark button to see a list of your bookmarks.

8 Click the **Library** button to return to your Library.

End

TIP

For Your Reading Pleasure One of the best parts about reading books onscreen, whether you're using your Mac or an iDevice, is that you can adjust the type and "paper" color to suit yourself—or to suit your aging eyes. When you click the **Appearance** button in the toolbar (Step 6), you can click the smaller and larger A buttons to reduce or increase the type size; click White, Sepia, or Black to change the page color; and choose from among seven different typefaces for the book's text. If you switch to black pages, the text automatically turns white. ∎

BUYING BOOKS FOR IBOOKS

If you've ever shopped in iTunes for music or videos, the iBooks Store is going to look awfully familiar. It works the same way and also requires your Apple ID for purchases.

Start

1. Open **iBooks**.

2. Click **iBooks Store**.

3. To see the bestselling books in the iBooks Store, click **Top Charts**.

4. To see free books, click **Free**, or click **Paid** to see books that are not free.

Continued

TIP

For the Collectors As your iBooks library grows, it may become unwieldy to scroll through. Rather than having to use search to find anything, consider dividing your books into collections. For example, perhaps it would make sense for you to create collections of Cookbooks, Beach Reading, and Kid Books. Click **Collections** at the top of the iBooks window to see your collections, and click **Add** at the bottom-left corner of the window to create a new collection. ■

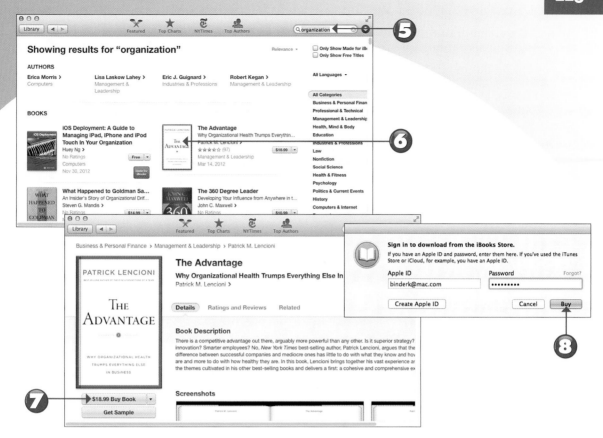

5 To locate a particular book or author, enter search terms in the **Search** field and press **Enter**.

6 Click a book's cover thumbnail to learn more about the title.

7 Click **Buy Book** to purchase the title and add it to your Library.

8 Enter your Apple ID and password and click **Buy** to confirm the purchase.

End

TIP

DIY iBooks iBooks supports both ePub and PDF formats, so if you like its interface for reading, feel free to add your own documents to it by dragging them into your library, including ePub books you've purchased elsewhere. ■

TAKING NOTES AND HIGHLIGHTING

Maybe you're a student, or maybe you're just an inveterate scribbler and page-corner-turner. Either way, iBooks is your dream come true. You can highlight as much as you want, and add marginalia to your heart's delight, without upsetting librarians or anyone else.

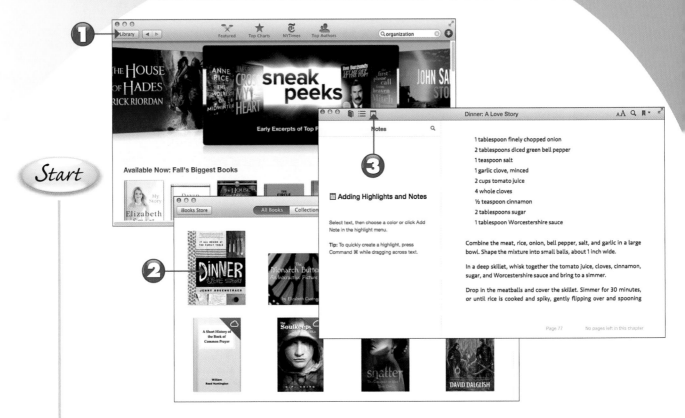

Start

① In iBooks, if you don't see your library of books, click **Library**.

② To open a book, double-click its thumbnail.

③ Click the **Show Notes** button.

Continued

TIP

The Definition of a Good eBook Reader Another great iBooks feature? A built-in dictionary. Select a word and choose **More**, **Define** from the pop-up menu. Instantly you're presented with the word's dictionary definition, including pronunciation. ■

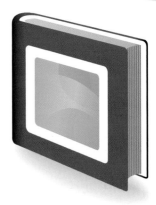

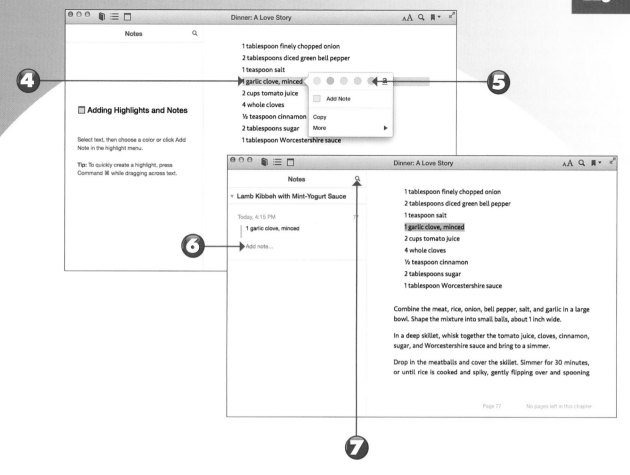

4 Select the text you want to highlight.

5 Choose a color for the highlight.

6 Click **Add Note** to make your own notes about the text.

7 Click **Search Notes** to search through for a specific term in the notes and highlights.

End

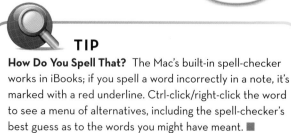

TIP

Speak to Me After you've marked text by highlighting it, you can have your Mac read it to you by Ctrl-clicking/right-clicking it and choosing **More**, **Start Speaking** from the contextual menu. ■

TIP

How Do You Spell That? The Mac's built-in spell-checker works in iBooks; if you spell a word incorrectly in a note, it's marked with a red underline. Ctrl-click/right-click the word to see a menu of alternatives, including the spell-checker's best guess as to the words you might have meant. ■

IMPORTING VIDEO FOOTAGE INTO IMOVIE

With iMovie, your home movies will reach new heights. You can add titles and credits, special effects, music and sound effects, and more. Then you can save your finished creations as small QuickTime files for emailing, high-quality DVD movies, or anything in between. The first step is to bring video from your video camera into iMovie.

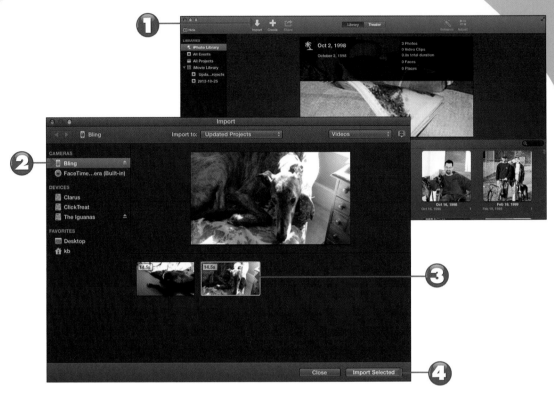

 In iMovie, click **Import**.

Make sure your camera or other device is connected to your Mac, and then click its name in the left column of the **Import** dialog.

Click to choose one or more clips to import, or leave the clips unselected to import all of them.

Click **Import Selected** (or **Import All**).

Continued

 NOTE

Trouble in iMovie Paradise Can't seem to get the camera to respond to iMovie's controls? Check to make sure the camera is in playback mode (VTR or VCR mode) rather than recording mode. ■

NOTE

Space Is Cheap If you find you're running out of disk space when you import video, consider buying an external hard drive just to store video files on. You can get quite a bit of space for well under $100. ■

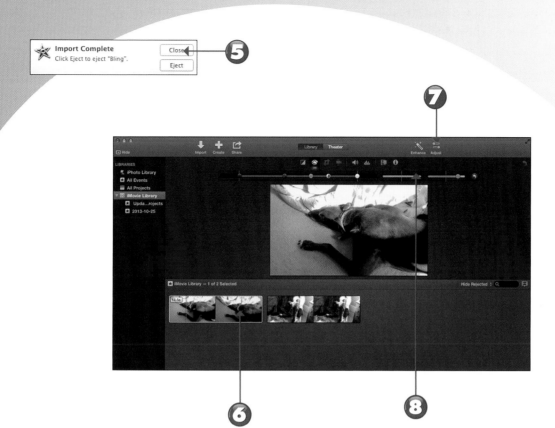

5 Click **Close** on the notification that your import is complete.

6 Click a clip to work with.

7 Click **Adjust**.

8 Drag the sliders to adjust the color and lighting in the selected clip. Your changes are saved automatically.

End

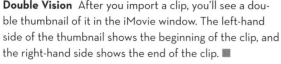

TIP

Double Vision After you import a clip, you'll see a double thumbnail of it in the iMovie window. The left-hand side of the thumbnail shows the beginning of the clip, and the right-hand side shows the end of the clip. ■

SAVING A MOVIE

When your magnum opus is complete—or at least when you're ready to share it with the outside world—you'll need to export it to a real movie format. This is an easy process, with only a few options to set.

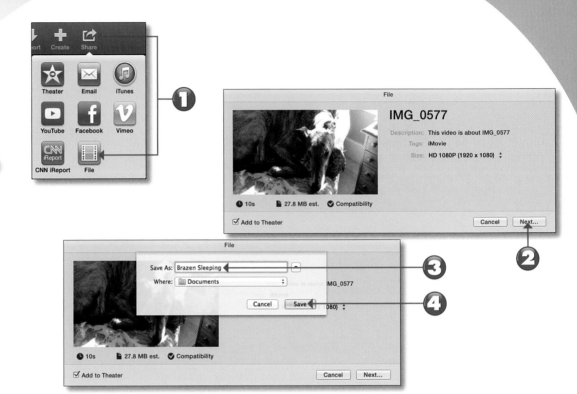

Start

Click **Share** and choose a format to create. If you don't have a specific destination in mind for your movie, click **File**.

2 Click **Next**.

3 Enter a name for your movie.

4 Click **Save**.

End

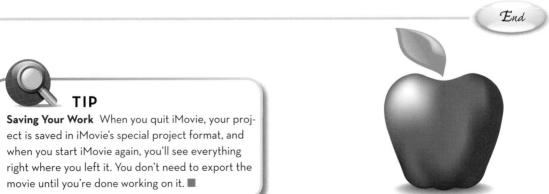

TIP

Saving Your Work When you quit iMovie, your project is saved in iMovie's special project format, and when you start iMovie again, you'll see everything right where you left it. You don't need to export the movie until you're done working on it. ∎

SENDING MUSIC TO YOUR STEREO OR TV

Even if you have expensive bookshelf speakers hooked up to your Mac, there are still times when you want to play your music with the power of a real stereo behind it—or maybe you just want to hear it in another room. With Apple TV and Airport Express, you can send music from your computer to speakers anywhere else in your house using a nifty feature called AirPlay.

Start

1 Find the music you want to play.

2 Click the **Choose Speakers** button.

3 Choose where you want the music to play.

4 To return the sound to your computer's speakers, go back to the Choose Speakers menu and choose **Computer**.

End

TIP

Under (Remote) Control After you've set your music free from your computer, feel free to follow it around the house. You can control playback with Apple's free Remote app, which works on any iOS device. You'll be able to choose what music you play and control the volume level using Remote, which you can find in the App Store. ◼

TIP

AirPlay for All You'll be pleased to hear that AirPlay works with your iPod, iPhone, or iPad as well as your Mac. You can also use AirPlay to send video to your Apple TV—turn to page 102 to learn more. ◼

SHARING YOUR MAC WITH MULTIPLE USERS

Mac OS X is designed to be a multiuser operating system, meaning each user of a single Mac has his or her own account. Each user is either a standard user or an admin user. Admin users can change preferences, install programs, and modify files—in other words, they can make changes that affect all users rather than just the user who implements them. Standard users can only read and modify their own files, and they can only change their own settings.

Your account can be customized with your choice of name, password, and login picture (used both in the login dialog box and for instant messaging with Messages). You also get your very own home folder, named with the short version of your login name. Your home folder is where you can put all your documents, music, pictures, and so on, and you can keep other users from reading, moving, or even seeing what files are in your home folder. When you do want to share files, you can put them in specific places where other users have access to them. Because customizations—such as the desktop picture, screen saver module, monitor resolution, and clock settings—apply only to the user who sets them up, you can also set up user accounts to create different configurations of your Mac for specific purposes, rather than for different people, if you want.

In this chapter, you'll learn how to create user accounts and change their attributes, as well as how to log in and log out. You'll also learn how to manage security with passwords.

ACCOUNT AND SECURITY SETUP

Change your
password, 238

Create and
delete users, 232

Share your files
with others,
240

Set your login
preferences, 236

CREATING AND DELETING USERS

Each user of a Mac gets his or her own account, with separate preferences, home folder, and login identity. Each account can have a customized level of access to system functions, and each account is password-protected so that only its user can change its settings.

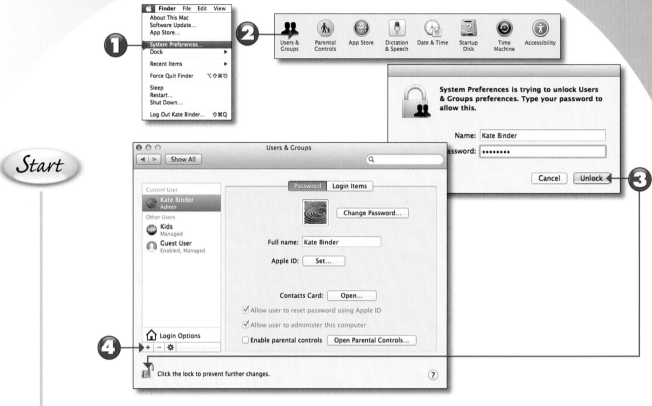

Start

1 Choose **Apple menu**, **System Preferences**.

2 Click **Users & Groups** to see the account's preferences.

3 If the preferences are locked, click the **padlock** button to unlock them; then enter an admin name and password and click **OK**.

4 To create a new user, click the **Add User** button.

Continued

TIP

Setting Limits When you create a new user account, you control the user's access to most functions. In the Password pane, click **Open Parental Controls**. On the Apps tab, choose the programs and functions you want to make available to the user. On the Web tab, turn on monitoring to limit access to adult content, and on the People tab, set limits on email and instant messaging use. The Time Limits and Other tabs contain controls for how much time the user can work on the Mac and for keeping track of what the user does. ∎

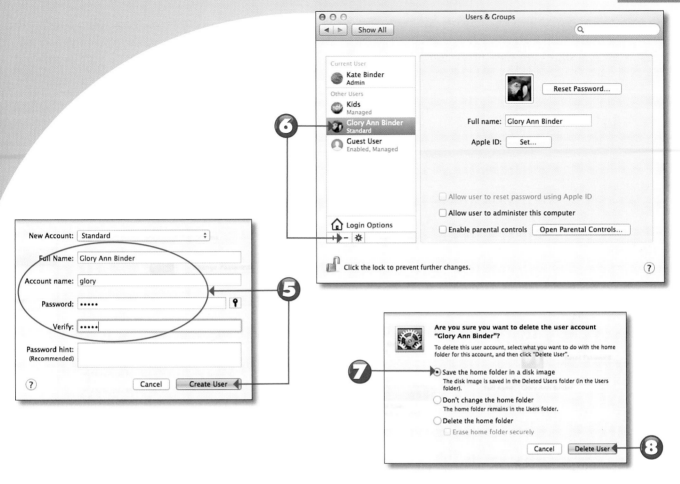

⑤ Enter the new user's name, a short version of the name (such as initials), and a password; then click **Create User**.

⑥ To delete a user, click a name in the list and then click the **Delete User** button.

⑦ Choose what you want to do with the user's files: archive them, leave them in place, or delete them.

⑧ Click **Delete User** in the confirmation dialog box.

End

TIP

The Stuff They Leave Behind When you delete a user, one of your options is to save the user's files as a disk image that's placed in the Deleted Users folder in the Users folder. Double-click the disk image to see the saved files. If the user was using FileVault, enter the user's password. FileVault or no FileVault, drag the disk image file to the Trash to delete the files. ■

MAKING A USER AN ADMIN

Each Mac has at least one admin user—the first user identity created on your Mac is automatically an admin. You can make any other user an admin as well, which allows that user to control system preferences and make changes to the Mac's setup.

Start

1 Choose **Apple menu**, **System Preferences**.

2 Click **Users & Groups** to see the account's preferences.

3 If the preferences are locked, click the **closed padlock** button to unlock them; then type an admin name and password and click **Unlock**.

Continued

NOTE

Admins Beget Admins Only admin users can create other admin users. If you're not an admin user, you'll need to ask someone who is already designated as an admin on your Mac to give you that status. ■

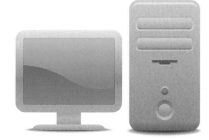

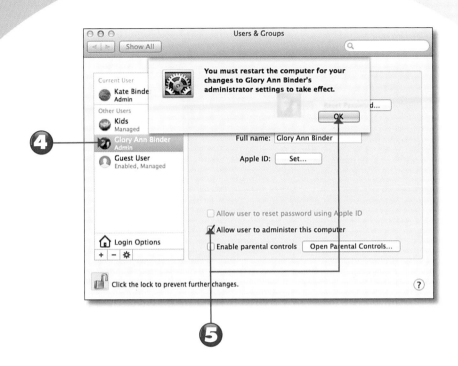

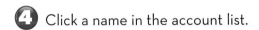

4 Click a name in the account list.

5 Click the **Allow user to administer this computer** check box and click **OK**. The next time you restart your Mac, the user will have admin privileges.

End

NOTE

Wherefore Admin, Anyway? To home users, the term *admin user* can seem strange. It's a result of Mac OS X's emphasis on accommodating multiple users of a single Mac. In most multiuser situations, such as computer labs, only authorized administrators should be able to change the Mac's setup. ■

LOGGING IN AND OUT

Depending on your preferences, you might need to log in to your Mac every day, or you might hardly ever see the login screen. Either way, you do need to remember your login name and password so you can log in when needed—after another user has logged out or after major changes are made to your system.

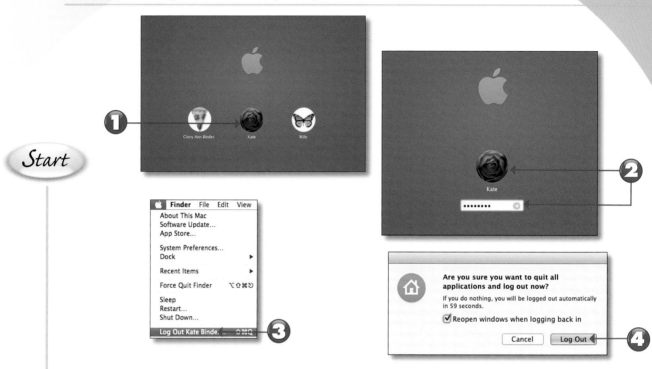

Start

End

1 In the Login dialog box, click your name in the list of users.

2 Type your password and press Enter or click the arrow at the right-hand end of the password field.

3 To log out, choose **Apple menu**, **Log Out**.

4 Click **Log Out** in the confirmation dialog box. All the applications quit, along with the Finder, and you're returned to the Login dialog box.

TIP

Skipping the Login Click **Login Options** at the bottom of the Users & Groups preferences panel in System Preferences; then choose a user from the **Automatically log in** pop-up menu. ■

TIP

Bring 'Em Back When you log out, your Mac asks if you want to open the same windows the next time you log in. Keep this box checked if you want to pick up exactly where you're leaving off, with all the same programs running and windows open. ■

SWITCHING USERS WITHOUT LOGGING OUT

When you share a computer, it may seem as though someone else is always coming along and wanting to jump on for a minute. If you had to log out (thereby quitting all your apps) every time another user needed access to your Mac, this could be a major hassle. Fortunately, you don't! That's what Fast User Switching is all about.

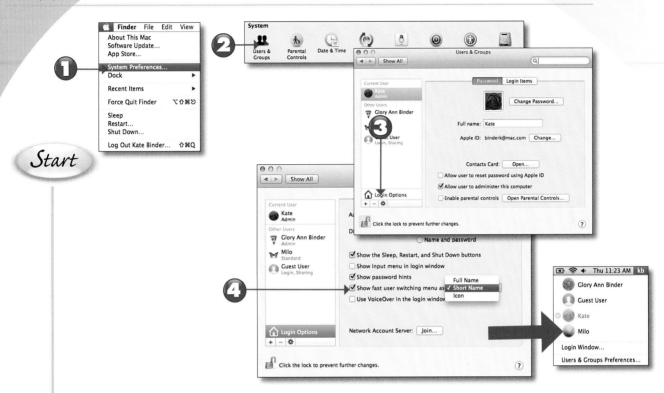

Start

1 Choose **Apple menu**, **System Preferences**.

2 Click **Users & Groups**.

3 Click **Login Options**.

4 Click the **Show fast user switching menu as** box and choose an option from the pop-up menu.

End

NOTE

Got Your Keys? If your Users & Groups preferences are locked, you'll need to click the padlock button and enter your username and password before you can change the Login Options settings. ■

TIP

I Can Only Do One Thing at a Time Your Mac can actually do a lot more than one thing at a time, but if you start to see it bogging down, check to see if another user is still logged in and running one of the programs you're using. Quit that program or log the user out to speed things up. ■

RESETTING YOUR PASSWORD

Because you need a password to access files on your Mac, be sure to choose a password you can't forget, and take advantage of the Hint feature to provide yourself with a memory-jogging phrase when you need it. If the worst does happen and you just can't figure out your password, here's how to remedy the situation.

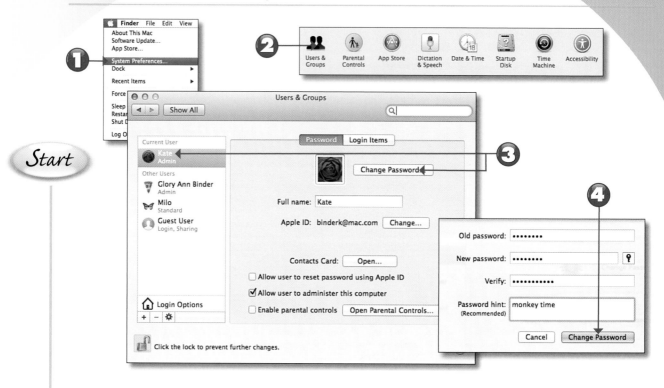

Start

1. If you just want to change your password, choose **Apple menu**, **System Preferences**.

2. Click **Users & Groups** to see the account's preferences.

3. Click your name in the list of users and then click **Change Password**.

4. Enter your old password and the new password and click **Change Password**.

Continued

CAUTION

Don't Make It Too Easy This might seem obvious, but if you enter a hint for your password, don't make the hint too obvious. Even if you're tempted to just use the password itself for the hint, don't! ■

NOTE

A Little Help from a Friend If you forget your password and can't log in or access your home folder (when you're using FileVault), an admin user can change the password for you. ■

 5 If you've forgotten your password, start up the Mac and click your name in the Login window.

6 Click the question mark at the end of the Password field to see a password hint.

7 To reset the password if you still don't remember it, click the arrow in the password hint box. This arrow only appears if you have an Apple ID.

8 Enter your Apple ID and password and click **Reset Password**.

End

 TIP
Identify Yourself Be sure that you enter your Apple ID in the Users & Groups pane of System Preferences and check the box marked **Allow user to reset password using Apple ID** so that you'll be able to perform steps 7 and 8. If you haven't done so, you won't have this option. ■

TIP
Give Me a Hint You did set a password hint when you created your password, didn't you? Make the hint something that is meaningful only to you, but make sure it's not too obscure for you to figure it out. If you don't have a password hint now, go to the **Users & Groups** pane of System Preferences and create one. ■

SHARING FILES WITH OTHER USERS

Some files are meant to be read and even modified by multiple users—a family calendar or a committee report in progress, for example. You can share these files in two designated places, with different results. And you can send copies of your files to other users via their Drop Box folders.

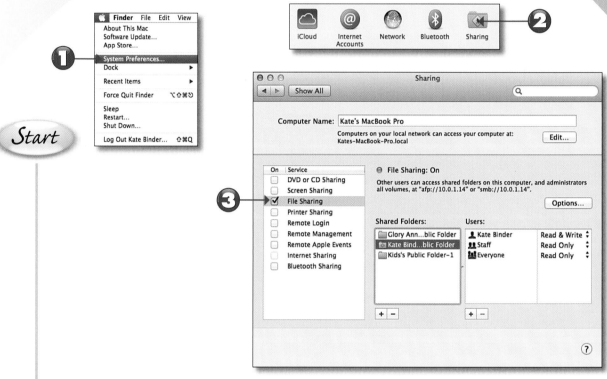

Start

1 Choose **Apple menu**, **System Preferences**.

2 To enable network users to access the Public folder in your home folder, click **Sharing**.

3 In the Services list, check the box labeled **File Sharing** to share files with other Mac users on your network.

Continued

NOTE

Skipping It Why all this rigmarole, you ask? The point is to keep your files as safe as you want them to be. If you want to skip the security routine, you can keep your Mac logged in with a single user account and give all users the password. ■

NOTE

It's Good to Share Files you might share in a Public folder or in the Shared folder within the Users folder include databases (of recipes, addresses, or clients, for example), templates for letters or memos that everyone uses, and logo graphics. ■

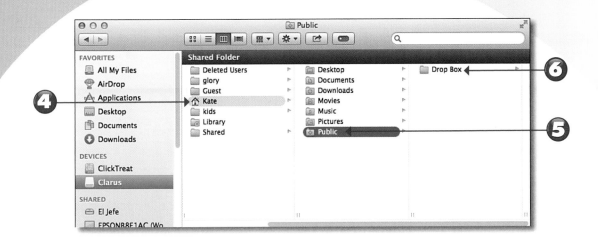

 4 Put files that you want all your Mac's users to be able to modify in the **Shared** folder in the Users folder.

5 Put files that you want all your Mac's users to be able to read but not change in the **Public** folder in your home folder.

6 To give another user of your computer a copy of a file, put the file in that user's **Drop Box** folder inside his or her Public folder.

End

NOTE

Flying Blind When you drag a file into another user's Drop Box, the Mac warns that you won't be able to see the result of the operation. This is its way of saying that you can't open another user's Drop Box folder to see what's in it. ■

CREATING A HOME NETWORK

A network, whether wireless or composed of physical cables, connects your computer with other computers so you can share files, play network games, and all use the same printers and Internet connection. The Internet, in fact, is simply a huge network comprised of many smaller networks. With OS X, setting up your own network in your home or office is easy.

Creating a network has two basic components. First, you need to make the connection by either hooking up your Macs (and Windows PCs, if you like) with Ethernet cables or installing AirPort cards and an AirPort base station so they can talk to each other wirelessly. Then, you need to tell your Mac how your network is set up so the system knows which connector and language to use to communicate with the other computers it's connected to.

In this chapter, you'll learn how to set up your network and turn on file sharing so both Windows users and other Mac users on your network can exchange files with you. You'll also learn how to share printers connected to your Mac with other users on your network. And you'll find out how to share a single Internet connection among all the computers on a network, as well as how to connect to an AirPort network and get online via a wireless AirPort connection.

SETTING UP AND USING A NETWORK

Set up the network
configuration, 244

Connect
to other
computers, 248

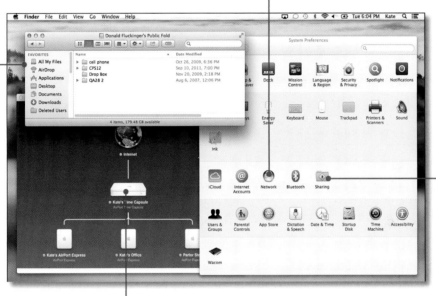

Share files,
printers, and
Internet
connections,
250–251,
255–256

Set up your own
wireless network,
244

CREATING AN AIRPORT NETWORK

You'll find Wi-Fi networks almost everywhere you go these days—coffee shops, airports, along your city's main street, even at McDonald's. Nice, isn't it? Why forgo such luxury at home? It's so easy to set up your own AirPort and provide Wi-Fi for yourself and your guests to use with computers, iPods, iPads, and all the countless other devices that now rely on Internet access to work, such as digital video recorders and Internet radios.

AirPort Utility

Start

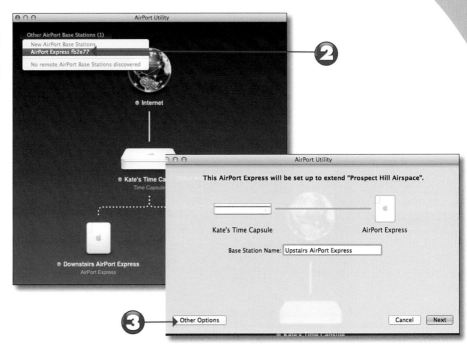

 Start up **AirPort Utility**, located in the Utilities folder within your Applications folder.

Click **Other AirPort Base Stations** and choose your new AirPort device from the pop-up menu.

To create a new network, click **Other Options**.

Continued

TIP

What's Your Name Again? Give your network a name you're sure you can remember—don't just default to Air-Port Network or something else generic. You need to be able to pick your network out of the crowd after all your neighbors get on the Wi-Fi bandwagon, too. ■

TIP

Speaking of Names Be sure to give your AirPort itself a name that identifies it clearly. You can add other AirPort devices to your network to extend it, and when you do that, you'll want to be sure which device is located where. ■

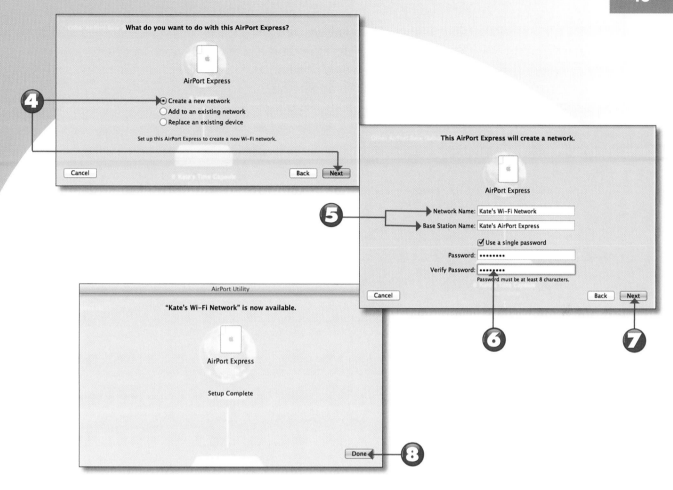

4 Choose **Create a new network** and click **Next**.

5 Enter a name for the network and a name for the AirPort base station.

6 Choose a password and enter it twice.

7 Click **Next**.

8 Click **Done**.

End

NOTE

Staying Secure In step 6, where you must choose a password, don't be tempted to skip it and leave your network unsecured. True, it can be a pain to remember and enter on multiple devices, but you need to shield your bank transactions and other private data from the outside world. Plus, do you really want the yahoos next door using up all your bandwidth downloading illegal movies? ■

JOINING A WIRED NETWORK

The first step to setting up a wired home network is this: Connect your computers with Ethernet cables (a regular one for newer Macs and a crossover cable for older Macs). If you have more than two computers, buy a hub and connect each computer to the hub; otherwise, connect your two Macs directly to each other.

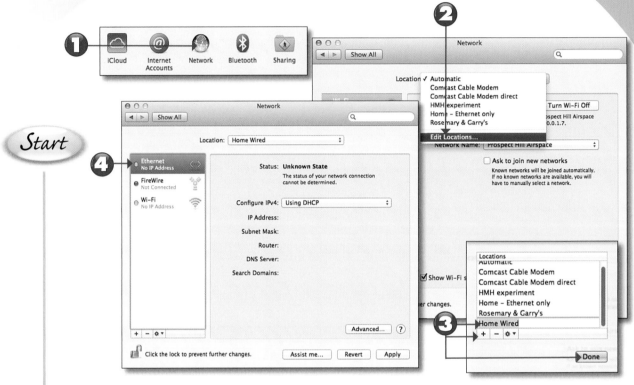

1 Open **System Preferences** and click the **Network** button.

2 Choose **Edit Locations** from the **Location** pop-up menu.

3 Click the **+** button, and then enter a name for the network configuration you're about to create and click **Done**.

4 Click the network port you want to use (usually either **Ethernet** or **AirPort**).

Continued

TIP

An Even Easier Way If network settings completely befuddle you, try using the Network Setup Assistant to get connected. Start up **System Preferences** and click **Network**; then click **Assist Me** and follow the instructions. ■

5 Set the **Configure** pop-up menu to either **Using DHCP** or **Manually** (check with your network admin).

6 If you choose **Manually** in step 5, enter settings for the IP Address, Subnet Mask, and Router.

7 Click **Revert** if you want to start over with the original settings.

8 Click **Apply** when you're satisfied with the settings to put them into effect.

End

NOTE

By the Manual When you choose **Manually** in the **Configure IPv4** pop-up menu, you must enter your Mac's IP address, your router's IP address, and the subnet mask. If all this is gibberish to you, go to Threemacs.com (www.threemacs.com) to learn about creating networks. ■

CONNECTING TO NETWORKED COMPUTERS

Networking has always been easy with Macs, but now the system's networking features are easier to use and more powerful than ever. You can connect to any Mac or Windows computer on your network using either AppleTalk or TCP networking, but all you need to know is the computer's name or IP address.

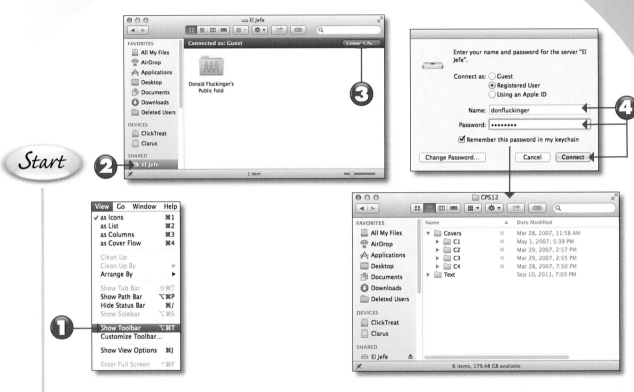

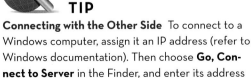

1 In the **Finder**, choose **View**, **Show Toolbar** to display the Places sidebar if it's not already visible.

2 Click a computer to connect to in the sidebar's **Shared** section.

3 Click **Connect As** to log into a user account on the network computer.

4 Enter your username and password and click **Connect**.

Start

End

TIP

Invisible Friends If the computer to which you want to connect isn't visible, you need to find out its network address (available in the Sharing section of System Preferences). Then choose **Go, Connect to Server** in the Finder and enter the address. ■

TIP

Connecting with the Other Side To connect to a Windows computer, assign it an IP address (refer to Windows documentation). Then choose **Go, Connect to Server** in the Finder, and enter its address in the dialog box in this form: smb://192.168.0.102. ■

MOVING FILES WITH AIRDROP

With AirDrop, Apple has virtually eliminated the need for the old-fashioned "sneakernet" method of walking files from one computer to another. You don't need a disk, a cable, or even an Internet connection—just two Wi-Fi-equipped Macs running Lion or a newer version of Mac OS, and you're good to go. Here's how it works.

Start

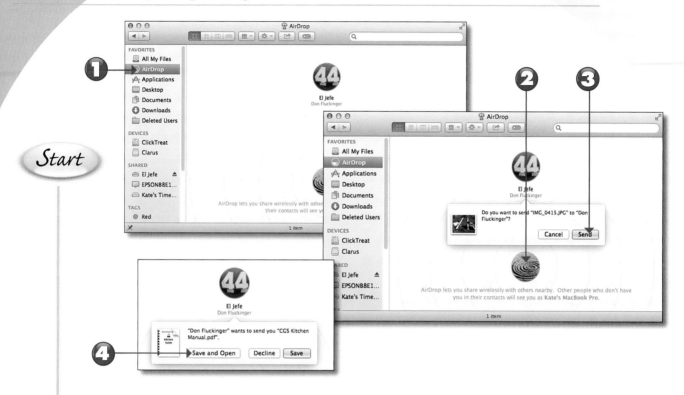

1. Click **AirDrop** in the sidebar of any Finder window.

2. Drag a file on top of the AirDrop icon for the computer to which you want to send the file.

3. Click **Send**.

4. To receive a file, click **Save** or **Save and Open**.

End

TIP
What's Up with That? Whenever files are transferring over AirDrop, you can see how far along they are and which file is copying at that moment by checking the Downloads stack in the Dock. ■

TIP
Let's Get a Move On Set up a queue to send files to more than one AirDrop user sequentially by dragging the files you want to transfer to each AirDrop icon in turn. As each batch copies over, the ones queued after it will display the message, "Waiting for transfer with [the first user's Mac] to complete." ■

SHARING FILES ON A NETWORK

When computers aren't networked, sharing files requires the use of sneakernet. Fortunately, creating a network is easy enough (see "Joining a Wired Network," earlier in this chapter) that Mac users rarely have to resort to sneakernet. Here's how to share your files on a real network.

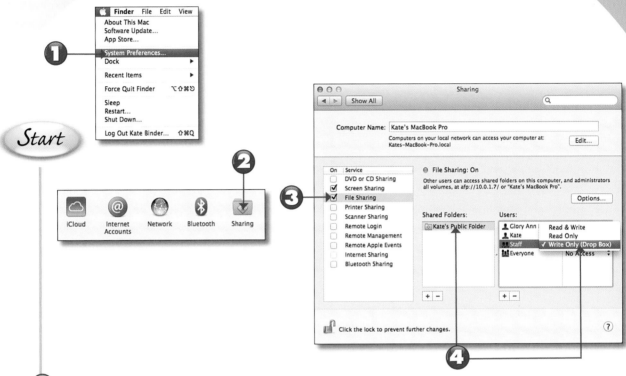

1 Choose **Apple menu**, **System Preferences**.

2 Click **Sharing**.

3 Check the box labeled **File Sharing**.

4 To change access privileges for specific users, click a user or group's name and change the privileges status in the column on the right.

TIP

When You Get There To connect to another Mac on your network, see the earlier task, "Connecting to Networked Computers." When you connect to another Mac, you'll see the home folders of that Mac's users. If you log in as a registered user of that Mac, you'll be able to access the same folders as if you were sitting in front of the Mac. Otherwise, you must connect as a guest; in this case, you'll be able to see only the contents of the user's Public folder (see "Sharing Files with Other Users," in Chapter 11, "Sharing Your Mac with Multiple Users"). ∎

SHARING DISCS

Some Macs have disc drives, and some don't. If yours doesn't, but you need to access files on a disc, you have two choices: hook up an external drive or share someone else's drive. Here's how you can share your own drive with a friend in need. Access to the files on the disc won't be as fast over the network as it would normally be, but it's much, much better than nothing.

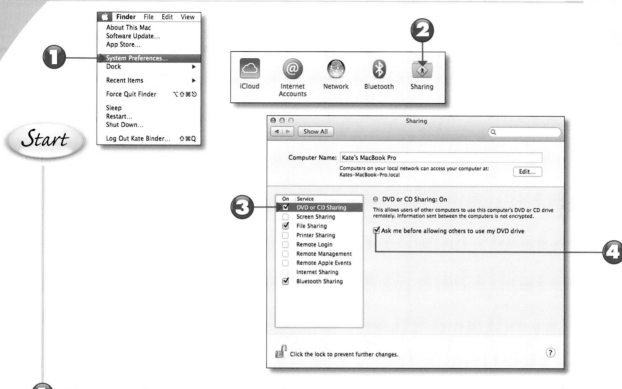

1 Choose **Apple menu**, **System Preferences**.

2 Click **Sharing**.

3 Click the box labeled **DVD or CD Sharing**.

4 Check the box labeled **Ask me before allowing others to use my DVD drive**.

End

NOTE

Out of Luck DVD and CD sharing doesn't work with copy-protected discs, such as some movie and game discs. ■

TIP

The Other Side To access a shared disc over a network, choose Remote Disc from the Devices section of a Finder window sidebar. You may have to click **Ask to use.** ■

CONTROLLING ANOTHER MAC

If you've ever wanted to reach right through the phone and grab someone else's mouse, screen sharing is for you. Starting with Leopard, this feature has been built right into OS X. It enables you to control the screen of any Mac on your local network, any Mac you can reach through Messages, and any Mac that's logged in to iCloud using your username.

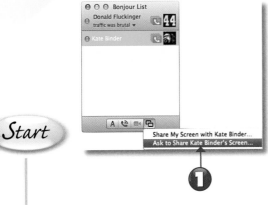

Start

① Click the **Screen Sharing** button at the bottom of the Messages window and choose **Ask to Share [User]'s Screen**.

② A dialog box tells you that your Mac is waiting for a response from the other user.

③ The other user must click **Accept** to begin screen sharing.

④ The other Mac's screen appears in a window; you can open folders, files, and programs as if you were sitting in front of the shared Mac.

Continued

TIP

Mother, May I? If you don't see a screen sharing button in Messages or in the Finder, open System Preferences and click Sharing; then click the box labeled **Screen Sharing**. The Mac to which you want to connect must also turn on screen sharing. ■

TIP

Find It in the Finder If you want to share the screen of a Mac on your local network, you don't need to use Messages. In the Shared section of a Finder window's sidebar, click the computer to which you want to connect; then click **Connect As**. ■

5 Click the double arrow to switch to full-screen view.

6 Click the **Capture Screen** button to save a picture of the shared screen.

7 Click **Fit Screen** to toggle between fitting the entire shared screen in the window and viewing it at actual size.

End

NOTE

Let's Share! You've probably noticed that Messages' Screen Sharing button also gives you the option of sharing your own screen with another user. The process works exactly the same way, except that the other user ends up controlling your Mac. ■

NOTE

If you need access to another of your own Macs, you can use iCloud to share screens no matter where your two computers are located. Turn to "Keeping Your Documents in iCloud," in Chapter 9, "Living Online," to learn more. ■

SEARCHING MACS

Searching with Spotlight brings the entire contents of your Mac right to your fingertips—and also the contents of other Macs on your local network. That's right; Spotlight can search, almost instantaneously, not only your hard drive but any drive you're connected to on a LAN.

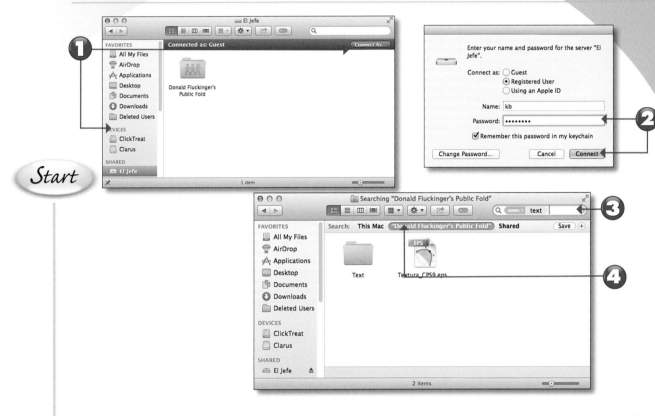

1. In the **Shared** section of the sidebar, click the computer to which you want to connect; then click **Connect As**.

2. Enter your username and password and click **Connect**. Click the check box if you want your Mac to remember your password so you don't have to enter it again.

3. Type the terms for your search in the Spotlight field.

4. Click the name of a shared drive to see the search results from network drives.

NOTE

Another Way You'll also see the Shared option in the menu of results that Spotlight shows when you use the Spotlight field in the menu bar. You can use either method to search—there's no difference in the results. ■

NOTE

The Mac Connection To learn more about connecting to other computers on your network, turn to "Connecting to Networked Computers," earlier in this chapter. ■

SHARING A PRINTER ON A NETWORK

You can share printers connected to your computer with other computer users on your network. Starting up printer sharing is simple; you can choose to restrict it to Mac users or enable Windows users to use your printers as well. Network users can add shared printers to their Print dialog boxes just like network printers.

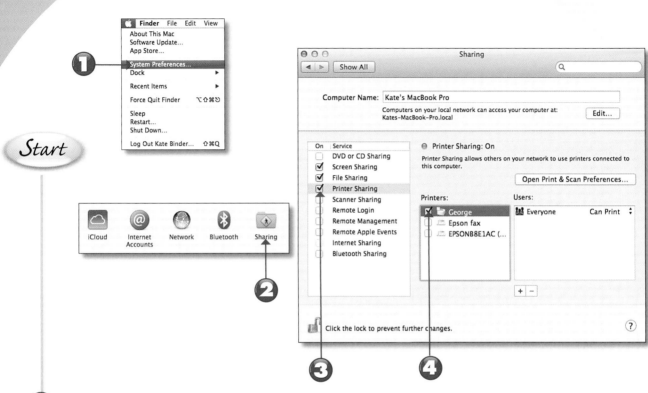

1. Choose **Apple menu**, **System Preferences**.

2. Click **Sharing**.

3. Check the box labeled **Printer Sharing**.

4. Check the boxes next to the printers you want to share.

End

TIP

Where in the Office...? To let other people know where shared printers are physically located, start Printer Setup Utility (in the Utilities folder in Applications). Select the printer and click **Show Info**; then add a description in the **Location** field. ∎

NOTE

What It's For Printers on your network are already shared, even if the printers are located in your office. Printer sharing gives network capabilities to devices such as USB inkjets, which don't usually have network connectors. ∎

SHARING AN INTERNET CONNECTION

If you've ever suffered through life with two Internet-capable computers and only one network connection, you'll appreciate the ability to share an online connection with all the computers in your house or office. And life gets even better when your connection is broadband, such as a cable modem or a DSL line.

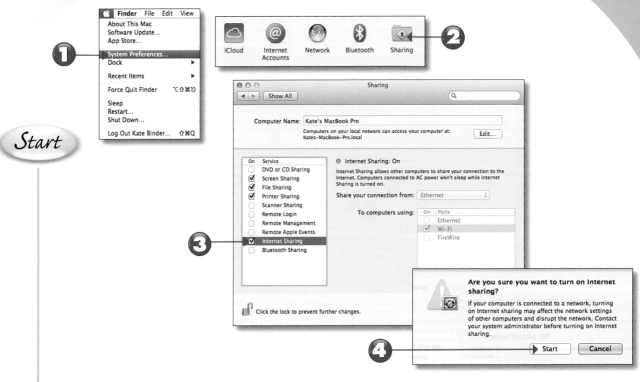

 Choose **Apple menu**, **System Preferences**.

Click **Sharing**.

Check the box labeled **Internet Sharing**.

Click **Start** in the dialog.

End

NOTE

When Not to Share If you connect to the Internet and your network via the same port, sharing your Internet connection can tell other computers to access the Internet through it when they shouldn't (such as when you take your laptop to the office). ■

NOTE

Another Way to Share If you're sharing an Internet connection through another Mac, you'll be able to get online only when that Mac is up and connected. If that doesn't work for you, consider buying a hardware router that can keep you online all the time. ■

JOINING A WI-FI NETWORK

With an AirPort card, you can get rid of those annoying network cables and connect to your network from wherever your computer happens to be, as long as you're close to a Wi-Fi connection point (either an AirPort base station, or another brand). AirPort is great for laptops—and it comes built into all of Apple's current laptops—but you can use it for desktop Macs, too.

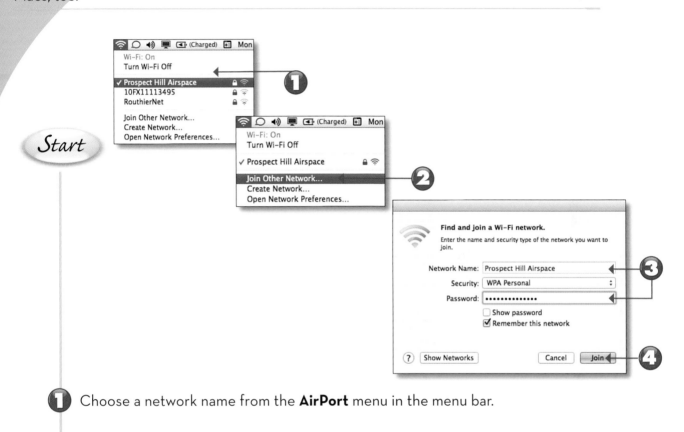

Start

1. Choose a network name from the **AirPort** menu in the menu bar.

2. To join a network that isn't shown, choose **Join Other Network**.

3. Enter the network's name and password in the login dialog box.

4. Click **Join**.

End

NOTE

AirPort in Your Menu Bar The AirPort menu also enables you to switch networks, turn AirPort on or off, or connect to other AirPort-equipped Macs. ■

TIP

Close to Home Base If AirPort is turned on but you can't get in touch with the network you're looking for, you might be out of range. AirPort base stations have varying ranges; you must be close enough to connect to the base station. ■

MAINTAINING YOUR MAC

Most of the time, your Mac just hums right along, cheerfully complying with your requests and sitting quietly in the corner when you're not using it. Every once in a while, however, even the best-behaved Mac needs a little maintenance or a minor repair. This chapter covers the basics of keeping your Mac happy and healthy.

In this chapter, you'll learn how to fix disk errors and reformat disks, both removable disks and hard drives. Also covered are updating your system software, setting the date and time automatically, and calibrating your monitor for accurate color. Some of these techniques are one-time jobs (calibrating your monitor) and others are things you'll do on a regular basis (formatting removable disks).

Along the way, you'll learn a variety of useful tricks, such as how to make sure you don't accidentally download harmful software and how to force quit programs when they're misbehaving. Whether you're a power user or a weekends-only Macster, the tasks in this chapter will teach you things every Mac user should know.

MAC MAINTENANCE AND REPAIR KIT

Calibrate your display, 268

Set the date and time automatically, 266

Avoid downloading harmful programs, 260

Update software, 264

Force programs to quit, 272

GUARDING AGAINST MALWARE

Real-world safety precautions include wearing your seatbelt and not letting children play with matches. In the world of computers, on the other hand, you need to watch out for *malware*—software that's intended to do bad things to your computer or your data for any of myriad reasons. The Gatekeeper feature can help ensure that you don't install any programs you can't trust to be safe.

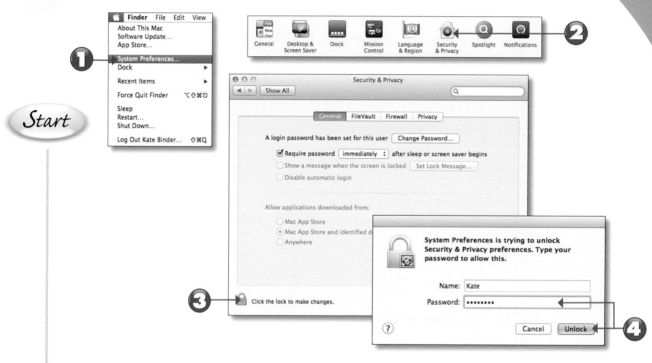

Choose **Apple menu**, **System Preferences**.

Click **Security & Privacy** to see your security preferences.

Click the lock so you can unlock the preferences.

Enter your user name and password and click **Unlock**.

Continued

TIP

Two for the Price of One Gatekeeper checks every program you download before running it, making sure that it doesn't contain any known malware and that it matches your preference settings—i.e., that it comes from either the App Store or a registered developer, if you have one of those options active. So it uses both a blacklist (of bad software) and a whitelist (of good developers) for a double dose of protection. If you want to run a program that you know is safe, but Gatekeeper says it doesn't pass these tests, you can always override Gatekeeper. ■

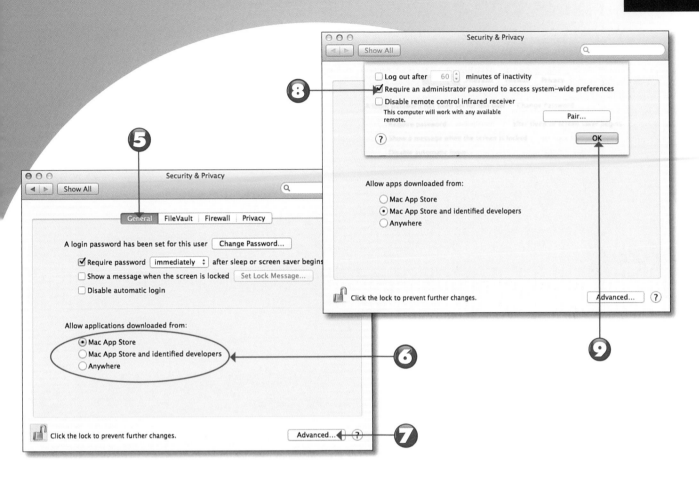

5 Click **General** in the Security & Privacy preferences pane.

6 Choose a Gatekeeper setting, or click the radio button marked **Anywhere** to turn Gatekeeper off.

7 Click **Advanced**.

8 Check the box marked **Require an administrator password to access system-wide preferences**.

9 Click **OK**.

End

TIP

Do It Anyway   If you try to open an app that doesn't qualify under the Gatekeeper setting you chose in Step 6, you'll see a dialog explaining that the app can't be opened. To bypass your Gatekeeper settings one app at a time, open it by Ctrl-clicking/right-clicking and choosing Open from the contextual menu. Then you'll see the same dialog, but this time with an **Open** button that you can click to move forward regardless. ■

FIXING ERRORS WITH DISK UTILITY

Over time and with use, the formatting structure of a disk can become scrambled, either slightly or seriously. If you have trouble reading files from, or saving files to a disk, or if you experience other mysterious problems, it's time to run the repair program Disk Utility. (To use Disk Utility on your startup disk, see the next task.)

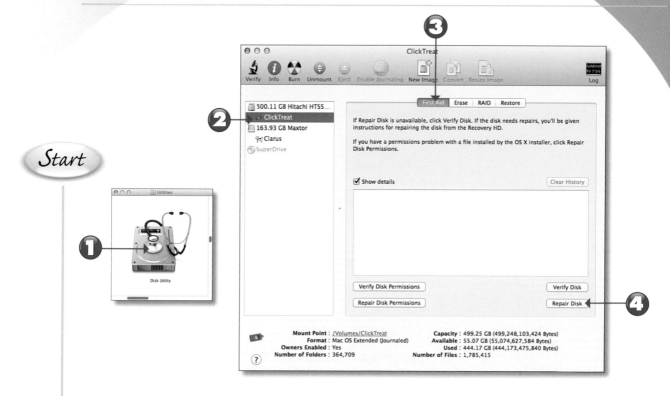

Start

1 Double-click **Disk Utility** to start it (it's in the Utilities folder within Applications).

2 Choose the disk to be repaired in the list.

3 Click the **First Aid** tab.

4 Click **Repair Disk**.

End

TIP

Verify or Repair? If you're concerned about modifying a disk in any way at all, you can check its status without making any repairs by using the Verify commands. And it's always good to have a current backup before you repair the disk. ■

NOTE

What Are Permissions? Each program, document, and folder in an OS X system has permissions describing who can open and modify it. Incorrect permissions can prevent programs from running or cause them to malfunction. ■

REPAIRING THE STARTUP DISK

Disk Utility can't repair the startup disk because the program can't modify the section of the disk that contains Disk Utility. If you have a second hard drive with an OS X system installed, you can start from that drive to run Disk Utility or you can use OS X's recovery partition, as described here.

 Choose **Apple menu**, **Restart**.

 Click **Restart**; then press ⌘-**R** while the Mac reboots to start it from its recovery partition.

3 Click **Disk Utility** and click **Continue**.

4 Choose your hard drive in the list, click the **First Aid** tab, and click **Repair Disk**.

NOTE

What's Going On? The Disk Utility program is just like the Disk Utility program installed in the Utilities folder on your hard drive. The only difference is that the one on the recovery partition can make changes to repair your startup drive. ■

TIP

Just in Case If you don't back up your hard drive regularly—and you really should!—at least do a backup before running Disk Utility. It's unlikely that anything will go wrong, but you'd rather be safe than sorry. ■

UPDATING PROGRAMS WITH THE APP STORE

Software Update checks with Apple over the Internet to see whether it finds updated versions of your system software and preinstalled programs. Then it can download and install updates for you. You enter an admin name and password when you update your software. OS X assumes only admin users are authorized to change software. Be aware that many system updates will require you to restart your Mac after they're finished installing.

App Store

Start

① Start up the **App Store** (it's located in your Applications folder).

② Click **Updates**.

Continued

TIP

Automatic App-dates The App Store is all grown up now—it has its very own pane in System Preferences. Here you can set the App Store to check for updates and install them automatically without bothering you—or, if you prefer to keep close track of what's happening on your Mac, you can turn off automatic updates. ■

 Click **More** to learn more about the specific features of an update.

Click **Update** to download and install the new software.

End

NOTE

Updating a New System Some updates don't show up until after other updates are installed. After installing system software from your original disk, update using the App Store repeatedly until it doesn't show any updates. ■

TIP

Don't Go First If you're not sure whether to install a system update, take a quick trip to MacFixit (**reviews.cnet.com/macfixit/**) to see whether other users who've already updated their Macs have reported any problems with the update. ■

USING THE DATE & TIME PREFERENCES

It's important that your Mac know what time it is. Every file on your hard drive is time-stamped, and the system uses that information to determine which files contain the most current data. Using the Date & Time preferences, you can ensure that the date and time stamps on your computer are accurate.

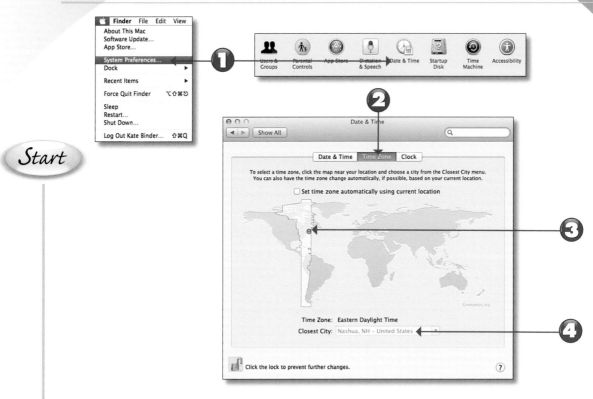

Start

1 Start up **System Preferences** and click the **Date & Time** button.

2 Click the **Time Zone** button.

3 Click the map near where you live.

4 Choose the nearest city from the **Closest City** pop-up menu.

Continued

TIP

Blink Blink Another useful setting in Date & Time preferences is located on the **Clock** tab. Check the box marked **Flash the time separators**. Then, if the colon stops blinking, you'll know your Mac is frozen and you can restart it. ■

NOTE

Today's Date Is... To see the full day and date, click the menu bar clock to reveal its menu. You can also open the Date & Time preferences here, as well as changing the menu bar clock to an analog icon instead of the standard digital display. ■

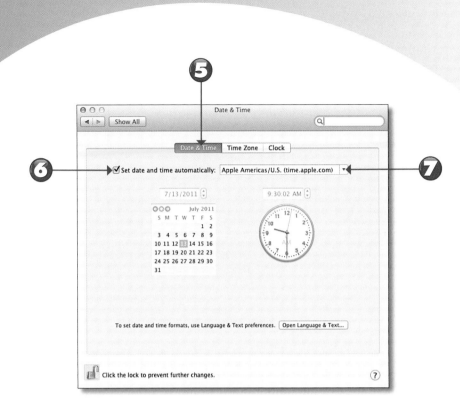

5 Click the **Date & Time** tab.

6 If you have a constant connection to the Internet, check the box marked **Set date and time automatically**.

7 Choose the nearest timeserver from the pop-up menu.

End

NOTE

More About NTP To learn more about how network timeservers work, you can visit the Network Time Protocol website at **www.ntp.org**. There you'll also find links to lists of alternative timeservers, including servers around the world. ▪

COLOR CALIBRATING YOUR MONITOR

It wasn't all that long ago that computers had grayscale monitors, but now it's all about color. To make sure color looks right on your screen, however, you need to calibrate your system. Here's how to create a color device profile that tells your Mac how your monitor displays color and makes appropriate adjustments.

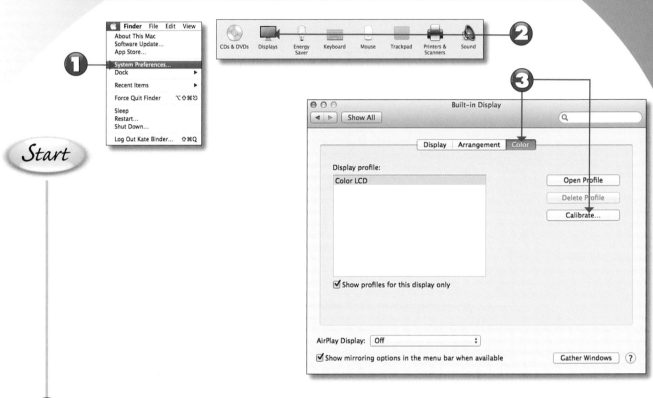

Start

Choose **Apple menu**, **System Preferences**.

Click the **Displays** button.

Click the **Color** button and click **Calibrate**. The Display Calibrator Assistant opens.

Continued

NOTE

Managing Color The software components that translate color between your Mac and your monitor comprise a color management system (CMS). In its full-fledged form, a CMS ensures consistent color throughout your system, from scanner to monitor to printer. ■

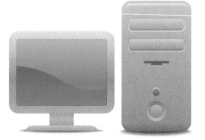

④ Click the **Expert Mode** box to create a more precise profile.

⑤ Click **Continue**.

Continued

NOTE

Where to Start The **Color** tab of the Displays preference pane includes a list of profiles. If one of those matches, or is close to, the monitor you're using, click to select that profile before you start the calibration process. You'll get a more accurate profile that way. ■

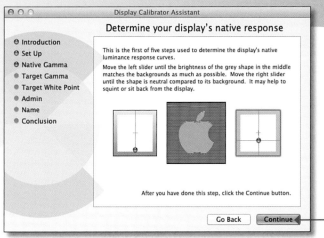

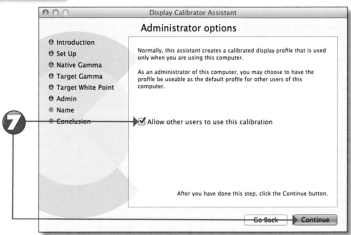

6 Follow the instructions on the **Native Gamma**, **Target Gamma**, and **Target White Point** screens, clicking **Continue** after each screen.

7 If you're an admin user, check the box to make the profile available to all users of this Mac; then click **Continue**.

Continued

NOTE

A Step Further If you're in the market for truly accurate color, you'll have to spend a little to get it. Look into a colorimeter such as i1Display (**www.xrite.com**), which sticks to your monitor to "see" the color itself as you create a monitor profile. ∎

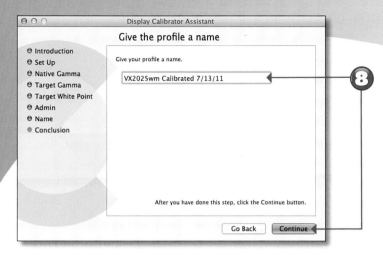

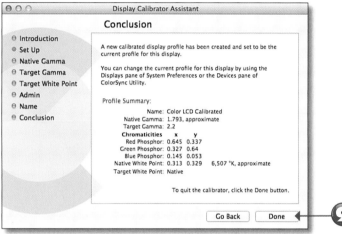

8 Enter a name for the profile and click **Continue**. The Display Calibrator Assistant saves the profile.

9 Click **Done**.

End

NOTE

Greek to Me The terms *Native Gamma*, *Target Gamma*, and *Target White Point*, used in the Display Calibrator Assistant, might sound very technical, but they simply refer to how your eye perceives the lightness, darkness, and overall color cast of your monitor's display. ■

FORCING AN APPLICATION TO QUIT

When a program isn't working right, your first tactic should be to quit and restart it. But sometimes a program is so off-track that the Quit command doesn't work. Then you can force the program to quit. This doesn't affect the other programs that are running, but unsaved changes in documents within the problem application are lost.

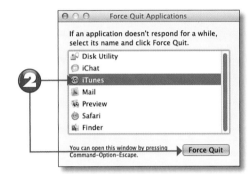

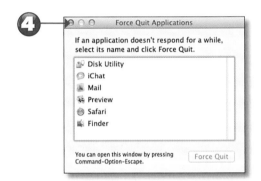

 Start

 End

Choose **Apple menu**, **Force Quit**.

Choose the program you want from the list and click **Force Quit**.

Click **Force Quit** again.

Click the **Close** button to dismiss the Force Quit dialog box.

NOTE

In the Olden Days Apple used to recommend that you restart your Mac after force quitting an application. But in OS X, each program runs in its own area of memory so that when it malfunctions, no other program is affected. No need to restart! ■

TIP

The Key to Force Quitting If you're a lover of keyboard shortcuts—they're definitely more efficient than using the mouse—then you'll be thrilled to know that the keyboard shortcut to get to the Force Quit dialog is ⌘+**Option+Esc**. ■

REFORMATTING A HARD DISK

There are three good reasons to reformat a disk. First, if you want to use the disk on a Windows or Unix computer, it will need a different format. Second, formatting a disk erases all data completely. And finally, reformatting a disk is a last resort if you're having problems opening or saving files on it.

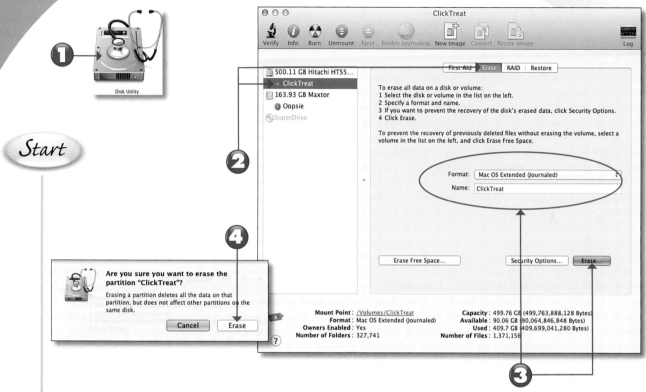

Disk Utility

Start

① Double-click Disk Utility to start it (it's in the Utilities folder within Applications).

② Choose the disk to be formatted in the list on the left and click the Erase button.

③ Choose a Volume Format option, type a name for the disk, and click Erase.

④ Click Erase again.

End

CAUTION

Sensitivity Training Disk Utility's Format menu contains six options, two of which you should definitely avoid. Mac OS Extended is the basic Mac disk format, and Mac OS Extended (Journaled) enables your Mac to keep a list of system operations so that it can restore your disk to its previous state. Mac OS Extended (Case-sensitive, Journaled) and Mac OS Extended (Case-sensitive) should only be used if you want to run UNIX programs that support case-sensitive file systems. The fifth and sixth options, MS-DOS (FAT), are used for Windows partitions that you use with Boot Camp, Apple's utility for running Windows on your Mac. ■

Glossary

A

access permissions See **permissions**.

accessibility The degree to which a device or **program** is usable by people with disabilities.

Action menu A **pop-up menu** that appears in **dialog boxes** and windows in the form of a gear **icon**. It provides access to commonly used commands.

admin user An administrative user of Mac OS X; a user who can read, write, and move some files that do not belong to her and who can change locked System Preferences settings and install new software.

AIFF Audio Interchange File Format is a sound file format used by iMovie and other multimedia programs.

AirDrop A method of transferring files via Wi-Fi on an ad hoc basis, without setting up access permissions ahead of time.

AirPort An Apple-branded combination of hardware (AirPort cards and the AirPort **base station**) and software with which computers can form a **Wi-Fi network** and communicate with each other and the **Internet** without wires.

alias A small file that, when double-clicked, opens the original file from which it was created.

App Store A program that enables you to buy programs directly from your Mac via download.

Apple ID A **username** for the Apple website and the iTunes Store.

Apple menu The **menu** at the left end of the Mac's **menu bar**, which is accessed by clicking the Apple logo; it contains commands such as Shut Down that work no matter which **application** you're using.

Apple TV A device that can display video from your Mac or from various Internet sources, including the iTunes Store, on a television.

application A program; usually refers to a fully featured program rather than a small accessory program or **widget**.

Application menu The **menu** that appears to the right of the **Apple menu** in each **program**; it's always labeled with the name of the program.

archive A compressed version of a file that must be unarchived before it can be opened.

B

back up To copy important files to a new location in case the originals are damaged or deleted.

base station A device that creates a **wireless AirPort network** in conjunction with Macs equipped with **AirPort** cards.

Bluetooth A short-range **wireless** technology that enables computers to communicate with other devices such as PDAs, keyboards, and mice.

bookmark A record of a **web** page's location, saved for future reference.

boot To start up a computer.

broadband A high-speed **Internet** connection such as **DSL** or a **cable modem**.

burn To write data to a disc; it usually refers to a CD or DVD.

burnable folder A folder whose contents will be burned to a CD or DVD when the user chooses.

button   Interface equivalent of the real-world object that triggers specified actions when clicked.

C

cable modem   A high-speed **Internet** connection that operates over your cable television line.

CD-R   Recordable CD, which can be recorded only once.

CD-RW   Rewritable CD, which can be erased and recorded again several times.

check box   Interface equivalent of the real-world object used to select options in a list or **dialog box**.

clip   A short section of video that can be combined with other clips in iMovie to create a movie.

Clip Shelf   The area of iMovie's window where individual video clips are stored before they're used in a movie.

Clip Viewer   The area of iMovie's interface where clips are combined with transitions, effects, and each other to form a movie.

collection   A group of **fonts**.

color management   The science of translating and adjusting scanned, displayed, and printed colors to produce consistent color from original art to final printout.

Column view   A **Finder** view in which columns of file and folder listings are placed from left to right, with the left columns representing folders closer to the **root** level of a drive.

compressed   Refers to a file that's reduced in size by manipulating its underlying data.

contextual menus   **Menus** that pop up wherever you click if you use a **modifier key**—specifically, the Control key. Their commands vary according to the context in which you're working.

Cover Flow view   A Finder view in which files are represented by large icons arranged similarly to the record album covers in a jukebox.

D

Dashboard   A user space containing small apps called **widgets**.

database   A data file in which each type of information is delimited in a field so the data can be sorted or otherwise manipulated based on categories.

desktop   The visual workspace in the **Finder**.

device profile   A file that describes the color reproduction characteristics of a printer, scanner, or monitor.

DHCP   Dynamic Host Configuration Protocol; a method of automatically assigning a personal computer an **IP address** so that the computer can connect to the **Internet**.

dialog box   A window in which you can click **buttons**, enter text, choose from **pop-up menus**, and drag **sliders** to determine the settings you want to make in a **program** or your **system software**.

dial-up   An **Internet** connection over a standard telephone line.

disclosure triangle   A **button** to the left of a **folder** or category name in a list; clicking it reveals the folder's or category's contents.

DNS server   A computer that translates **URLs** (such as www.apple.com) into the domain name system (DNS) numeric addresses where **web browsers** can find the files that make up websites.

Dock   The panel at the bottom of your Mac OS X **desktop** that contains an icon for every running program, as well as **icons** for any other **programs**, **folders**, or documents you want to access quickly.

download To copy files from the **Internet** to the computer you're currently using.

dragging and dropping Clicking a file's **icon** and dragging it into a **dialog box**, on top of an **application's** icon, into the **Dock**, or elsewhere.

Drop Box A folder within your **Public folder** that other users can use to give files to you; you are the only person who can see the contents of your Drop Box folder, but each user has his or her own Public folder and Drop Box.

drop-down menu A menu accessed from the **menu bar**.

DSL Digital Subscriber Line, a high-speed **Internet** connection that operates over your phone line.

DVD Digital video disc; a CD-like medium that holds several times as much data as CDs and that is generally used to distribute movies.

E

email Electronic mail that travels from your computer to another computer, across the **Internet** or over a local network, or **LAN**.

Ethernet A **networking** technology that enables you to transfer data at high speeds.

export To store data in a new file, separate from the currently open file.

extension See **filename extensions**.

F–G

FaceTime Apple's video chat program.

file sharing A system feature that enables you to transfer files from your Mac to other computers and vice versa; it can also enable other users to access your files if you allow it.

filename extensions Three-letter (usually) codes placed at the end of filenames to signify the type of file. These may not be visible in the **Finder** or in **application dialog boxes**.

FileVault A feature that encrypts the contents of a user's **home folder** so they can't be accessed without a password.

Finder The part of Mac OS X that displays the contents of your **hard drives** and other drives in windows on your **desktop**.

FireWire A type of connector for digital camcorders, **hard drives**, and other devices.

flash drive A keychain-sized storage device with no moving parts that plugs into a **USB** port.

folder A system-level equivalent of a real-world file folder, in which you can store files and other folders to help you organize them.

font The software that enables your Mac to represent a particular typeface.

format To prepare a removable disk or **hard drive** to accept data.

function keys The "F" keys at the top of a keyboard are used for performing special functions that vary depending on the **program** being used.

Game Center A program that displays your game scores next to your friends' scores and connects to the App Store so you can download new games.

Gatekeeper The name given to Mac OS X's ability to prevent installation of applications that are not created by registered Apple developers.

H

hard drive A device for data storage, usually found inside a computer.

hardware router A device that shares an **Internet** connection across a local network, or **LAN**.

home folder The folder in your Mac OS X system in which you can store all your personal files.

HTML   Hypertext Markup Language, which is the coding language used to create **web** pages.

hub   A device that connects multiple individual computers to form a network.

I–K

iCloud   An online service available to any Mac user that includes an **email** address and **web** storage space, among other features.

icon   A picture indicating a file's contents or type.

Icon view   A **Finder** view in which files are represented by graphic **icons** rather than just lists of names.

iLife   Apple's bundle of entertainment **programs**, including iMovie, iPhoto, and Garage-Band.

IMAP   The Internet Message Access Protocol, which is a less common method of connecting to a mail **server**.

import   To retrieve data from a file using a format other than the program's own format.

instant messaging   A method of communicating over the **Internet** in which users type short messages and instantly send them to other users.

Internet   The global network of computers that encompasses the **World Wide Web**, **instant messaging**, **email**, and many other ways to communicate and share data.

IP address   A numerical code that identifies the location of each computer on the **Internet**, including your Mac.

iPod   Small, portable Apple device for playing music in **MP3** format.

ISP   **Internet** service provider, a company that provides access to the Internet.

iTunes Store   Apple's online content store, accessible via iTunes, which offers music, podcasts, and video both free and for sale.

JPEG   A graphic file format (Joint Photographic Experts Group) commonly used for photos displayed on the **World Wide Web**.

L

label   A color applied to a file **icon** in the **Finder**.

LAN   Local area **network**, which is a small network enclosed entirely within one building.

Launchpad   A grid of application icons designed to give quick access to all of the Mac's programs.

List view   A **Finder** view in which each **window** displays the contents of a single **folder** or drive in the form of a list of files.

local network address   An identifier of a computer on a **LAN**.

log in   To identify yourself as a particular user by entering a **username** and password.

login icon   A picture representing an individual user that is displayed when that user **logs in** or uses Messages.

M

mail server   A computer that directs **email** to and from a local computer on the **Internet**.

memory   See **RAM**.

menu   A list of commands that appears when the user clicks a keyword or **icon**.

menu bar   The wide, narrow strip across the top of the screen that contains **drop-down menus** in the **Finder** and in applications.

menu screens   Screens on a DVD containing buttons that lead to other screens or open movies.

minimized   A **folder** or document **window** that has been placed in the **Dock**, where you can see a **thumbnail** view of it.

Mission Control   An "eagle's eye" view of all Spaces currently in use, including the Dashboard.

modem   A device that enables your computer to connect to the **Internet** over a standard phone, **DSL**, or **cable** line.

modifier keys   Special keys (such as Shift, Option, ⌘, and Control) that enable you to give commands to your Mac by holding them down at the same time as you press letter or number keys or the mouse button.

monitor   A computer's display.

motion menus   DVD menu screens that incorporate moving video in their backgrounds.

mount   To connect to a disk drive (either one connected to your Mac or one connected to a **network** computer) so you can access its files in the **Finder**.

MP3   A compressed music file that's very small but that retains very high quality.

multiwindow mode   **Finder** mode in which double-clicking a **folder** displays its contents in a new **window** rather than in the same window.

N–O

network   A group of computers linked together so that they can exchange information and share functions.

network locations   Groups of **network** settings for specific situations or locations, such as an office **LAN**.

network port   Computer hardware interface used to connect the computer to a **network**.

NTP Server   See **timeserver**.

Notification   An error message or alert that appears in the upper right-hand corner of your screen and in a list of Notifications called the Notification Center.

operating system (OS)   The software that enables a computer to run.

P

pane   A separate page in a **dialog box**, usually accessible by choosing from a **pop-up menu** or (as in the case of System Preferences) clicking a **button**.

pathname   The address of a file on a **hard drive**; it lists the nested **folders** in which the file resides.

PDF   See **Portable Document Format**.

peripheral   A device that connects to your Mac, such as a printer, scanner, tape backup drive, or digital camera.

permissions   File attributes that determine which user owns each file and which users are authorized to read it and make changes to it.

pixel   Picture element; a square on the screen made up of a single color.

Places sidebar   A column of disk and **folder icons** that appears on the left side of each **Finder** window in **multiwindow mode**.

playlist   A collection of songs in iTunes.

PNG   Portable Network Graphic format, a graphic file format used on the **World Wide Web**.

POP   Post Office Protocol, the most common method of connecting to a mail **server**.

pop-up menu   A **menu** that appears in a **dialog box** or other interface element rather than dropping down from the **menu bar** at the top of the screen.

Portable Document Format   The file format used by Adobe Reader (formerly Acrobat Reader) and its related software, as well as Apple's Preview. PDF documents look just like the original documents from which they were created.

PPP   Point-to-Point Protocol, a method of connecting to the **Internet** via a phone modem.

PPPoE   PPP over Ethernet, a method of connecting to the **Internet** via a **DSL** modem.

preview   Small or low-res view of a file's contents.

printer driver   A file that describes the characteristics of a printer and enables **programs** to use the printer's features.

processor   The core of a computer; its brain.

profiles   Data files that characterize how a device reproduces color. *See also* **color management**.

program   A file containing thousands or even millions of instructions in such a way that a computer can follow them to perform some useful function for the user.

project   A collection of files used to produce a movie in iMovie or a DVD in iDVD.

protected memory   An **operating system** feature that places barriers around the areas of a computer's memory (or **RAM**) being used by each program, so that if one program crashes, the other programs are unaffected.

proxy preview   A **thumbnail** version of a document, usually in a **dialog box**, that can be manipulated to change the real document in the same way.

Q–R

queue   The list of documents waiting to be printed.

QuickTime   Apple's proprietary video format.

RAM   Random access memory, which is the part of a computer that stores the currently running **programs** and the currently open documents so you can work with them.

Reader Mode   A feature enabling web page text to be displayed in a highly readable black-on-white form without ads or other extraneous content.

reboot   To restart the Mac.

removable disk   Any media that can be ejected from its drive and used in another computer.

resolution   The number of pixels per inch contained in a graphic or displayed on a monitor.

rip   To convert songs on a CD to files on a **hard drive**.

router address   The **IP address** of the computer or device that is providing a shared **Internet** connection.

RSS   Really Simple Syndication, an XML format for distributing **web** content such as news headlines, events listings, and excerpts from discussion forums.

RTF   Rich Text Format, a format for word processor documents that retains information about bold, italic, and other formatting in a form that almost all word processors can understand.

S

screen name   A nickname by which Messages users are identified.

screen saver   A moving display that covers the screen to prevent monitor burn-in.

screen sharing   Feature that enables network users to see another Mac's screen on their own screens and, if authorized, to control the other Mac.

screen shot   A picture of the computer's screen.

script   A simple program that can be created and customized by a user; the Mac OS's built-in scripting language is AppleScript.

search field   Text entry field at the top of a **window** where users enter search parameters.

select   To choose or designate for action; for example, the user must click a file to select it in the **Finder** before he can copy the file.

server   A computer that provides a service to other computers via a **network**, such as forwarding **email** or streaming video.

Services   A set of commands to access programs' features while those programs are not running.

single-window mode   The **Finder** mode in which double-clicking a **folder** displays its contents in the same **window** rather than in a new window.

sleep   A state in which the Mac is still powered on but consumes less energy because it's not being used.

slider   A **dialog box** control for choosing a value along a continuum.

smart folder   A **folder** that collects files from all over the user's **hard drive** based on search criteria set by the user.

smart group   A Contacts group whose contents are updated automatically based on user-determined criteria.

smart mailbox   A mailbox in Mail that displays **email** messages that are actually filed in other mailboxes, based on user-determined criteria.

Space   Custom screen layout that hides extraneous **windows** and **programs**, showing only what's in use at the time.

spam   Junk **email**.

speech recognition   A technology by which the Mac can understand spoken commands.

Stack   An alternate view of a **folder**'s contents accessed by dragging the folder into the **Dock** and then clicking its Dock **icon**.

startup items   **Programs** or documents that open automatically when a user **logs in**.

storage media   A type of computer media used for data storage rather than active information exchange.

submenu   A **menu** that extends to the side from a command in a **drop-down menu**.

SuperDrive   An internal drive for writing CDs and DVDs.

sync   To synchronize data between a computer and a device such as a PDA or cell phone.

system software   See **operating system (OS)**.

T

tag   A color-coded category that users can assign to files in the **Finder** or in Save dialogs to organize documents

TCP/IP   Transmission Control Protocol over Internet Protocol, the **networking** method Mac OS X uses; it is an industry standard.

text buttons   **Buttons** in iDVD that don't have video or photo images.

themes   Sets of **menu** and **button** designs that can be applied to iDVD projects.

thumbnail   Miniature image.

TIFF   A graphic file format (Tagged Image File Format) used for images destined to be printed.

timeserver   A computer on the **Internet** that transmits a time signal your Mac can use to set its clock automatically.

title bar   The part of a **window** that displays the **folder**'s or document's title.

toolbar   A row of **buttons** for common functions that appears at the top of a **window** in Preview or another **program**.

transition   A special effect inserted between scenes in iMovie.

Trash   The holding location for files or **folders** you want to delete.

U–V

URL   Uniform Resource Locator, an alphanumeric address that points to a specific location on the **Internet**, such as www.apple.com for Apple's website.

USB   Universal serial bus, a type of computer connector.

username   An alphanumeric identifier of a single user.

vCard   A small file containing contact information that can be attached to an **email** message.

video buttons   **Buttons** in iDVD that have video images.

virus   A **program** that damages a computer or the computer's files in some way and then reproduces itself and spreads via **email** or file transfers.

W–Z

Web   *See* **World Wide Web**.

web browser   A **program** used to view websites. Safari is the **web** browser that comes with OS X.

webcam   A small, digital camera used with Messages or to provide a constantly updated image over the **World Wide Web**.

WebDAV   A type of **server** that makes iCal calendars available to subscribers over the **Internet**.

widget   A small program that can be accessed using **Dashboard**.

Wi-Fi   The type of **wireless** networking used by Apple's **AirPort** hardware and software and by other manufacturers' similar devices.

window   A defined rectangular area on the computer screen displaying files or data.

wireless   The capability to communicate without cables; for example, AirPort is Apple's *technology* for creating a wireless network between multiple Macs. *See also* **AirPort** and **Bluetooth**.

word processor   A program used for composing, laying out, and printing text.

World Wide Web   A computerized information source consisting of text, images, and other data displayed on "pages" organized into "sites" that are linked together such that clicking a word or image on one page displays a different page.

A

C

D

F

G

H

I

S

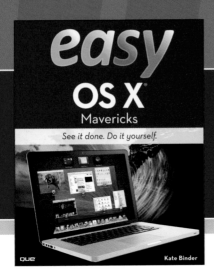

FREE
Online Edition

Your purchase of **Easy OS X® Mavericks** includes access to a free online edition for 45 days through the **Safari Books Online** subscription service. Nearly every Que book is available online through **Safari Books Online**, along with thousands of books and videos from publishers such as Addison-Wesley Professional, Cisco Press, Exam Cram, IBM Press, O'Reilly Media, Prentice Hall, Sams, and VMware Press.

Safari Books Online is a digital library providing searchable, on-demand access to thousands of technology, digital media, and professional development books and videos from leading publishers. With one monthly or yearly subscription price, you get unlimited access to learning tools and information on topics including mobile app and software development, tips and tricks on using your favorite gadgets, networking, project management, graphic design, and much more.

Activate your FREE Online Edition at
informit.com/safarifree

STEP 1:   Enter the coupon code: HIJZQZG.

STEP 2:   New Safari users, complete the brief registration form.
Safari subscribers, just log in.

If you have difficulty registering on Safari or accessing the online edition,
please e-mail customer-service@safaribooksonline.com